VEHICLES

Vehicles
Cars, Canoes, and Other Metaphors of Moral Imagination

Edited by
David Lipset and Richard Handler

Published by

Berghahn Books

www.berghahnbooks.com

© 2014 David Lipset and Richard Handler

All rights reserved. Except for the quotation of short passages for the purposes of criticism and review, no part of this book may be reproduced in any form or by any means, electronic or mechanical, including photocopying, recording, or any information storage and retrieval system now known or to be invented, without written permission of the publisher.

Library of Congress Cataloging-in-Publication Data

Vehicles : cars, canoes, and other metaphors of moral ambivalence / edited by David Lipset and Richard Handler.
   pages cm
   Includes index.
   ISBN 978-1-78238-375-8 (hardback : alk. paper) —
   ISBN 978-1-78238-376-5 (ebook)
   1. Vehicles—Social aspects—Case studies. 2. Transportation—Social aspects—Case studies. 3. Material culture—Case studies. I. Lipset, David, 1951– , author, editor of compilation. II. Handler, Richard, 1950– , author, editor of compilation.
   GN438.V45 2014
   629.04'6—dc23

2013050719

British Library Cataloguing in Publication Data

A catalogue record for this book is available from the British Library

Printed on acid-free paper

ISBN: 978-1-78238-375-8 hardback
ISBN: 978-1-78238-376-5 ebook

CONTENTS

List of Figures — vii

Acknowledgments — ix

Introduction. Charon's Boat and Other Vehicles of Moral Imagination — 1
David Lipset

Part I. Persons as Vehicles

Chapter 1. Living Canoes: Vehicles of Moral Imagination among the Murik of Papua New Guinea — 21
David Lipset

Chapter 2. Cars, Persons, and Streets: Erving Goffman and the Analysis of Traffic Rules — 48
Richard Handler

Part II. Vehicles as Gendered Persons

Chapter 3. "It's Not an Airplane, It's My Baby": Using a Gender Metaphor to Make Sense of Old Warplanes in North America — 69
Kent Wayland

Chapter 4. Is Female to Male as Lightweight Cars Are to Sports Cars?: Gender Metaphors and Cognitive Schemas in Recessionary Japan — 88
Joshua Hotaka Roth

Part III. Equivocal Vehicles

Chapter 5. Little Cars that Make Us Cry: Yugoslav Fića as a Vehicle for Social Commentary and Ritual Restoration of Innocence — 111
Marko Živković

Chapter 6. "Let's Go F.B.!": Metaphors of Cars and Corruption
  in China   133
    Beth E. Notar

Chapter 7. *Barrio* Metaxis: Ambivalent Aesthetics in
  Mexican American Lowrider Cars   156
    Ben Chappell

Chapter 8. Driving into the Light: Traversing Life and Death in
  a Lynching Reenactment by African-Americans   178
    Mark Auslander

Afterword. *Quo Vadis?*   194
    James W. Fernandez

Notes on Contributors   209

Index   211

FIGURES

1.1. Murik canoes docked along the shore of at a rural market off the Sepik River, August 2012. Photo: David Lipset. 26
1.2. Dama'ii Mask, 1982. Photo: David Lipset. 27
1.3. Human canoe-bodies getting into a second canoe, 1988. Photo: David Lipset. 29
1.4. A mask mounted on a cane "canoe" frame, 2008. Photo: David Lipset. 31
1.5. Lizard canoe prow, 1988. Photo: David Lipset. 33
1.6. A bus named after a lineage outrigger, 2010. Photo: David Lipset. 38
1.7. The model canoe being brought to present to Sir Michael Somare, 2008. Photo: David Lipset. 39
3.1. Texas Raiders. Photo: Kent Wayland. 72
3.2. China Doll. Photo: Kent Wayland. 73
3.3. Yellow Rose, Today. Photo: Kent Wayland. 74
3.4. Man-Woman Control Box. 83
4.1. Danger map. Photo: Joshua N. Roth. 92
4.2. No sidewalks in the 2000s. Photo: Joshua N. Roth. 93
4.3. A husband and a wife. The yellow license plate indicates a K-car. Photo: Joshua N. Roth. 95
5.1. Trabi as an extended wedding limo in Kusturica's Drvengrad on Mokra Gora, Serbia, 2007. Photo: Marko Živković. 113
5.2. Trabi and Fića on a Belgrade street, 2003. Photo: Marko Živković. 113
5.3. A rigged-up cart on a Belgrade street, 2013. Photo: Marko Živković. 121

5.4. Lined-up Fićas of the Fića Lovers Association at the 2008 Fićiad in Šabac. Note both the souped-up cars and those more or less faithfully restored to their "factory condition." Photo: Marko Živković. 123

5.5. The Fića-shaped glass bottle for brandy displayed prominently in a Yugo-nostalgia exhibition in Belgrade, 2013. Photo: Rea Mucović. 125

6.1. "Public Servant." Woodcut by Ding Cong, *Zhoubao* 23 (Feb. 9, 1945). 138

6.2. "Impatience" (Ji bu ke nai 急不可耐). Cartoon by Zhang Leping, *Sanmao the Vagabond*, vol. 1 (1948). 139

7.1. "Gypsy Rose" on display at the Petersen Automotive Museum. Photo: Petersen Automotive Museum, Los Angeles. 159

7.2. "Chavez Ravine" on display at the Petersen Automotive Museum. Photo: Petersen Automotive Museum, Los Angeles. 160

7.3. Mr. Cartoon's Lowrider Ice Cream Truck on display at the Petersen Automotive Museum. Photo: Petersen Automotive Museum, Los Angeles. 161

7.4. Alamo truck mural, San Antonio, Texas. Photo: Ben Chappell. 164

7.5. Smile now/cry later truck, Austin, Texas. Photo: Ben Chappell. 167

7.6. Zapata/luxury truck, Houston, Texas. Photo: Ben Chappell. 171

8.1. Moore's Ford reenactment, July 2009. Photo: Ellen Schattschneider. 187

ACKNOWLEDGMENTS

As ethnographers, and members of a discipline in a perpetual state of intellectual crisis, most of us live amid, or perhaps at the forefront of, change. Nevertheless, the inspiration for and development of this volume, which focuses on the metaphoric value of vehicles for identity, history, and society, arose from an abiding kind of creativity, a kind that utilized a conventional anthropological practice.

It originated from radical, cross-cultural comparison. Email exchanges took place between the co-editors, David Lipset and Richard Handler, concerning, on the one hand, Erving Goffman's work on changing concepts of the person found in traffic rules, traffic, and vehicles in mid-twentieth-century North America, and, on the other, canoe metaphors for personhood in Melanesia. This virtual dialogue in turn yielded the realization that symbolic anthropology, material culture studies, semiotics and metaphor theory had not recognized the significance of transport vehicles as a category of metaphor for moral thought.

Deciding to explore the empirical and analytic value of this insight, we recruited junior fieldworkers who had done research in sites around the world to write essays analyzing vehicles as signifiers of moral order and/or disorder. And we asked a distinguished scholar, James Fernandez, to write an afterword. The rich, fine-grained quality of the chapters, as well as their manifest thematic integrity attested to the fruitfulness of the vehicle metaphor.

We would like to thank several people who inspired, read, and commented on individual chapters: Carole Atkinson, Daphne Berdahl, Elaine Engst, Beth Notar, Ami Terachi, Gloria Tsang, and Wu Han.

INTRODUCTION

Charon's Boat and Other Vehicles of Moral Imagination

David Lipset

Marx and Engels regretted the consequences of the "icy waters of egotistical calculation" on moral order ([1888] 1969: 11). The solidity and sacredness of meaning were melting away and being profaned by bourgeois capitalism. At the same time, they viewed the change as potentially diagnostic. "Man" might now be "compelled to face with sober senses, his real conditions of life, and his relations with his kind" (12). However, more than 150 years later, it seems that their qualms, rather than their bittersweet optimism, abide in modern social thought.

What has won conceptual privilege? *Absence.* Absence is perceived in metaphors and significations of the moral, of community, personhood, and other collective forms of experience. According to idealist (e.g., poststructuralist, postcolonial, feminist, queer, postmodern aesthetic) critiques of realism, the very relationship between signifier and moral object has been called into question. Changes in capitalist production, from a decline in industrial production to the rise of finance capitalism independent of labor power, state devolution as well as multiculturalism have exposed gaps, indeterminacies, and instabilities in meaning (Mulvey 1993). Referentiality itself has come to be viewed as infinitely deferred: it is discursive, relative, and recursive rather than determined and real. Difference and simulacra—the desert of the real—are all that remain of the moral (Baudrillard [1985] 1994).[1]

In this volume, however, we adopt what could be called a position of methodological ambivalence about referentiality. Metaphors of the social, in our view, may be both exemplary yet problematic, but not null or void. However immersed in, or degraded by, capitalism they may have become, signifiers of the moral—like love—are nevertheless credible and persuasive (see Illouz 1997). Indeed, they may comprehend the signifying process itself (see Seidel 2000).[2] While we concede that the signifying hyphen may no longer be drawn authoritatively, that is, in gold, or by the state, and thus falls short of constituting comprehensive or totalized meaning, signifiers exist that do draw together, elaborate, and conceptualize the *presence and absence* of the moral (cf. Ortner 1973). They may not inspire the certainty that the body of Christ evokes to his faithful, but their elicitive capacity can hardly be lamented as having been drowned by rationality.

Our focus in this volume is on one such class of objects: *vehicles*. Why vehicles? For us, the significance of boats, carts, cars, airplanes, trains, etc. not only arises from their functional utility—e.g., they literally transport people and goods through space; it is also caused by the metaphor or trope they provide to imagine the social, and in particular to imagine its movement across and askew moral boundaries, a mobility that is depends, in turn, on human, or at least humanoid, agency.

In other words, vehicles lend themselves as phenomenological images for both the mobility of persons through society and space, as well as for the movement of meaning across semantic domains in general, and moral ones in particular. Fixing upon the vehicle *qua* metaphor, we notice, also has etymological and theoretical virtue. The Greek root of metaphor means "to transfer" or "carry over," which not only suggests that the synthesis or integration of two ideas into one involves topographic movement through semantic space, but intention as well (Wheelwright 1962; see also Fernandez 1986: 37).

In semiotics, literary theory, and symbolic anthropology, moreover, a vehicular view of signification and metaphoric association is well-known. Peirce's signs were composed of three elements: a sign-vehicle; the object for which the sign-vehicle stands; and the *interpretant,* the consequent understanding of the sign-vehicle/object relation. Although the two theorists differ considerably (Petrilli 2004), recall that Morris (1938) also divided semiosis into the same three components: "Semiosis is accordingly a mediated-taking-account-of. The mediators are sign vehicles; the takings-account-of are interpretants; the agents of the process are interpreters; what is taken account of are designata" (Morris 1938: 4). For his part, I. A. Richards (1936) divided metaphoric meaning into a double unit: the "vehicle," which was the "figure," and the "tenor," which was the principle subject. The relationship between the two was social/interactive and contextual.[3] And not least, Victor Turner, invoking or adopting a concept of semiosis to symbols whose "multivocality enables a wide range of groups and individuals to relate to the same signifier-vehicle in a variety of ways" that motivate action in public culture (1975: 155).[4]

If both metaphor and the signifying process may be conceptualized as a vehicular movement of meaning through semantic space, notions of totemic descent propose a useful contrasting view, one which is not vehicular, but embodied. That totemic signifiers are understood in and through ideas of reproduction, reincarnation, consubstantiality, etc. reminds us that vehicles may not just be abstract, semiotic images, but more specifically, they express the social via the social. Take one of the most celebrated examples—Wollunqua, the rainbow serpent. In central Australia, the Uluuru moiety of the Warramunga tribe claim ancestry back to Wollunqua, the rainbow serpent, who slithered through the landscape trying to wend his way back to his subterranean home. As he did, he left behind Uluuru spirit-children who "came out of his body" (Spencer and Gillen [1899] 2010: 229; Durkheim [1912] 1995: 380). In other words, the hyphen, linking signifier to signified, is conceptualized as filial, rather than vehicular. Now, although vehicles may or may not signify common descent, they seem to possess totem-like qualities. Not only do they comprehend how metaphor works to bring together dissimilar pairs of ideas and phenomena in semantic and cognitive senses; they are also understood to provide the agency by which the moral boundaries of collective life may be traversed (see Lakoff 1993).

The anthropology of material culture has contributed many insightful and creative studies of particular vehicles (see, e.g., Munn 1973; Miller 2001; Tilley 1999). Indeed, the linguists, Lakoff and Turner (1989) analyzed the *machines as people* metaphor as well. However, the signifying value of vehicles, as a whole category, seems to have gone unrecognized up to this point. The following two sections of this introductory chapter, on boats and cars, are thus meant to propose something of extent of the metaphoric capacity of vehicles to cross, or travel along, the moral edges of society, which is the volume's general theme. Both sections start with a brief overview of ordinary usages of these two vehicles before going on to discuss a few examples in detail (see also Whorf [1939] 1964: 145–46).

Boats

Boats are often used to express various scales of moral order, e.g., the "ship of state," being a well-known metaphor for governmental sovereignty. But perhaps more elaborate is the *person as boat* metaphor from which attributes of ships and other vessels are imputed to identity and face-to-face solidarity, as well as to states of being. One's background can thus be "anchored" in the values of a traditional upbringing. Whether or not one is literally entering a boat, "Welcome aboard!" is a common enough salutation acknowledging a person's joining a group for the first time. Being "on deck" may refer to times when one is responsible for what is taking place in a social setting. Similarly, when adhering to a common set of goals or agenda, people speak of being "on board" with it. Or, a group of co-workers may be called a "crew." People caught in a shared or collective predicament are sometimes said to be "in the same boat." Persons express desire to participate in a group activity by wanting to "put their oar in." One can "launch into" a discussion or an agenda. The admonition not to "rock the boat" is an injunction against defying norms or a collective status quo, a status quo over which leaders may "take the helm" by "changing or staying its course." People, advised to improve their performance, may be admonished to "shape up or ship out."

By contrast, people confess to being "up a creek without a paddle," when they lack resources or agency. "Two ships passing in the night" refers to people who have failed to start or maintain a relationship. "That ship has sailed" usually denotes someone who has missed an opportunity. Or, to be "foundering" on "rocky seas" or to be "on the rocks" express experiences of difficulty. To find a "port in a storm" may refer to getting help during a time of uncertainty. People who abruptly quit a group may be accused of "jumping ship." Lastly, boats have served as a metaphor for the passage of persons across gaps in moral order. The "journey to the … Isles of the Dead … [is] found in the beliefs of ancient Egypt, Assyro-Babylonia, the Greeks in various times and regions … These beliefs undoubtedly are the reason for the practice of giving the deceased a real or miniature boat and oars" (van Gennep [1914] 1960: 153).

Charon's Boat

In ancient Greece, Charon, the ferryman of Hades, transported shades of the dead—newly arrived from the world above into the lower world across the unbridged River Styx. A coin to pay Charon for passage was sometimes placed in or on the mouth of a dead person (Grinsell 1957). But those who could not pay the infernal ferryman's fee, or whose bodies were left unburied, had to wander the shores for one hundred years. By contrast, heroes—such as Heracles, Orpheus, Aeneas, Dionysus, and Psyche—travel to the underworld, but are returned, still alive, by Charon's boat.

In his comparison of Charon's Boat narratives in classical antiquity to later appearances in Dante through the mid seventeenth century, Terpening divides the story into distinct narrative units (1985: 11–12). Motivations for the hero's or the soul's descent to hell may vary, but they inevitably arrive at an obstacle, which is not necessarily a river. The boatman appears there. Dialogue may take place. A prerequisite, like proper funerary rites, having been fulfilled, the ferry is boarded. By one means or another, the boat then crosses the river. Passengers pay a fee and disembark, and the ferry returns for another crossing. Death is thus construed as a vehicular movement across a barrier, a moral *aporia*. The gloomy, fierce oarsman drags boatloads of recalcitrant souls across the River Styx in his little ferryboat. The boat, as van Gennep observed, serves as a metaphor for the transition of persons across one of the preeminent boundaries of society—between life and death—which Charon mans.

British Naval Ships

In addition to the *person as boat* metaphor, the personified image, *boat as person*, appears in launches of British Royal Navy ships. According to Sylvia Rodgers, launchings resemble rites of passage, as if the new ship were a liminal person passing across space, from land to water, changing from an inanimate thing into an animate, moral being—namely, a woman. Far from becoming a numbered object when launched, the ship receives a name, which is to say, an individual, social identity, with life essence, luck, and femininity (Rodgers 1984: 2).

The ocean being understood as big, unpredictable, and unforgiving in the West, seafaring has been often portrayed as masculine. Maritime activity requires physical strength and endurance, and it involves adventure and danger. In taking to the seas, a man risks his life, battling the elements, using science and the best technology to improve his chances, while always challenging nature. These are "manly" struggles. Yet sailors refer to a ship by the feminine pronoun. In the Royal Navy, as well as the merchant navies, sailors talk about a ship as having a life, a soul, and a character of "her" own. These qualities are not always attributed, and the terms are used interchangeably. What is constant is the gender of the ship. In the English language, which otherwise only assigns gender to human beings and animals of determinate sex, it is nonetheless the rule to refer to a ship as "she" or "her."

The metaphor *ship as woman* is legally encoded in naval and legal documents, and it is celebrated in poetry and prose. But what kind of woman is "she"? A ship is imagined as possessing the moral attributes of more than one kind of woman. Two images predominate: the all-powerful mother who nurtures and offers womb-like protection; and the enchantress of whom a man can never be certain. Figureheads that are no longer affixed to British ships were looked upon as particularly efficacious in the sheltering capacity, especially if bare-breasted (Kemp 1976). There are some grounds for concluding that "she" symbolized the mother who suckled the infant god of the sea, and that this made her a powerful guardian, especially against the devil.

The metaphoric relationship of women to ships made by mariners continues to inform meaning in British fleets. At launching, the two most important personages are feminine: the ship and "her" patron. It is the role of the latter, a woman of high rank, to exercise mystical powers that imbue the ship with agency by naming her in accordance with strict adherence to ritual procedure: she should strike the ship with a bottle just as it begins to move and pronounce "her" name (to give luck and life)—all in a moment (Rodgers 1984).

The Titanic

Žižek (1989) developed an intriguing (Lacanian) view of the sinking in 1912 of the great ship, not as a vehicular metaphor of human agency or id, but, of course, as loss. In psychoanalysis, although the meaning of symptoms may be discovered retrospectively, such insight is limited by what Žižek and Lacan call "the Real," e.g., the trauma that resists being, and ultimately may never be, signified, but at the same time may never be removed, or at least domesticated, by being talked over. The wreck of the Titanic, Žižek argues, was this kind of collective and historical symptom. The age of progress and stable class distinctions was ending and society was threatened by labor movements, anti-Semitism, nationalism, and war. For Žižek, the great ocean liner was a signifier of order, stratification, gentility, and so forth whose meaning has been supplemented not just by its destruction, but now, by the contemporary sighting of its remains at the bottom of the sea:

> By looking at the wreck we gain an insight into the forbidden domain, in a space that should be left unseen: visible fragments are a kind of a coagulated remnant of the liquid flux of *jouissance* [pleasure], a kind of petrified forest of enjoyment ... The wreck of the Titanic ... functions as a sublime object: a positive, material object elevated to the status of the impossible Thing ... permeated with ... [terror and] enjoyment. (1989: 71)

Now Žižek argues that the Titanic was such a self-evident symbol of moral order and its ruin that a novelist had already imagined the sinking of a transatlantic ocean liner about fifteen years *before* it sank. The figural conspicuousness, and efficacy, of a great ocean liner I would add, consisted in its very vehicularity. The ship was not just an mode of prestigious transportation for elites and an image of progress; it was a material metaphor that transported these meanings across icy waters. The sunken wreckage becomes no less of a vehicular metaphor, not of moral order, but inexpressible trauma.

Cars

Like boats, the metaphor *person as car* has a lot of usage in daily language, for example, to express agency. To "hand the car keys" over to somebody means to let him or her make decisions. Tough negotiators "drive a hard bargain." We talk about "switching gears" when changing the subject in conversation. When people want to stop doing or talking about something, they may say that they are "applying the brakes." A person who is exhausted may allude to being "out of gas." To "get a lot of mileage" out of a project, object, or idea is to work at or exploit it for a long time. A person may "drive something into a ditch," by which is meant that he or she has wrecked it. A person may be "ticketed" or penalized, for having committed a wrong. People who feel a sense of failure, or helplessness, may speak of "spinning their wheels." Alternatively, a person who has been deceived by a falsehood or defrauded by a scam is said to have been "taken for a ride." If the *person as car* metaphor appears to convey familiar aspects of agency or its lack in face-to-face spaces, reciprocally, the *car as person* metaphor has assumed no less communicative and conceptual importance phenomenologically. But it also has a become refractory signifier of compound forms of modern relations with technology as well as of modern identities, both individual and collective, both insubordinate and glorified.

Automobility

Urry has nominated the automobile as one of the principle socio-technical institutions in contemporary life (Urry 2000; Sheller and Urry 2000: 738; Featherstone 2004). It is a manufactured object, an item of individual consumption, an economic complex, an environmental agent, as well as, of course, a form of mobility. "Automobility" is his term for a set of political institutions and practices that organize, accelerate, and shape the spatial movements and impacts of cars, while simultaneously regulating their many consequences. Automobility is also an ideological or dialogic formation (see Basquet/Gorz 1973) in the sense that cars are imagined to possess human qualities and attributes. They are associated with ideals of freedom, privacy, and autonomy, ideals that are celebrated and/or analyzed in popular and academic discourses alike. What is more, automobility entails, a set of ways of experiencing the world, that both serve to legitimize its cultural dominance and unsettle taken-for-granted boundaries separating human from nature, from technology and so on. Diverse as the elements that comprise automobility are, Urry insists that they are not reducible to *the* automobile itself.

Urry employs automobility in a double-sense. On the one hand, "auto" refers reflexively to the self, as in "auto" in autobiography. On the other hand, "auto" refers to objects or machines that possess a capacity for movement, as expressed by automatic, automaton, and especially automobile. This dual meaning of "auto" suggests that the car-driver is a "hybrid," a fetishized assemblage, not simply of autonomous persons, but simultaneously of machines, roads, buildings, signs, and entire cultures of mobility (Haraway 1991; Thrift 1996: 282–84). The car becomes an extension of the driver's body, creating new subjectivities organized around the disciplined "driving body" (Hawkins 1986: 63; Morse 1998, cf. Brottman 2001: xxv). It becomes a metonym for the person, and, simultaneously, the person becomes a metonym for the car (see also Latour 1999).

The car can be thought of as an extension of the senses; the car-driver can feel its contours, shape, and relationship as a hybrid of human and metallic skin. So the driver is habitually embodied within the car as an assemblage, a "driver-car" that becomes an aspect of bodily experience carried into taken-for-granted perceptions of and engagements with the material world (Dant 2004: 61). The car does not simply afford the driver mobility or independent agency; it enables a range of embodied actions available only to the driver-car. The driver-car is neither a thing nor a person; it is an assembled social being that takes on properties of both and cannot exist without both.

As people inhabit, and interact through, moving cars, automobility makes instantaneous time and the negotiation of extensive space central to how such life is configured. Automobility extends the individual into realms of freedom and flexibility whereby inhabiting the car can be positively viewed, but can also be constraining. Car "users" live in spatially stretched and time-compressed ways. The car, Urry worries, is a literal version of Weber's "iron cage" of modernity. Automobility is a world of anonymous, violent machines occupied by the other who is moving too fast to know directly or especially to see through the eye.

Car as Nation

While images of desire and sexuality, adventure, freedom, and rebellion splash across the mass media in the West, they also circulate globally as car cultures become increasingly internationalized. Still, cars belong to nations (Inglis 2004). Cars denote national identity (Edensor 2004: 103, Sedgwick 1970). They are well-known, iconic objects arising from historic systems of production and expertise.

Between World War I and World War II, overcoming France's lead in production, the car became a necessary feature of middle-class British life (Church 1979, 1994; Foreman-Peck et al. 1995; O'Connell 1998; Richardson 1977). Germany lagged behind, which prompted Hitler to argue that the modern nation was by definition a motorized nation (Koshar 2004; Nolan 1994).[5] By contrast, as Barthes remarked in 1963, the automobile was a vehicle for nostalgia and anxiety about the integrity of French national identity. Despite its symbolic omnipresence in society, the automobile tended to be perceived by intellectuals and others as a foreign, colonizing influence on French life. Baudrillard's view of tail-fins ([1968] 2002) indicated that objects like birds and shark fins were being appropriated into the design of cars. De-natured, they were reduced to little more than a series of abstract and artificial signifiers of sleek movement through space. In this way, the car-commodity was destroying an older and more apparently French environment, in favor of a wholly man-made setting in which natural phenomena only appeared as stylized parodies.

Americans, in turn, shamelessly drive their national values without qualms. In particular, cars are viewed as allowing independence from schedules and the desires of others: "the car is experience as the ultimate tool of self-reliance" (Lutz and Fernandez 2010: 15). Obtaining the first drivers' license is as revered a moment in the passage to independent maturity as there is for American teens. "Carless adults" must cope with anxiety or guilt about having to ride with others and the shame of seeming immature, inadequate, or incompetent (Lutz and Fernandez 2010: 15). Americans imagine themselves as driving to unexplored places, crossing the frontier, as it were, even if they are only going to the supermarket. Model names—such as the Expedition, the Explorer, the Sierra, and the Mustang—invite drivers to see themselves as trailblazers in a "fantasy that another life is possible down the road, just over the horizon, or in some faraway exotic locale" (Lutz and Fernandez 2010: 17). If cars are vehicles of freedom, they also become vehicles for American anti-stateism according to which seat-belt regulations, speed limits and gas taxes are fiercely opposed and resisted, however beneficial they may be, as governmental interference. That is, as Daniel Miller has observed, cars "become more a means to resist alienation than a sign of alienation" (2001: 3).

What do Urry's anxiety-ridden view of automobility as a new "iron cage" and Charon's boat ferrying souls to hell have to tell us about vehicles? Where, that is to ask, do vehicles take the myriad meanings that they convey? What kind of cultural work does this metaphor perform? Both automobility and Charon's boat, I would say, illustrate that vehicles pull the moral imagination along so as to express the disquiet and apprehension that pervades social life, uncertain as it is. In elaborate and diverse ways, vehicles transport the moral in no single direction. That is, while they provide material forms of movement and convey restive unease, they are also useful to think with—about important ethical issues, problems, and questions as they arise in the course of the historical moment.

Rather than by vehicle-type, history, or geography, we have therefore divided up this volume around the general theme of how vehicles are used to express constructions of the moral. Specially, the collection consists of fine-grained, ethnographically informed analyses of canoes, airplanes, and cars in relation to three, interrelated topics: 1) vehicular constructions of personhood in general, 2) vehicular constructions of gender in particular and 3) of vehicles that express equivocal views about the nation-state as well as bittersweet attitudes of minorities oppressed within it. We prefer this thematic order for several reasons. At the same time as we want to foreground the cultural variability of the vehicle metaphor, we want to magnify the degree to which vehicles may serve cross-culturally as master-signifiers of the moral. We want to disrupt self-evident historical binaries, like tradition-modernity. And lastly, we want to highlight the critical attitudes which vehicles may express.

The Vehicles

The first part of the volume thus focuses on vehicle metaphors in two rather different settings, rural Papua New Guinea and mid-twentieth-century North America. Lipset introduces cosmological and postcolonial canoe metaphors among the coastal Murik of the Sepik estuary. Among the Murik, the "body is a canoe" that transports and protects spirit-passengers through otherwise hostile space. However, these vehicles are also personified: the "canoe is a body" whose ornately decorated prow is its head that defends its safe passage. Although the scene then shifts in an unexpected direction, to the urban street in North America, Handler discovers a strikingly resonant conceit there. In his chapter on the twentieth-century history of traffic codes, pedestrians and cars come to be viewed as "vehicular units" that possess morally equal bodies. Negligence by either (as jaywalkers or reckless drivers) could result in their being held legally responsible for causing crashes. Lipset and Handler tie the emergence of these vehicle-metaphors to unrelated processes of technological and political history. Lipset looks to the prehistory of coastal Papua New Guinea while Handler discusses interest-group politics led by automobile insurance companies. Together they document that vehicles—canoes and cars—serve as an important trope for changing concepts of moral personhood in their respective settings.

Part II recalls the gendered image of British Naval ships as providing sailors support and protection on the high seas that we introduced above. In the first of its two chapters, Wayland analyzes meanings of the metaphor, "airplanes are women," as used by retired North American men who restore and fly World War II legacy warplanes. These vehicles, alternately viewed as affectionate, nurturing, and demanding, are decorated with erotic pinup art on their 'noses.' One restorer even allowed that airplanes had "menstrual periods" when several things went wrong with them at once, especially after long intervals of working well. Like Murik persons whose bodies are vehicularized, these men also think and talk about "women as airplanes." Wayland argues that the metaphoric gender of World War II airplanes serves broader historical and norms. And he goes on to draw a useful conclusion: the airplane-woman metaphor all but precluded restorers' consideration of the violence these vehicles once inflicted.

In Japan, as Roth then discusses, cars express moral differences between male and female. Not only do men and women drive different types of car; the way they are expected to drive them conforms to gender roles and stereotypes in the society at large. Men typically experience driving as an activity that frees them, if just temporarily, from the constraints of workaday masculinity. This possibility is embodied in the Mazda RX-8 or other sports cars, which are impractical for daily use but appeal to ideals of speed and power. In contrast to the sports car, the compact, or the even smaller K-car, typifies practicality. Women drive these tiny, fuel-efficient vehicles for shopping or to take children to and from school. Rather than providing a release from routine, K-cars tie women to domestic duties. No less than the "airplane as woman" metaphor, in other words, the homology between cars and gender maps out and sustains this moral status quo.

The chapters of Part III focus on cars in Serbia and China, as well as among Mexican-Americans and Afro-Americans in the United States, four cars that are all construed in terms of decidedly ambivalent attributes and sentiments. Though these vehicles represent quite distinct cultures, they make the general point that cars may express morally equivocal, rather than conservative or uniformly critical, views of the historical transformations through which they are driven.

Živković teases out multiple meanings in contemporary Serbia of the Fića, a little vehicle that is at once considered to be "kin" as well as a kind of souvenir of and for family history. In addition, the Fića has wider significance. It signifies the make-do *zeitgeist* of life in the former state of Yugoslavia, and for a kind of nostalgia about the present in which life is less given to reciprocity and has become more rationalized, and alien, than it is recalled to have been during the communist past.

If Serbian cars evoke nostalgia, and imply a critical view of the capitalist present, the careful investigation of images of cars in contemporary "capitalist" China that Notar carefully analyzes, suggest no love lost for the past as well as no straightforward commitment to the present. Here, as elsewhere, the human body can be vehicularized: a poor man is portrayed as a vehicle that transports wealthy elites who "ride" him. Or, cars may also be personified as gas-guzzling sports utility vehicles that caricature public officials. Yet, as more consumers in China become able to afford their own cars, cars are being morally differentiated between transgressive "public" cars that signify official corruption and "private" cars that belong to and signify the purposes of a rising middle class, recreational or otherwise.

The final pair of chapters focus on vehicles among two different minority groups in the United States. In Chappell's essay, which is an exegesis of lowrider automobiles that Mexican-Americans customize, ambivalences are conveyed about the status of Mexican-Americans on the outside of a dominant society. Concentrating on what he calls a "lowrider aesthetic sensibility," Chappell argues that these flamboyant cars should be viewed as rich and authentic expressions of the dual loyalties of Mexican-Americans. In lowrider iconography, Chappell perceives a "both-and" logic of identity in such problematic images as the Alamo chapel, as well as in a "Smile Now/Cry Later" motif that also seems to comment on moral contradictions in *barrio* life as well.

Lastly, Auslander recalls the Fića in contemporary Serbia, when he turns our attention to another trouble-prone, morally equivocal, vehicle, which, in his case, is a vintage Lincoln Town Car. This vehicle appears during an annual re-enactment of a 1946 mass lynching in the rural American south to transport four African-American victims to their deaths. Auslander argues that although the car evokes terrifying memories, its role in the reenactment nevertheless serves as a potent metaphor of moral redemption. Among its several references, the Town Car seems to convey the story of African-American martyrdom, from whose moral force no one can claim to be excused. That is, the immoral past is not gone by any means, but it is being reclaimed and remade by this vehicle, in addition to much else.

A Capacity to Move the Moral

At the beginning of this introduction, I suggested that by privileging the vehicle metaphor, we were adopting a position of methodological ambivalence with respect to the politics of representation, one that was not entirely given over to poststructural nihilism. Like the rainbow serpent of the Arunta, that is to say, vehicles serve as totemic metaphors for moral personhood in society and history. However, the way they do so combines action with collective forms of identity, nation, gender and the ancestors. Being manufactured, maintained, and driven, the moral reference of vehicles requires agency (Osgood [1957] 1978). By the same token, the cultural work of making vehicles metaphorically meaningful would seem to address an absence, lack, or indeterminacy of meaning that must be crossed, or remedied (Gibbs 1994: 124ff). Linguists have called this view of metaphor, the inexpressibility hypothesis (Fainsilber and Ortony 1989; Ortony 1975). But, as cultural anthropologists, we adhere to Durkheim. The lack between the vehicle and its signified is not just any lack, it is a lack in and of the social. Vehicle metaphors seem to convey moral *lacunae* of one sort or another in response to which something figural is done to imagine that transportation across the missing relationships is possible, if not necessarily secure. Vehicles thus carry shifting, often equivocal, viewpoints about moral identity in society, as well as the moral identity of society.

Now of course this collection is not meant to be encyclopedic. We do not, nor would we seek to, examine the moral signification of every kind of vehicle. No chapters, for example, on carts or trains are included in the volume, although both these vehicles call to mind two rather fundamental moments in Western moral imagination. I refer to the "road rage" of Oedipus, who inadvertently kills his father after they quarrel over right of way on the path to Thebes, or the railway cars now used as monumental metaphors in museum exhibits for the Holocaust. No, the ethnographic accounts that now follow are meant to evocative, not exhaustive. They are meant to indicate a little bit of the strong referential capacity of vehicles to convey the moral, whether in normative, contrary, egregious, or ambivalent registers.

NOTES

1. At the same time, of course, there are political and theoretical constituencies that continue to assert essentialist positions in which the real is unproblematic. The right insists that God, the state, patriarchy, and the family are immune from, and should not be infected by, global modernity. From their points of view, man and nature, man and technology, and territorial sovereignty remain distinct and dichotomous. Human agency remains unilateral and autonomous. The signifier refers to a signified rather than to a lack of one.
2. See also Levi-Strauss ([1962] 1966); Tambiah (1969); Gibbs (1994); Buchli (2002).
3. In contemporary theory, Glucksberg and McGlone (1999) also divide metaphors into constituent parts that they call the "metaphor topic" and "vehicle." The two may share "candidate properties" which determine meaning through a process of attribute identification and selection arising from the context of the utterance.
4. Sapir and Crocker (1977: 6) developed a view that metaphor consists of a process involving three constituent moments: departure, intermediary, and arrival, which again connotes an image of action and movement in a vehicle.
5. For example, in 2002, Jeremy Clarkson, "doyen of laddish commentary on motor matters," remained so annoyed about the German purchase of the Rolls-Royce company four years earlier that he was prompted to complain: "The whole point of the Rolls was the brylcreemed men in Crewe. German-built Rolls-Royces make as much sense as *sushi* at a Buckingham Palace garden party" (cited in Edensor 2004: 104).

REFERENCES

Barthes, Roland. (1963) 2002. "Mythologie de l'automobile: la voiture, projection de l'ego." Reprinted in *Oeuvres Completes*, vol. 2. Paris: Editions de Seuil.

Baudrillard, J. (1968) 2002. *The System of Objects*. Translated by James Benedict. London: Verso.

———. (1985) 1994. *Simulacra and Simulation*. Translated by Sheila Glaser. Ann Arbor: University of Michigan Press.

Bosquet, M. [Andre Gorz]. (1973) 1977. *Capitalism in Crisis and Everyday Life*. Translated by John Howe. Hassocks, Sussex: The Harvester Press.

Brottman, Mikita. 2001. *Car Crash Culture*. New York: Palgrave Press.

Buchli, V. 2002. *The Material Culture Reader*. Oxford: Berg.

Church, Roy. 1979. *Herbert Austin: The British Motor Industry to 1941*. London: Europa.

———. 1994. *The Rise and Decline of the British Motor Industry*. London: Macmillan.

Dant, Tim. 2004. "The Driver-Car." *Theory, Culture and Society* 21, no. 4/5: 61–79.

Durkheim, Emile. (1912) 1995. *The Elementary Forms of Religious Life.* Translated by Karen E. Fields. New York: The Free Press.

Edensor, Tim. 2004. "Automobility and National Identity: Representation, Geography and Driving Practice." *Theory, Culture and Society* 21, no. 4/5: 101–20.

Featherstone, Mike. 2004. "Automobilities: An Introduction." *Theory, Culture and Society* 21, no. 4/5: 1–24.

Gibbs, Raymond. 1994. *The Poetics of Mind: Figurative Thought, Language and Understanding.* New York: Cambridge University Press.

Glucksberg, Sam, and Mathew S. McGlone. 1999. "When Love Is Not a Journey: What Metaphors Mean." *Journal of Pragmatics* 31, no. 12: 1541–58.

Grinsell, L. V. 1957. "The Ferryman and His Fee: A Study in Ethnology, Archaeology and Tradition." *Folklore* 68, no. 1: 257–69.

Haraway, Donna. 1991. "A Cyborg Manifesto: Science, Technology and Socialist-Feminism in the Late Twentieth Century." In *Simians, Cyborgs and Women: The Reinvention of Nature*, edited by Donna Haraway, 149–82. New York: Routledge.

Hawkins, R. 1986. "A Road Not Taken: Sociology and the Neglect of the Automobile." *California Sociologist* 9, nos. 1–2: 61–79.

Fernandez, James.1986. *Persuasions and Performances: The Play of Tropes in Culture.* Bloomington: Indiana University Press.

Foreman-Peck, James, Sue Bowden, and Alan McKinley. 1995. *The British Motor Industry.* Manchester: Manchester University Press.

Ilouz, Eva.1997. *Consuming the Romantic Utopia: Love and the Cultural Contradictions of Capitalism.* Berkeley: University of California Press.

Inglis, David. 2004. "Auto Couture: Thinking the Car in Post-war France." *Theory, Culture and Society* 21, nos. 4/5: 197–219.

Kemp, Peter. 1976. *The Oxford Companion to Ships and the Sea.* Oxford: Oxford University Press.

Koshar, Rudy. 2004. "Cars and Nations: Anglo-German Perspectives on Automobility Between the World Wars." *Theory, Culture and Society* 21, nos. 4/5: 121–44.

Lakoff, George. 1993. "The Contemporary Theory of Metaphor." In *Metaphor and Thought*, edited by Andrew Ortony, 202–51. Cambridge: Cambridge University Press.

Lakoff, George, and Mark Johnson. (1980) 2004. *Metaphors We Live By.* Chicago: University of Chicago Press.

Lakoff, George, and Mark Turner. 1989. *More Than Cool Reason: A Field Guide to Poetic Metaphor.* Chicago: The University of Chicago Press.

Latour, Bruno. 1999. *Pandora's Hope: Essays on the Realities of Science Studies.* Cambridge, MA: Harvard University Press.

Levi-Strauss, Claude. (1962) 1966. *The Savage Mind.* Chicago: University of Chicago Press.

Lutz, Catherine, and Anne Lutz Fernandez. 2010. *Carjacked: The Culture of the Automobile & Its Effect on Our Lives.* New York: St. Martin's Press.

Marx, Karl, and Frederich Engels. (1888) 1969. "The Communist Manifesto." Reprinted in *Marx/Engels Selected Works,* vol. 1. Translated by Samuel Moore. Moscow: Progress Publishers.

Miller, Daniel. 2001. *Car Cultures.* New York: Berg.

Morris, C. W. 1938. *Foundations of the Theory of Signs.* Chicago: University of Chicago Press.

Morse, M. 1998. *Virtualities: Television, Media Art and Cyberculture.* Cambridge: Cambridge University Press.

Mulvey, Laura. 1993. "Thoughts on Theories of Fetishism in the Context of Contemporary Culture." *October* 65:3–20.

Munn, Nancy. 1973. "The Spatiotemporal Transformation of Gawan Canoes." *Journal de la Société des Océanistes* 33:39–52.

Nolan, Mary. 1994. *Visions of Modernity: American Business and the Modernization of Germany.* New York: Oxford University Press.

O'Connell, Sean. 1998. *The Car in British Society: Class, Gender and Motoring 1896–1939.* Manchester: Manchester University Press.

Ortner, Sherry. 1973. "On Key Symbols." *American Anthropologist* 75, no. 5: 1338–46.

Ortony, Andrew. 1975. "Why Metaphors Are Necessary and Not Just Nice." *Educational Theory* 25:45–53.

Ortony, Andrew, and Lynn Fainsilber.1989. "The Role of Metaphors in Descriptions of Emotions." In *Theoretical Issues in Natural Language Processing,* edited by Yorick Wilks, 181–84. Hillsdale, NJ: Erlbaum.

Osgood, Charles, G. J. U. Suci, and P. H. Tannenbaum. (1957) 1978. *The Measurement of Meaning.* Chicago: University of Illinois Press.

Petrilli, Susan. 2004. "From Pragmatic Philosophy to Behavioral Semiotics: Charles W. Morris after Charles S. Peirce." *Semiotica* 148, no. 1/4: 277–315.

Richards, I. A. 1936. *The Philosophy of Rhetoric.* London: Oxford University Press.

Richardson, Kenneth. 1977. *The British Motor Industry, 1896–1939: A Social and Economic History.* London: Macmillan.

Rodgers, Sylvia. 1984. "Feminine Power at Sea." *RAIN* 64:2–4.

Sapir, J. David, and J. Christopher Crocker. 1977. *The Social Use of Metaphor: Essays on the Anthropology of Rhetoric.* Philadelphia: University of Pennsylvania Press.

Sedgwick, Michael. 1970. *Cars of the 1930s.* London: B. T. Batsford.

Seidel, George J. 2000. *Knowledge as Sexual Metaphor.* Cranbury, NJ: Associated University Presses.

Sheller, Mimi, and James Urry. 2000. "The City and the Car." *International Journal of Urban and Regional Research* 24:737–57.

Spencer, Baldwin, and F. J. Gillen. (1899) 2010. *Native Tribes of Central Australia.* Cambridge: Cambridge University Press.

Tambiah, Stanley. 1969. "Animals are Good to Think and Good to Prohibit." *Ethnology* 7:423–59.
Terpening, Ronnie. 1985. *Charon and the Crossing: Ancient, Medieval, and Renaissance Transformations of a Myth.* Lewisburg, PA: Bucknell University Press.
Thrift, N. 1996. *Spatial Formations.* London: Sage.
Tilly, Christopher Y. 1999. *Metaphor and Material Culture.* Oxford: Blackwell Publishers.
Turner, Victor. 1975. "Symbolic Studies." *Annual Review of Anthropology* 4: 145–61.
Urry, John. 2000. *Sociology Beyond Societies.* London: Routledge.
———. 2004. "The 'System' of Automobility." *Theory, Culture and Society* 21, nos. 4/5: 25–39.
van Gennep, Arnold. (1914) 1960. *The Rites of Passage.* Translated by M. B. Vizedom and G. L. Caffee. Chicago: University of Chicago Press.
Wheelwright, Philip. 1962. *Metaphor and Reality.* Bloomington: Indiana University Press.
Whorf, Benjamin Lee, and John B. Carroll. (1939) 1964. "The Relation of Habitual Thought and Behavior to Language." Reprinted in *Language, Thought and Reality,* edited by John B. Carroll, 134–69. Cambridge, MA: MIT Press.
Žižek, Slavoj. 1989. *The Sublime Object of Ideology (Phronesis).* New York: Verso.

PART I

Persons as Vehicles

CHAPTER 1

Living Canoes
Vehicles of Moral Imagination among the Murik of Papua New Guinea

David Lipset

Utilizing Bourdieu's concept of *habitus* (1977) I make two related ethnographic-theoretic points in this chapter. First, it orients my discussion of how canoes are metaphorically deployed as moral bodies among the Murik of Papua New Guinea (PNG). And then second, I adapt it to elucidate a characteristically postcolonial circumstance, namely, how this local *habitus* informs the way modernity is perceived and morally evaluated.

To begin: a brief methodological aside about *habitus*. It consists in self-evident, routine practices, forms of comportment, and commonsensical assumptions or ideas through which actors unconsciously reproduce fields of inequality in society. Now I admire Bourdieu's theoretical ingenuity and solution to the problem of structure and agency that provoked its invention. I no less endorse the virile analytical register in which he privileges action and embodiment in the *habitus*. Still, as I indicated above, I must modify the boundaries of Bourdieu's view of agency and structure, and not insubstantially so.

As I go on to show, long before the invention of the automobile, the body was imagined in composite terms that were not somatic. In Murik, we will see that the body takes the form of a canoe that transports its subject-passenger. The embodied person, acting in his or her *habitus*, is not necessarily a physical, or a physically self-evident, being but must admit the influence of a third idea, namely, material culture (see Urry 2000). I want to claim that the polyvalent concept of automobility does not go far enough in its conception of the "driver-car." In Murik, the body is understood as an assemblage, and action, in particular, is not merely habitually embodied in its vehicle. It is indivisibly a vehicle for the subject who cannot be understood separately from it.

If the body need not be a physically bounded entity, its *habitus* may not necessarily be synonymous or isomorphic with its society (Ignatow 2009: 99). Instead of embodied actors moving in a single *habitus* (cf. Abu-Lughod 1989 and Starrett 1995), actors will be seen to act in vehicles in plural *habituses*, those in their non-capitalist culture and of postcolonial modernity. Living in a double, and discontinuous, pair of *habituses*, I argue, the Murik desire to encompass modern vehicles within what they continue to regard as their own moral categories, which is to say that their relationship to the two *habituses* is contradictory: self-evident yet emergent. A discursive effort is made to compose one in terms of the other. It fails: the Murik vehicle-body does not succeed to construct the postcolonial world in its entirety.

To develop this view of the vehicle-body in discordant, plural *habituses* and societies, I first turn to the body in the Murik *habitus*. Here, the body is a vehicle that transports the subject-passenger in society and space. I trace this distinctive notion back in regional prehistory, where I fix its source in the Austronesian *habitus*, the Austronesians being mariners from insular Southeast Asia who voyaged to Melanesian shores in outrigger canoes some 4,000 years ago, before moving on to settle the islands that became Polynesia some 3,000 years later (Kirch 2010). To begin, I therefore trace the regional setting of this metaphor in insular Southeast Asia. I then introduce the Murik *habitus*, which bears an uncanny resemblance to that of the Austronesians. Lastly, I discuss contemporary Murik usages of canoe metaphors within the modern *habitus* in order to argue that the cultural significance of vehicles in Murik is part of a wider, trans-Pacific discourse that seeks to make modernity in its own image in the aftermath of colonial subordination and now in the midst of global encroachments.

The Austronesian *Habitus*

In a useful historical survey of the pre-colonial, or very early colonial, Austronesian *habitus* in insular Southeast Asia, Manguin arrives at the conclusion that in addition to its maritime functions, "the boat" served as "a metaphor for the ordered social group" (1986: 187; see also Ballard et al. 2003: 390; Crumlin-Pedersen and Thye 1995). Today, for example, the husband, elder brother, and masculinity are all called "rudder" and "aft" in Eastern Indonesia. In the southeast Moluccas, villages continue to be arranged around centrally placed stone enclosures or platforms that are shaped like canoes decorated with carved prows. These "stone canoes" represent the original settlement of its ancestors; they signify a community grounded in terrestrial space (de Jonge and van Dijk 1995). On Sawu, Kei, and Tanimbar Islands, leaders have assigned seats in literal boats, a pattern replicated in canoe-shaped meeting spaces that are complete with "prows and sterns." The Malay Sultanates were "fond of fully fledged boat metaphors to express their own perception" of the state (Manguin 1986: 193). Perak Malays viewed the

> *negeri* explicitly as a ship, with the ruler as her captain … and some of the ministers as members of the crew: they were said to be as the mate … whose station is forward, as the helmsman … , i.e., sitting nearest to the part of the ship occupied by the Raja, … as the poler of the ship, or as "the person who bales the ship if she leaks" … i.e. who removes any danger threatening the country (Manguin 1986:193).

If boats were metaphors for the body politic at all scales of the Austronesian *habitus,* they also appear to have informed shifts in social status. The *tampan* "ship cloths" of the Lampung region in South Sumatra are used in rites of passage as a "concrete symbol of conveyance to a new state of being" (Gittinger 1972: 202). The metonymic deployment of ships as vehicles of transition was also applied to the "movement" undergone during divination rites in which shamans "travel" in search of the spirit of a supplicant (Gittinger 1972: 63). With reference to death, boat burials were widespread, boats and coffins being called by the same word in Java. The "ship of the dead" or the "flying ship," whether a proper coffin or a scale-model, was loaded down with images—of toothy monsters, the hornbill, the chthonian snake, among others—that invoked cosmological order. Additionally, boats for the dead were no less associated with rank and perhaps gender than in the society of the living. In Borneo, the Kayan people built large wooden structures on poles, in which a deceased chief, his followers and slaves were placed, together with his war canoe (Crystal 1985: 142–43; Manguin 1986: 197).

Ship metaphor clearly informed a range of contexts and media in the Austronesian-speaking world. In Tanimbar, ritual dances are staged in the shape of a canoe, and songs celebrate the canoe mapped on the ground. One of the lead dancers announces its name and is himself called its "prow" (McKinnon 1988: 163). Canoe metaphors are also applied to objects. "Houses … are either described in terms of the structure of a ship or fashioned after the form of ships" (Ballard et al. 2003: 391). The Malay *puan,* or *sirih* (container), is used in marriage rites, particularly those of ranked persons. The term *puan* does not refer to a canoe; but the vessel-like container is often fitted with a kind of rack called *dandan*, a term that also refers to the prow and stern platforms on local canoes. Betelnut containers are referred to as canoes in Bali and Old Javanese. Bronze Dong Son drums produced in the Red River Delta in northern Vietnam and southern China beginning about 600 BC were decorated with friezes of scenes featuring canoes and warriors wearing elaborate feather head-dresses. Textiles, tattoos, combs, and head ornaments also featured ancestors in canoes. Zoomorphic images associated with ship forms appearing in rock art or on prow and stern designs included lizards, crocodiles, and birds. And rock art that features "the ship of dead appears to be associated with the distribution of Austronesian-speaking particularly in the Moluccas and along the coastline of Western New Guinea" (Ballard et al. 2003: 395).

All of which is to say this: boats shaped meaning in the Austronesian *habitus*. They signified the moral body—in marriage, siblingship, descent, rank and leadership, community, the state, as well as in cosmological transitions of the subject. And it is to say that vehicle imagery was extended to material culture, whose objects thus became associated with moral bodies as well. There is one final, but crucial point, one which McKinnon has labeled a "puzzling contradiction in terms" (1988: 152), to be made about the Austronesian *habitus*.

Throughout the Indonesian archipelago, boats voyaged both at sea and on the land. I mentioned that houses and village space were constructed and imagined as boats. The ritual centers of many villages were also marked by stone monuments associated with ancestors, cosmological powers, and boats—petrified on the land. To a certain degree, power was understood as sustaining a relationship between attributes of maritime and terrestrial vehicles. However, according to McKinnon, the guarantor of their meaning, their fixed point of reference, stemmed from the relationship between the landed, stone boats, and the maritime ones (1988: 158). That is, the latter "anchor," and provide a permanent space of occupancy and access point to ancestral power by uniting the ancestors with their living descendants as the crew of the same metaphoric boat.[1] But this relationship can only be realized through the voyaging process. "Between the sailing boat and the stone boat there lies an essential dialectic—which is central to Tanimbarese culture—between mobile and immobilized states of existence" (McKinnon 988: 167).

When Austronesian seafarers voyaged from island Southeast Asia to seaboard Melanesia,[2] the version of the boat *habitus* they took with them is a matter of conjecture (see Bellwood, Fox, and Tryon 1995). However, their influence on Melanesians is clear, if somewhat elusive.[3] Drawing from linguistic, ceramic, and genetic data, Kirch has argued that "intrusive populations not only interacted with pre-existing ... communities, but intermarried with them as well" (2010: 137). On beaches, archaeologists have discovered remains of large settlements, a diversified marine/horticultural economy, as well as Lapita, their famous ceramics (see Kirch 1996; Allen 1996). That the Austronesians brought vehicle technology with them is attested by detailed reconstructions of Proto Oceanic vocabulary and culture, from which I take an important datum: canoes were called *wangka* (Pawley and Pawley 1993; see also Doran 1981).[4]

The Murik Lakes people, to whom I now turn, seem to have been relative latecomers to the north coast of New Guinea, the heartland of Austronesian influence in this region (Swadling 1997, 2010; Lipset 1985). They certainly did not encounter the Austronesian mariners, but rather established overseas, hereditary trade relations, called "routes" or, today, "roads" with their descendants (see Handler, this volume). Nevertheless, Murik represent an exemplary, if not the quintessential, case of a non-Austronesian speaking (Laycock 1973), seaboard culture that not only adopted the Austronesian boat *habitus* but was given to elaborate upon it.

Wankau and the Murik *Habitus*

The Murik Lakes are a big coastal system of mangrove lagoons located just to the west of the mouth of the Sepik River, on the north coast of PNG. The five Murik villages (total population, approximately 3,000) are built on the narrow barrier beaches that divide that Pacific Ocean from their shallow mangroves (Lipset 2011). In 1988, I collected a version of the "Two Brothers" legend. Vincent Tanep told me the story, and, among other things, it seemingly acknowledges the influence of Austronesian-speaking peoples upon indigenous residents of this area. Two spirit-men appear in the tale as elder brother, whom Tanep called Wankau, and Arena, his younger brother. The plot turns on the cuckolding of Wankau, either due to his wife's seduction of, or her seduction by, the younger brother. Either way, Wankau pursues Arena, after he takes flight, seeking retribution. The elder brother visits village after village in the region on the trail of his sibling. While the story admits of tensions in social life, as I say, it also seems to recognize the acquisition and significance of Austronesian technology, whose key vehicle, *wangka,* is introduced to the Murik *habitus* by the vengeful hero. Vincent Tanep allowed that

> Wankau went ashore at [the hamlets today called] Kaup. He gave us the first outrigger canoe, also named Wankau, which was his canoe, as well as the magic to build it . . . He gave us names for other canoes, their prows and ornaments. He explained to us how to trade with the islanders. "They are just like you," he said. "I have made them just like you already."

Now, during the early postcolonial moment, perhaps some readers might be skeptical about my assertion that the Murik go on living in the Austronesian *habitus* that Wankau, the elder brother-spirit, gave them. But their contemporary economy (1981–2011) still consists of aquatic foraging, intertribal visiting trade, and a small-scale fishery, all of which involves dugout canoe- and boat-based work. And culturally, whether Christian or animist, they continue to know themselves as "spirits" (*nabran*) who travel through the region in "canoe-bodies" (*gai'iin*).

This concept, of a transported subject moving through society and the environment in a vehicle, also has a second meaning. While the significance of the *body as canoe* metaphor is no less widespread in Murik than it was in prehistoric Austronesian cultures, in Murik the canoe is also a body. This is to say, the body is a canoe and vice versa: the *canoe is a body*. Action occurs in a canoe-*habitus:* choices are made and intensions pursued that reproduce this construction of culture and society (Figure 1.1). I will first discuss the *body as canoe* vector of this metaphor in Murik totemism (see Lipset 2005), where it appears in unambiguous terms.

Figure 1.1. Murik canoes docked along the shore of at a rural market off the Sepik River, August 2012. Photo: David Lipset.

Body as Canoe

Murik society was and is made up of cognatic lineages and ritual matrilineages and patrilineages. Proprietors of the latter used to keep large, wooden masks of ancestor-spirits (*brag sebug*) in their houses, masks they propitiated with food and tobacco in return for magical guardianship. The extended, phallic noses and powerful foreheads of the masks, by which motifs they are today well-known in primitive art circles, cannot be said to suggest that a realist orientation guided the representation of these spirits in this cosmology. Nevertheless, *brag* masks were unadorned in their pre-state forms, except for a single, zoomorphic figure, which might have been carved with a degree of dimensionality up and down the middle of their foreheads (Figure 1.2). If the mask was understood "to be" the "face" of the ancestor-spirit, this latter figure was said to be a second part of his body. The forehead figure was called the "canoe" (*gai'iin*) in which the spirit traveled through space.[5]

In the pre-state, pre-Christian era, what measure of "being" was attributed to this image? Was the bird imagined to be the literal "canoe" of the spirit, or was it a carved *representation* of its "canoe"? The bird was both, from what I can gather. On the one hand, the forehead figure was (and remains) distinguished from its spirit. That is, in the case of Dama'ii, the *brag* spirit depicted in Figure 1.2, the little black cormorant (*munimunik*) carved on the forehead, is said to be a "canoe" for that spirit, rather than Dama'ii himself. However, on the other hand, the bird is not said to be a mere representation of, or vehicle for, the ancestor, but rather the ancestor itself. In these two senses, the bird was simultaneously a vehicle

Figure 1.2. Dama'ii Mask. Photo: David Lipset, 1982.

for and an embodiment of the *brag*'s spirit. Today, I would venture to say, Murik men emphasize its analogic properties: how the spirit's "canoe" provides it with the same sort of agency afforded to and exerted by human beings in the canoes they build and use in daily work. The spirit, Dama'ii, may fly through space in his waterbird "canoe" in the way a wooden dugout transports people through water (see Lipset 1997: 192–94).

Both spirits and people move through their *habitus* in canoes for moral purposes. When traveling in and about the Murik Lakes or elsewhere in the region, the zoomorphic "canoe" of a spirit might appear and convey a warning or a message of support to its kin. Should a member of Dama'ii's lineage travel by canoe—for example, to visit kin—and see this bird "canoe" flying in a contrary direction, or see it perched along the way, he or she might conclude it prudent to turn back, either because to proceed was hazardous or because the kinsman was not home. By contrast, should the bird fly in front of or follow his canoe, then one might be encouraged that his or her way was secure and people were expecting and prepared for the visit.[6]

In addition to the signifying powers of their "canoes," the *brag* spirits possessed warriors and imbued them with military agency. Before war parties departed, mothers' brothers brought masks to the Male Cult Hall, where they "fed" them tobacco and a ceremonial porridge (*aragen*). One of the spirits might then possess a senior man, his trance-state being likened to "setting out in a canoe; one has to get into it (Figure 1.3). And so the ... [spirit] 'gets into' the *gai'in*—to tell about the future events and exploits" (Tamoane 1977: 176).[7] Shamans were thus called "canoes." But warriors were also said to be "canoes" for spirits who possessed them prior to battle (Lipset 1997). That is, their aggression was construed as an ego-alien state of being which they entered into by voyaging out of the domestic *habitus* (see also Harrison 1993). In 1982, Anenbi of Darapap village told me a story about the first time two brothers called Bwase and Kabaga went into battle with their father:

> Before leaving, their mother's brother gave them spears and bespelled the brothers with the magic of Painse and Tarego [their *brag* spirits]. The youth put two birds in baskets in the Male Cult Hall, named the birds after their *brag* spirits, and paddled off with their father and the war party.
>
> Kabaga went to one side of a channel and Bwase climbed up the other. They began to throw spears and called, "Painse! Tarego!" the names of their war spirits, as they did. After a time, they switched sides of the canal and went on killing and yelling [the names of their *brag* spirits].

Figure 1.3. Human canoe-bodies getting into a second canoe, 1988. Photo: David Lipset.

> "Let a canoe go home to beat the slit-drum and tell the story!" their father finally screamed. But the two boys ignored him and went on attacking.
>
> A few rear canoes escaped and fled back to their village.

In this episode, the two boys name the birds after war spirits to augment their magical agency. The birds make them nimble, while their namesakes, the *brag* spirits, make them fierce and invulnerable. The boys do not listen to their father because, having become vehicles for, that is to say, having become possessed by, the spirits, their ears have been "closed" to the voices of others. They thus call the names of their *brag* spirits when they spear the enemy, the enemy who is also referred to as a "canoe," a vehicle of human communication, one of which should be allowed to return home to "tell the story." The story thus becomes an effective précis of several points about the construction of moral agency in this *habitus*: body and subject are imagined as a canoe. They travel, communicate, and may be possessed by spirits who take them to war. Lastly, some spirits, at least, also have a mimetic, but still vehicular, association with the agency of birds.

Upon returning home from a successful raid, a celebration might ensue. *Brag* masks might then be attached to conical cane scaffoldings and decorated with dogs' teeth headbands and shell ornament vests, as well as a leafy bunting. A masker would position himself inside the scaffolding so that it rested on his shoulders; the framework was called a "spirit canoe" (*brag gai'iin*) (see Figure 1.4).[8] However ritually charged, the person then enacted a completely ordinary practice: he became a double canoe, a canoe transporting a canoe. During this victory celebration, the masker's body was no longer just a "canoe" for his own spirit. In the moment, his body, a "canoe-body," bore the "canoe"—the scaffolding—for his war spirit-mask.

The colonial administration "pacified" the Sepik estuary during the years just prior to World War I. In 2001, this intricate, redundant concept of vehicular embodiment was no longer staged in honor of military victory. Moreover, the mask spirits no longer possessed people.[9] But, as I say, Murik men and women routinely climb into canoes and paddle through the lakes to fish, gather other resources, or visit kin (Figures 1.1 and 1.3).

Clearly, canoes carry a surplus of meanings that define or inform embodiment in the Murik *habitus*. Recall Manguin's conclusion that the "boat" served as a metaphor for an ordered social group in the Austronesian *habitus*. Similarly, heads of Murik lineages are called "canoes" for the sacred, corporate insignia (*sumon*) they are said to "steer." In large measure, their control consists in staging rites of passage and reconciliation that bring the moral body together around these *sacra* and figures of canoes. The platform on which a retiring insignia holder is seated together with kin and affines is built and partly decorated with paddles to invoke a canoe (see Lipset 1997: 128). Within the lineage, five siblings are sometimes called a "canoe" by parents, of whom the first-born may be referred to his father's or mother's "canoe-prow son/daughter"

Figure 1.4. A mask mounted on a cane "canoe" frame, 2008. Photo: David Lipset.

(*gai'kev goan/ngasen*). A husband may refer to his wife as his "canoe" or his "outrigger float." A group of initiates, upon being released from isolation in the Male Cult House, come outside decorated in lineage ornaments are also called a "canoe." A dance troupe, moreover, that enters a performance ground is led by its "canoe prow."

The canoe is not only a metaphor for moral relationships and collectivities; I also want to argue that it signifies uncertainty aroused upon traversing moral boundaries. That is, the canoe expresses the ambiguity that mobility through social space creates. The residents, for example, who live at the tip of a small peninsula that is most vulnerable to the sea in one village is said both to be and to reside on its "canoe prow." If canoe-bodies are exposed to the edges of moral space in this way, it is interesting that many objects are also understood as "canoes," or to possess their attributes. The handles of the big wooden slit-drums—which are given personal names and are understood to be subjects who communicate with kin—are called "prows" (*kev*). Moreover, the handles of hand drums, bowls, plates and headrests are all called "prows" as well. Like canoe-prows, these handles are decorated by the canoe-bodies in which ancestor-spirits in their anthropo- and zoomorphic canoe-bodies travel as guardians of their human kin. In short, they are inscribed by a cluster, or flotilla, of moral bodies that would protect the subject from the perils of action—sleeping, eating, and performance. In Murik, the body is not just a "canoe" that travels; the body also carries a subject, a spirit. That is to say, Murik people view the canoe both as a literal vehicle as well as an ordinary and extraordinary mode of *reflexivity*. If its vehicularity constitutes a *habitus* of action, it is also a discourse about the vulnerability of embodiment.

In the *body as canoe* metaphor, zoomorphic, masked, and human "canoes" ferry spirits through space for moral purposes. They provide agency that protect and support kin. It is also the case, however, that canoes are bodies. "The canoe is a man," an informant once said while discussing the etiquette of visiting trade according to which it should dock bearing goods. If so, I will now reverse figure and ground.

Canoe as Body

Just as human bodies are vehicularized, so canoes are personified in Murik thought. They have "stomachs" (*sar*) which are their interiors. The stomach has a "belly button" (*sapwera'kap*), which is rendered by a triangular motif incised on the forward floor. They have two "hands" (*gai'bubaug*), short strakes that run lengthwise along either side of the upper exterior hull for a yard or so from the prow and are meant to keep water out. Most significantly, they have heads, which are their prows (see also Wayland, this volume). Of the two main types of dugout canoes—lineage owned, ocean-going outriggers; and lake canoes—the Murik differentiate the latter by their prow designs (*gai'kev*). One is called the "Fog Man Nose" (*Wau Nor Da'ur*), while the other is known as the "Lizard" (*Jagreb*) (Figure 1.5). The two prows duplicate each other along the exterior hull and I have elsewhere discussed the details of the bird and teeth motifs that appear there in an exegesis of the "Fog Man" design (Lipset 2005). Here, I just focus on the eponymous chain of figures on the Lizard prow, a chain that portrays, with sublime virtuosity, precisely what I have been arguing about the vehicular construction of the moral body in the Murik *habitus*.

What the Lizard prow confirms is this: canoes are not inert, value-neutral objects but they possess embodiments and capabilities that make them no less moral than sentient human spirits. No less than human beings, they are canoe-bodies. A condensed, complex conceit about the capacities and attributes of the embodied person is given a graphic expression here, of which the most obvious, yet perhaps most elusive, idea is that canoes, like people, possess multiple canoe-bodies. The prow depicts an ardent, tried-and-true world of a morally supportive, enchanted enchainment of vehicles (see Wayland, this volume).

How is virtue secured, according to the Lizard prow? Moral agency is made up of interconnected canoe-bodies bound together by common descent and technology. As he or she makes his or her way through the

Figure 1.5. Lizard canoe prow, 1988. Photo: David Lipset.

dangerous space of the other, a human subject, the passenger-spirit who appears seated inside the canoe prow, is protected by a flotilla of ancestor-spirits. Of course, it would be analytically naïve to fail to acknowledge that as a nodal point of signification, the Lizard prow embodies and expresses a desire, if only to prevent unbound, untied elements of meaning from floating away. But before turning to an exegesis of this implicit desire, which is perhaps its starting point, I want to look at the visible imagery on the Lizard prow thoroughly.

From the inside-out, rather than from the oblique angle depicted in Figure 1.5, a human figure (which has male genitalia in some versions of this prow) appears sitting in the canoe. Facing toward its interior where passengers sit, he has a short, humanoid nose, as if he were everyman, a passenger. The lizard's tail extends down his forehead to the bridge of his nose. The association of the lizard figure both to the man but also to the canoe now becomes explicit: its legs grip the gunwales. The head of the lizard faces outward; its eyes gaze abroad. The tail of a small bird attaches itself to the lizard's nose. The bird's head also gazes outward and is engraved as a forehead motif on a *brag* spirit-mask that has been carved into the tip of the prow, its eyes no less wide open than the man's, the lizard's, and the bird's. Bird motifs are duplicated on either side of the prow, adding more eyes to the task of surveillance.[10]

Given the Murik *habitus*, the meaning of the Lizard prow could hardly be mistaken for anything less than a graphic statement about what is inside the "head" of the canoe-body. Depicted here is an image of a transubstantial relationship of humanoid spirits to their zoomorphic vehicles, in other words, an image of ancestor-spirits riding through space in multiple canoe-bodies. This is no image of a nodal point on the land that may guarantee stability to sea voyagers at risk as we see in the stone canoes of Tanimbar (McKinnon 1988) or on canoe prow imagery in the Solomon Islands (Tilly 2002: 36). Rather, the Lizard prow is a figure of human mobility, of vehicular transition, somatic transformation but, above all else, of a head full of eyes watching, gazing, or "plunging," as Foucault once remarked about a different context, "into the space that it has given itself the task of traversing" (1973: 133). What is fixed in this image is not the land, but a multiplicity of eyes deciphering the moral character of space, reckoning whether it harbors, or will harbor, friend or foe.

A word about the risks of pre-state travel in the lakes. The neighboring inland, horticultural groups with whom the Murik exchanged fish for garden produce were also enemies—as were, for that matter, certain rival factions on the Murik coast (Lipset 1985). The Hobbesian context of *warre* posed the moral question that the Lizard prow answered, a question that continues to be asked when the wooden hull of a new canoe is singed with fire to seal and waterproof it. A mock battle scene may then be staged. In 1982 the "lakes people," played by a group of young boys dressed up in battle decorations, blackened their faces with soot. They sang loudly as they took the new canoe into the water. On shore, a second group of boys, the "land people," waded out and tried to tip it over. This was play. But it was also a performance that commemorated the moral uncertainty that crossing lacustrine boundaries once entailed.

If totemic combine with human spirits in the Lizard prow to safeguard the canoe from the dangers of travel, its imbricated imagery, and its imagery of imbrication, expresses the social and symbolic instability of the transition (van Gennep 1960: 15f). Zoomorphic motifs are bound together with humanoid ones in labile, figure-ground reversals. The prow does not depict a morally certain body, but one oriented toward a condition, like birth and dying, of being unfinished. That is to say, it evokes a human subject, sentient, generative, moving through space, transgressing its boundaries. This is not the head of a body that is "differentiated from the world, but [one that] is transferred, merged and fused with it" (Bakhtin 1984: 339). Its abundant imagery is thus both sensible, yet extraordinary. It merges with the other; the other is assimilated into it. Its agency defies the closed, impenetrable surface of the jural body. It is a body becoming, rather than complete and separate. The Lizard prow acknowledges moral uncertainty and insecurity, on the one hand, and expresses a desire for mastery, on the other. Mastery through what? Through a fleet of allied canoe-bodies, their eyes wide open.

The Murik and the Austronesian Habitus

Thus far, I have argued that the Murik canoe *habitus* was thoroughly influenced by the *habitus* brought to Melanesian shores by the Austronesian voyagers. I would also suggest that the ethic of support and protection, and the vehicular constitution of the social, was motivated, or at least subverted, by an apprehension of uncertainty and vulnerability that the very mobility and agency their vehicles made possible. While the Austronesian and the Murik *habituses* closely resemble one another, I want to suggest an important distinction between one and the other before going on to discuss the contemporary moment.

In light of Bourdieu's high opinion of non-reflective action, what is curious about the Murik canoe *habitus* is that action is not automatic and unreflexive, but apprehends itself. The canoe metaphor entails a kind of ethno-semiosis. It accounts for the movement of meaning from signifier to signified. It is a metaphor, that is to say, for metaphoricity. As temporary passengers, spirits are habitually transported across moral boundaries in canoe-bodies for moral purposes, which semantic movement they recognize.

Unlike metaphor theory and semiotics whose broad project may in general be said to be motivated by abstract, or perhaps bureaucratic, desire—for intellectual or scientific mastery (see, e.g., Jakobson 1956), the canoe meta-metaphor explicitly derives from the social. It is aroused by a desire for collective agency and moral integration that is jeopardized by the moral boundaries it traverses, boundaries where that self-same agency and integration are called into question. The *habitus* of Murik canoe-bodies is challenged by the vulnerability to which the mobility it affords gives rise. The canoe-body opens up a moral *aporia*, a discontinuity that it cannot suture. It is paradoxical: it exposes an irreducible void, an unobtainable something, whose symptoms are moral identity, agency, and a saturation of enchanted meanings (Žižek 1989). Thus the exquisite Lizard prow involves a dense relational-differential interplay, quilted together by figure-ground reversals. But the presence it asserts is absent, the moral emptiness in the water it cuts through. What lies beyond the prow must remain an unknown other that cannot be negated because it escapes metaphoric accessibility. The prow denies but reveals this fundamental lack in the Murik subject, a lack beyond its prow. The pervasiveness of this paradox throughout the Murik *habitus* attests to its utter significance in Murik identity. This significance is confirmed by the contemporary deployment of canoe imagery in the ambient Melanesian modernity, a modernity that has given rise to vulnerable passages crossing new moral boundaries, but also gives rise to one and the same desire—that Murik passenger-spirits be protected from vulnerability.

"Canoes" in a Melanesian Modernity

No less than their lakes, the Murik view the *habitus* of Wewak, the provincial capital and market town located about 40 miles west along the coast, as involving movement and travel in canoe-bodies, canoe-bodies that are functionally similar to indigenous ones in that both transport passengers through space. Both require power and the agency of a driver. Both constitute a temporary relationship among passengers who join together in a temporal sequence of boarding, departing, traveling, arriving and disembarking from a vehicle. Now, the Murik recognize that their canoe metaphor is imperfect. More often than not, persons travel among strangers rather than kin in town. Passengers must pay a fare when riding buses. On the one hand, they express ambivalence about urban canoes. Urban

Murik spare no effort to find rides from kin or friends who have cars. On the other, they charge fares to ferry both kin and nonkin to and from Wewak town in the small, 19–23 foot fiberglass boats that replaced lineage-owned outriggers in the 1990s. What is more, the safety of the former on the open seas is no longer seen to depend upon local agency and personhood, e.g., upon ancestor spirits traveling in zoomorphic canoes or the chastity of the helmsman's wife, as the safety of sailing outriggers once did. Rather, the passage of boats is understood in secular-rational terms. There must be sufficient gasoline, engine maintenance, sparkplugs and, not least, a skilled driver. Nonetheless, the Murik have imported modern vehicles, cars, canoes, and airplanes into their pre-existing vernacular category, not exactly with the detail that the Apache used to refer to automobile parts as limbs and organs (Basso 1967), or to the extent that the Kewa of the PNG Highlands have also done (Franklin 2003), but as the basis for a general folk taxonomy.

The Murik differentiate among canoes, ships, cars, and airplanes in the way that they differentiate among their own dugouts, by function, size, and owner. The fiberglass boats powered by outboard motors are simply called "canoes" (*gai'iin*) of course. But likewise, larger passenger or tourist boats, tuna trawlers, and timber ships that anchor in Wewak harbor are also called "canoes" and are distinguished by these same three criteria. The Fokker 100s and the Dash-8 airplanes in which Air Niugini transports people and cargo to Boram Airport in Wewak are "bird canoes" (*pise gai'iin*).[11] And all the cars and trucks that clog the roads in town are "modern, white man's canoes" (*yabar gai'iin*). In Wewak in 2008, I saw a bus, owned by a Murik man, transporting fare-paying passengers about town. He had emblazoned Diskum, a lineage outrigger-canoe name, in large green and yellow letters on its hood, its "prow" (Figure 1.6). This semantic extension and the canoe taxonomy, I would argue, expresses an involuntary desire to sustain the Murik *habitus* where it is being impugned, invalidated, and repudiated by modernity.

Another expression of this desire caught my attention in September 2008. A festival was then staged in Wewak by the East Sepik Province in honor of the Prime Minister, Sir Michael Somare's 40th year in PNG politics. Now Sir Michael is universally recognized as one of the "founding fathers" of the postcolonial state. He is both a native son of the region, and, more importantly for my purposes in this chapter, Murik (Somare 1975).

Some thirty-five or more villages sent dance troupes to stage performances in his honor. Arapesh, Abelam, and Iatmul were among the Sepik groups represented. Schouten Islands groups, among others, also found their way to Wewak for the event. No less than five Murik villages had dispatched troupes where they were joined by an urban troupe. Each Murik

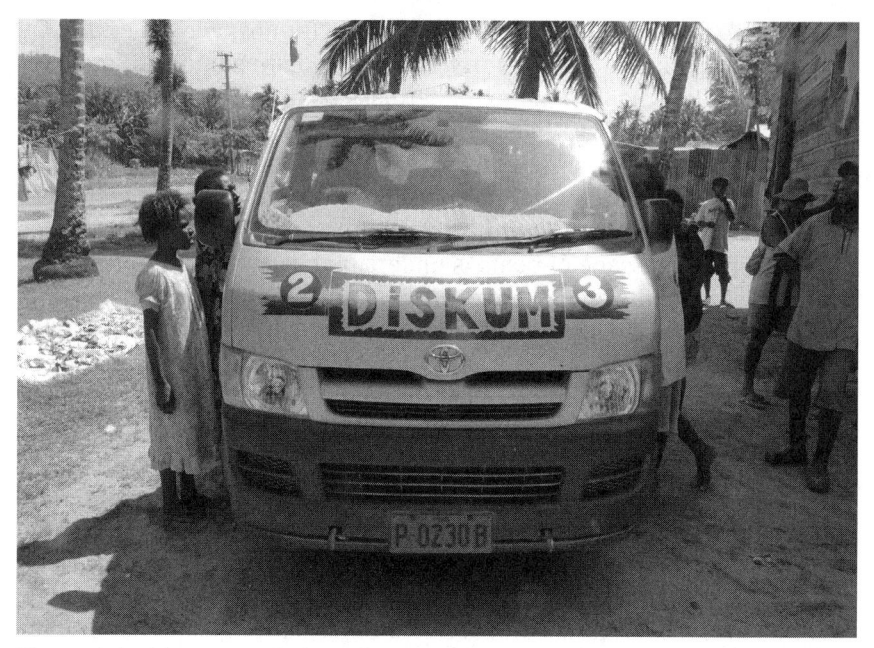

Figure 1.6. A bus named after a lineage outrigger. Photo: David Lipset, 2010.

group rehearsed a different show of course. The village of Mendam had resolved to present the prime minister with several gifts at the climax of the festivities, the centerpiece of which was to be a model outrigger canoe (*bun gai'iin;* see Figure 1.7).[12] In the days prior to the show, I paid several visits to "Number Two Bay," one of the peri-urban camps where employed Murik live permanently or board while marketing, visiting kin, or getting medical care, to watch the preparations and rehearsals.

Mendam men told me about their intentions with gusto. They brought out the delicate little outrigger, which had been covered with a sheet of plastic, so I could photograph it. Its construction had clearly received detailed attention. They pointed out its twin prows, each of which represented one of the "Two Brothers," whose narrative I cited as evidence of Austronesian influence earlier in this chapter. The model canoe, they now declared, was a reproduction of Wankau, the first Murik canoe, which took its name from the elder brother who had given its design to their ancestors.

I went to the dance ground on the day of the Somare Festival. Dance troupes began to off-load themselves from big trucks in the late morning, and then seek privacy of one sort or another to get dressed. Performances began around midday, under a blazing, equatorial sun. The ground quickly filled up with simultaneous performances of dancers

Figure 1.7. The model canoe being brought to present to Sir Michael Somare, 2008. Photo: David Lipset.

dripping in shell and teeth valuables, feathers, and leaves, as well as magnificent headdresses. Each troupe was surrounded by well-wishers and choruses of kin who sang and beat hand drums. Stalls, from which vendors sold snacks, tobacco, soda pop, and flavored ices, bordered the large field. Perched on a hill in the shade of a temporary wooden structure that had been decorated with streamers, the prime minister sat with his wife, Veronica, and their two daughters, Betha and Dulciana, as well as other provincial dignitaries.

Toward the end of the day, formalities ensued. Speeches were made to a huge audience and several communities staged a kind of command performance for the PM. Notable were the Wogeo Islanders whose (ethnographically) famous *Lewa* mask danced (Hogbin 1970, 1978; Anderson 2003). The Wogeo also favored Somare with two huge pigs together with a large pile of their garden produce, bananas, taro, and *canarium* almonds. The men of Kopar village, from the very mouth of the Sepik, no doubt made the most spectacular impression with their Dragon dance, whose great monster was hefted by some twenty youth dancing in two lines inside it. Not to be outdone, the Murik villagers from Mendam were last to make their entrance.

Led by several elders bearing lineage emblems, they climbed up the steps to where the PM's genial party stood. Before the gaze of an emergent nation, Felix Yamuna, speaking in Tokpisin, delivered a short, vigorous speech in the belligerent manner of customary Murik oratory. Essentially, Yamuna recognized Somare's Murik identity and his specific membership in the Sait lineage. Wangi, a very senior Sait headman, then presented Somare with insignia (*sumon*) that consisted of a ceremonial spear, a medallion made of boars' tusks and bright yellow bird of paradise plumage, and the little outrigger canoe (Figure 1.7). In response, Somare concluded the proceedings. Speaking in the Murik vernacular, he thanked Yamuna and Wangi by name, both for the lineage insignia as well as for all the support he had received from Murik people over the many years of his long career.

Next day, I made my way back to "Number Two Bay" to canvas opinion about how the festival had gone. Expecting that Sir Michael would have taken the model canoe with him as a souvenir, I was startled to find it toppled over, foundering on a low platform, like a broken toy. What, I asked, was the model canoe doing there? "No," Felix Yamuna answered, "it was just an image, a picture. He couldn't take this canoe. He just took the idea. He took the image of … our power, we beach people."[13] What then *was* this little vehicle? What kind of a model was it?

For Max Black (1962), thinking about Western science, scale-models serve the purposes of realism. They assert a relationship to an original, in which relative proportions are preserved. A model, Black avers, is an icon, in Peirce's terms, which claims: "this is how the original looks or looked!" It brings the unknown into the present, middle-sized existence. However, what we learn from this incident is that in addition to their representative purposes, scale-models may serve other ends of which Black was not aware, namely, they may have a totemic, participatory, or consubstantial, association with an original signified, which is collective in origin and practice. Even though the PM did not take the scale-model canoe, he nevertheless took "it." There is no question that the end of outrigger canoe production rendered the model canoe an expression of nostalgia for a prelapsarian past (Stewart 1993), for that time when use-values prevailed and the big Murik canoes still plied trading partners with goods. At the same time, the little canoe was not just a symptom of melancholia, of irresolvable loss. Nor was it merely a kitschy miniature, an object frozen in time and space. It remained a vital, living body. Before the gaze of the spectacle, it was no fiction (to the Murik). It remained an embodiment that transported spirit-agency and identity to the PM. The canoe's display-value, as a scale-model, belied its persisting position as master-signifier not only in, but for, the Murik *habitus*.

However eminent and powerful its recipient may have been, the *sacra* presented to the PM did not belong to any single individual, so Felix Yamuna seemed to declare. The PM had as much as acknowledged its collective significance in his speech. The model outrigger canoe was and was not a replica. It was and was not an allusion to a temporal rupture. It was not a souvenir/commodity, to be brought home and moved into a private time and space. Still, "it" had indeed replaced the full sized version that was gone. Once its vehicular/metaphoric work was finished, the model canoe evidently became irrelevant; it lost referential and aesthetic value. It was discarded because it was no longer needed to transport its mystical cargo, the sacred agency of the lineage. The *habitus* it transported had not become an exotic curiosity in need of false promises of restoration; the canoe-body, like the *habitus* for which it stood, had nevertheless suffered miniaturization. Its moral agency, while still present, was no longer what it once was.

In one way or another, many, if not most, postcolonial Papua New Guineans now live in this kind of a double *habitus* that is made up of adverse combinations of amoral, bureaucratized, and technological objects, on the one hand, and their scaled down "canoe-bodies," their abridged, vernacular concepts of moral agency in society, on the other. That is, the postcolonial subject is not synonymous with the structures that produced this *habitus*. Rather than enthralled by its gleaming signifiers of progress, the taken-for-granted moral action and thought that he would exempt from modernity not only make him appear a little quixotic, but alienated from their promise of the good life.

Coda: Reviving the Austronesian *Habitus* in the Postcolonial Pacific

What I saw in Papua New Guinea in 2008 is being expressed throughout the contemporary Pacific, where a comparable moral vision—of launching metaphoric canoes on modern seas—is having its moment (compare Auslander, Chappell, and Živković, this volume). Perhaps Epili Hau'ofa (1993) put it passionately but cogently. The postcolonial Pacific, as he saw it, was becoming a "sea of islands" again. That is, its inhabitants were returning to their ancestors' concept of mobility in oceanic space to advantage themselves of resources, material and social, however far-flung they might appear to be to Western eyes. They were casting off the colonial "islands in the sea" view of the Pacific, which had reduced it to a modified kind of Hobbesian primitivism where moral life was not "small, brutish and short," but its islands were small, poor and isolated.

In French Polynesia, for example, a poet advocated that a "canoe (*va'a*)" of stories, dances, chants, and oratory reconnect interisland relations shattered by colonization. The canoe's travels, she went on, could be facilitated by "a technological *va'a* with all the courage it took centuries ago to face open-ocean voyages and unknown horizons" (Stewart quoted in Mateata-Allain 2008: 618; see also Iding, Skouge, and Peter 2008: 14–15). Reflecting upon her experience teaching Pacific culture to islanders, Teaiwa (2005) adopted a view of the lecture hall as outrigger canoe on which she served as "helmsman" and "navigator." Students, who had to cooperate in order to reclaim indigenous knowledge, were "crew." Then in a dissertation on language revitalization among the New Zealand Maori, King reported that one-third of her informants, when speaking Maori, referred to their vernacular as a "canoe" in which custom could move forward (2007: 155f). Somewhat improbably perhaps, Ramsey (2008) argued that "from the dug-out Pacific *waka* with outrigger and/or sail to the bark canoes of the North American 'First Nations,' the canoe has become a contemporary symbol" both of the value of indigenous identities and for a capacity to transcend essentialist constraints of ethnicity and national particularity (2008: 560–61). Like the Murik gift to the PM of Papua New Guinea, these canoe metaphors express a contradictory desire that Pacific Islanders be transported forward into a postcolonial *habitus* where the Austronesian vehicle of their heroic maritime history might voyage anew.

NOTES

1. See also Hocart (1952: 33–38) and Tambiah (1985: 303) on the anchoring of supernatural powers in stone which become stabilized points of access to these powers in the Trobriands and elsewhere.
2. Green (1991) argues that the Pacific should be divided between what he calls Near and Remote Oceania and that the tripartite categories, Melanesia, Micronesia, and Polynesia, be abandoned, the new division being based on greater time depth of human settlement in the former southwestern region. I use them here as nothing more than shorthand terms for geography.
3. On Austronesian social and political structure, see also Murdock (1949), Goodenough (1955), Blust (1980), and Sahlins (1963).
4. In Proto Oceanic, the subgroup that historical linguists associate with Austronesian influence in island Melanesia and Polynesia, "*waga* (phonetically [*wankga*] with [ng] being a single phoneme) is a generic term for a canoe, or canoe with a hull, as opposed to a raft" (Pawley and Pawley 1994: 336).
5. The Dama'ii mask was carved in Watam village on the east side of the mouth of the Sepik River. It was imported to Karau village from Watam, four generations before the early 1980s, as a mortuary gift some time during the 1870s.
6. The kin of Dama'ii regarded his spirit and cormorant "canoe" as having descended from a single, consubstantial body, a common ancestor. They therefore trusted its portents. They were obliged to observe a dietary restriction against "eating his canoe," the cormorant. In other words, while they were objects of nurture within the household, the *brag* spirits did not offer themselves as food to, and demanded a certain degree of discipline from, their devotees. These canoes were ancestors and guardians to their kin. They were not symbolic mothers, however. Their bodies were androgynous.
7. The author, Matthew Tamoane, was raised in the Seventh-day Adventist Church. He attended a national high school and later took a degree in linguistics at the University of Papua New Guinea during the late 1970s. This is excerpted from an elegiac chapter he contributed to an anthology on prophets in Melanesia (Trompf 1977) about Jari, the spirit-woman, who selected Kamoai, one of Tamoane's grandmothers, to serve as her "canoe" in 1931. There were several shamanic canoes practicing in Darapap village in those days, offering cooperative or supplemental oracular information to cure or divine sorcery or, as I say, to forecast the outcome of collective enterprises, such as warfare, fishing, or hunting. A highlight of Kamoai's career as a shaman was her prediction of the Allied bombing raid on Darapap in 1944; as a result of her prediction, at least some of the villagers fled in advance of it.
8. There are other issues about masculine identity at stake here. In the ritually charged state, such a man must also obey sexual taboos that quarantined him from the sexual impurities of young women.

9. But the Murik still perform and trade dances in the Lower Sepik and North-coast region (see Lipset 2009) which include spirit-figures attached to this kind of scaffolding.
10. See my discussion of the iconography of the prow sides in Lipset (2005).
11. This recalls the flying canoes in the Trobriands Islands (Malinowski [1922] 1978) and Gawa (Munn 1977).
12. In the past, such model canoes were made for children as toys and for mortuary rites, as psychopomp vehicles for ghosts to use to travel to the spirit world. Lately, they have been made as gifts and commodities.
13. *Em piksha tasol. Em i no inap kisim dispela gai'iin. Em kisim idea tasol. Em kisim piksha bilong powa bilongem na bilong mipela long nambis.*

REFERENCES

Abu-Lughod, Lila. 1989. "Zones of Theory in the Anthropology of the Arab World." *Annual Review of Anthropology* 18:267–304.

Allen, J. 1996. "The pre-Austronesian Settlement of Island Melanesia: Implications for Lapita Archaeology." In *Prehistoric Settlement of the Pacific,* edited by W. H. Goodenough. Philadelphia: Transactions of the American Philosophical Society 85 (5):11–27.

Anderson, Astrid 2003. "Landscapes of Sociality: Paths, Places and Belonging on Wogeo Island." In *Oceanic Socialities and Cultural Forms: Ethnographies of Experience,* edited by Ingjerd Hoem and Sidsel Roalkvam, 51–70. New York: Berghahn Books.

Ballard, Chris, Richard Bradley, Lise Nordenborg Myhre, and Meredith Wilson. 2003. "The Ship as Symbol in the Prehistory of Scandinavia and Southeast Asia." *World Archaeology* 35, no. 3: 385–403.

Bakhtin, M. 1984. *Problems of Dostoevsky's Poetics.* Translated by Caryl Emerson. Minneapolis: University of Minnesota Press.

Basso, Keith. 1967. "Semantic Aspects of Linguistic Acculturation." *American Anthropologist* 69, no. 5: 471–77.

Bellwood, P., J. Fox, and D. Tryon. 1995. "The Austronesians in History: Common Origins and diverse Transformations." In *The Austronesians: Historical and Comparative Perspectives,* edited by P. Bellwood, J. Fox, and D. Tryon, 1–16. Canberrra: Australian National University.

Black, Max. 1962. *Models and Metaphors: Studies in Language and Philosophy.* Ithaca, NY: Cornell University Press.

Blust, R. 1980. "Austronesian Etymologies." *Oceanic Linguistics* 19, nos. 1 & 2: 1–181.

Bourdieu Pierre. 1977. *Outline of a Theory of Practice.* Translated by Richard Nice. Cambridge: Cambridge University Press.

———. 1984. *Distinction: A Social Critique of the Judgement of Taste.* Translated by Richard Nice. Cambridge, MA: Harvard University Press.

Camic, Charles. 1986. "The Matter of Habit." *American Journal of Sociology* 91, no. 5: 1039–87.
Crumlin-Pedersen, O., and B. Thye, eds. 1995. *The Ship as Symbol in Prehistoric and Medieval Scandanavia.* Copenhagen: National Museum.
Crystal, E. 1985. "The Soul that is Seen: the Tau Tau as Shadow of Death, Reflection of Life in Toraja Tradition." In *The Eloquent Dead: Ancestral Sculpture of Indonesian and Southeast Asia,* edited by J. Feldman, 129–46. Los Angeles: Fowler Museum of Cultural History.
Durkheim, Emile. (1912) 1995. *The Elementary Forms of Religious Life.* Translated by J. W. Swain. New York: The Free Press.
———. 1951. *Suicide: A Study in Sociology.* Translated by John A. Spaulding and George Simpson. New York: The Free Press.
Eliade, M. 1964. *Shamanism: Archaic Techniques of Ecstasy.* London: Routledge and Kegan Paul.
Fortes, Meyer. 1973. "On the Concept of the Person among the Tallensi." In *La Notion de Personne en Afrique Noire,* no. 544, edited by G. Dieterlin, 283–319. Paris: Colloques Internationaux du Centre National de la Recherche Scientifique.
Foucault, Michel. 1973. *The Birth of the Clinic: An Archaeology of Medical Perception.* Translated by A. M. Sheridan-Smith. London: Tavistock.
Franklin, Karl. 2003. "Some Kewa Metaphors: Body Parts as Automobile Parts." SIL International, http://www.sil.org/silewp/2003/silewp2003-005.pdf.
Gittinger, M. S. 1972. *A Study of the Ship Cloths of South Sumatra: Their Design and Usage.* PhD thesis, Columbia University. Ann Arbor: University Microfilms International.
Goodenough, Ward. 1955. "A Problem of Malayo-Polynesian Social Organization." *American Anthropologist* 57:71–83.
Green, R. C. 1991. "Near and Remote Oceania: Disestablishing 'Melanesia' in Culture History." In *Man and A Half: Essays in Pacific Anthropology and Ethnobiology in Honour of Ralph Bulmer,* 491–502. Auckland: The Polynesian Society.
Harrison, Simon. 1993. *The Mask of War: Violence, Ritual and the Self.* Manchester: Manchester University Press.
Hau'ofa, Epili. 1993. "Our Sea of Islands." In *A New Oceania: Rediscovering Our Sea of Islands.* Suva: University of South Pacific Press.
Hocart, Arthur M. 1952. *The Northern States of Fiji.* Occasional Publications 11. London: Royal Anthropological Institute.
Hogbin, H. Ian. 1970. *The Island of the Menstruating Men: Religion in Wogeo, New Guinea.* Melbourne: Melbourne University Press.
———. 1978. *The Leaders and the Led: Social Control in Wogeo, New Guinea.* Melbourne: Melbourne University Press.
Hoskins, Janet. 1988. "The Drum is the Shaman, the Spear Guides his Voice." *Social Science and Medicine* 27, no. 8: 819–28.
Iding, Marie, James Skouge, and Joakim Peter. 2008. "The Computer and the Canoe: Web-based Communities Across the Pacific Islands." *International Journal of Web Based Communities* 4, no. 1: 5–16.

Ignatow, Gabriel. 2008. "Why the Sociology of Morality Needs Bourdieu's Habitus." *Sociology Inquiry* 79, no. 1: 98–114.

Jakobson, Roman, and Morris Halle. 1956. *Fundamentals of Language.* The Hague: Mouton and Co.

Kirch, Patrick. 1996. "Lapita and its Aftermath: Austronesian Settlement in Oceania." In *Prehistoric Settlement of the Pacific,* edited by W. H. Goodenough. *Transactions of the American Philosophical Society* 85, no 6: 57–70.

———. 2010. "Peopling of the Pacific: A Holistic Anthropological Perspective." *Annual Review of Anthropology* 39:131–48.

Laycock, Donald. 1973. "Sepik Languages—Checklist and Preliminary Classification." *Pacific Linguistics Series* C: 1. Canberra: Australian National University Press.

Lipset, David. 1985. "Seafaring Sepiks: Ecology, Warfare and Prestige in Murik Trade." *Annual Review of Research in Economic Anthropology* 7:67–94.

———. 1997. *Mangrove Man: Dialogics of Culture in the Sepik Estuary.* Cambridge: Cambridge University Press.

———. 2005. "Dead Canoes: The Fate of Agency in Twentieth-Century Murik Art." *Social Analysis* 49, no. 1: 109–40.

———. 2009. "A Melanesian Pygmalion: Masculine Creativity and Symbolic Castration in a Postcolonial Backwater." *Ethos* 37, no. 1: 50–77.

———. 2011. "The Tides: Climate Change and Masculinity in Coastal Papua New Guinea." *Journal of the Royal Anthropological Institute* (N.S.) 17:20–43.

Malinowski, Bronislaw. (1922) 1978. *Argonauts of the Western Pacific.* London: Routledge & Kegan Paul.

Manguin, Pierre-Yves. 1986. "Shipshape Societies: Boat Symbolism and Political Systems in Insular Southeast Asia." In *Southeast Asia in the 9th to 14th Centuries,* edited by David G. Marr and A. C. Milner, 373–400. Canberra: Australian National University.

Mateata-Allain, Kareva. 2008. "*Metissage* and Migration Through the Metaphor of the *va'a,* or Canoe: Intellectual Cross-fertilization of Ma'oli Literature within an Oceanic Context." *International Journal of Francophone Studies* 11, no. 4: 601–21.

McKinnon, Susan. 1988. "Tanimbar Boats." In *Islands and Ancestors: Indigenous Styles of Southeast Asia,* edited by J. P. Barbier and D. Newton, 152–69. New York: The Metropolitan Museum of Art.

Munn, Nancy. 1977. "The Spatiotemporal Transformations of Gawan Canoes." *Journal de la Societé des Oceanistes* 33, nos. 54–55: 39–53.

Murdock, George Peter. 1949. *Social Structure.* New York: Macmillan.

Pawley, A., and M. Pawley. 1994. "Early Austronesian Terms for Canoe Parts and Seafaring." In *Austronesian Terminologies: Continuity and Change,* edited by A. K. Pawley and M. D. Ross, 329–61. Pacific Linguistics C-127. Canberra: Australian National University.

Sahlins, Marshall. 1963. "Rich Man, Poor Man, Big Man, Chief: Political Types in

Melanesia and Polynesia." *Comparative Studies in History and Society* 5, no. 3: 285–303.
Somare, Michael. 1975. *Sana: The Autobiography of Michael Somare.* Hong Kong: Niugini Press.
Starrett, Gregory. 1995. "The Hexis of Interpretation: Islam and the Body in the Egyptian Popular School." *American Ethnologist* 22, no. 4: 953–69.
Stewart, Susan. 1993. *On Longing: Narratives of the Miniature, the Gigantic, the Souvenir, the Collection.* Durham, NC: Duke University Press.
Swadling, Pamela. 1997. "Changing Shorelines and Cultural Orientations in the Sepik-Ramu, Papua New Guinea: Implications for Pacific Prehistory." *World Archaeology* 29:1–14.
———. 2010. "The Impact of a Dynamic Environmental Past on Trade Routes and Language Distributions in the Lower-Middle Sepik." In *A Journey Through Austronesian and Papuan Linguistic and Culture Space: Papers in Honour of Andrew Pawley*, edited by John Bowden, Nokolaus P. Himmelmann, and Malcolm Ross, 141–57. Canberra: Pacific Linguistics.
Tambiah, Stanley J. 1985. *Culture, Thought and Social Action: An Anthropological Perspective.* Cambridge, MA: Harvard University Press.
Tamoane, Matthew. 1977. "Kamoai of Darapap and the Legend of Jari." In *Prophets of Melanesia*, edited by G. Trompf. Port Moresby: Institute of Papua New Guinea Studies.
Teaiwa, T. 2005. "The Classroom as Metaphorical Canoe: Cooperative Learning in Pacific Studies." *World Indigenous Nations Higher Education Consortium.* http://www.win-hec.org/docs/pdfs/Journal/Teresia%Teaiwa-Final.pdf.
Tiesler, Frank. 1969–1970. *Die intertribalen Beziehungen an der Nordkust Neuguineas in Gebeit der kleiner Schouten-Inseln.* Translated by K. Barlow. Abhandlungen und Berichtet des Statlichen Museums fer Volkerkunde. Dresden: Academie Verlag.
Tilly, Christopher. 2002. "The Metaphorical Transformations of Wala Canoes." In *The Material Culture Reader*, edited by Victor Buchli. Oxford: Berg.
Trompf, Gary, ed. 1977. *Prophets in Melanesia.* Port Moresby: Institute of Papua New Guinea Studies.
van Gennep, Arnold. 1960. *The Rites of Passage.* Translated by Monika B. Vizedom and Gabrille L. Caffee. Chicago: University of Chicago Press.
Žižek, Slovoj. 1989. *The Sublime Object of Ideology.* New York: Verso.

CHAPTER 2

Cars, Persons, and Streets
Erving Goffman and the Analysis of Traffic Rules

Richard Handler

In email conversations that preceded this volume, David Lipset and I were discussing Erving Goffman's descriptions of vehicles. David told me that when he was learning to drive in 1967, he inherited Goffman's late-1950s black Volkswagen beetle from his father, who had bought it second-hand from Goffman when they were colleagues at Berkeley.[1] This anecdote sent me back to *Behavior in Public Places,* to one of the few vignettes in the Goffman corpus in which an interacting ego is the driver of a car. Goffman is analyzing "exposed positions," in which individuals cannot protect themselves from being engaged by strangers. One type of exposed position, Goffman says, is being "out of role," a concept he illustrates with an anecdote which we can now surmise he experienced more than once: "As might have been predicted, the first persons in America to drive Volkswagens laid themselves open to face engagements from all and sundry, since they did not seem to be seriously presenting themselves in the role of driver, at least as a driver of a serious car" (Goffman 1963a: 127).

Goffman gives us no further details, but it seems fair to assume that he was referring both to driver-driver and to driver-pedestrian interactions, and that he was using himself as his primary informant, as he often did (Schegloff 1998). While drivers and cars are more or less out of sight in Goffman's work, we should keep in mind that the "relations in public" and the "behavior in public places" that he analyzes with Talmudic intensity were set in an urban spatial system in which pedestrians and cars had long since become inured to one another. The mid-century equilibrium between cars and pedestrians on city streets was at that time an unstable one (as it is today); it had resulted from decades of struggle between walkers, cyclists, carters and teamsters, motorists, policemen, safety advocates, traffic engineers, city managers, automobile clubs, auto dealers, and auto manufacturers (Norton 2008). At issue were the relative rights of various kinds of individuated entities (persons with bodies, teamsters with horses, drivers with cars) to move freely on and in the most basic of all public spaces, city streets.

This chapter gives a glimpse of the history of traffic rules in North American cities from the mid nineteenth century to the mid twentieth, when Goffman was writing. At issue is what we might call the co-construction (with "construction" understood to be of the cultural sort) of cars, persons, and streets. There is a growing literature on cars and drivers, with a focus on the machine-human interaction. And there is an enormous technical literature on traffic engineering and road construction. Goffman's work prompts us to bring these topics together in a new way, to emphasize some of the basic features of modern, individualist culture that become visible when we analyze the traffic rules that guide the interactions of cars, drivers, and pedestrians on city streets (see Roth, this volume). With his usual make-the-familiar-strange techniques, Goffman offers us a useful opening into this analysis with his startling insights into the cultural construction of human persons as "vehicular units" on mid-century North American streets.

Body as Vehicle, Self as Driver

We begin with two texts: Goffman's essay "The Individual as a Unit," which is the first chapter of *Relations in Public* (1971); and the second chapter ("Introductory Definitions") of *Behavior in Public Places* (1963a). In these chapters, Goffman is concerned with "traffic codes" (1971: 5), both those bearing on the physical safety of individuals who must coordinate their movements through public spaces, and those pertaining to what we might call the moral safety provided by the "communication traffic order" (1963a: 24), which regulates access between co-present selves, stipulating who can speak to whom, when, where, and how.

In "The Individual as a Unit," Goffman conceptualizes the analytically separable aspects of personhood that cannot be captured by the standard sociological treatment of status and role (Handler 2009: 291–93). To do so, he distinguishes between the individual as a "vehicular unit" and as a "participation unit," in order to examine the fact that individuals can simultaneously participate in conversations (governed by one set of rules of order) and negotiate locomotion in public spaces (governed by another set of rules). While Goffman's work focuses far more on participation units than vehicular units, my topic in this essay is the latter (see also Lipset, Chapter 1, this volume). In the discussion of vehicular units, Goffman is concerned with traffic rules and the "techniques that pedestrians employ ... to avoid bumping into one another" (1971: 6). The avoidance of collisions is effected, Goffman argues, by pedestrian traffic rules that most people follow unconsciously, which is why they are free to focus on all sorts of other social exchanges while they walk.

A vehicular unit, Goffman explains, "is a shell of some kind controlled (usually from within) by a human pilot or navigator." In the modern cities Goffman wrote about (and which we continue to inhabit), vehicular units travel on "a set of thoroughfares"—roads and streets—that can accommodate "shells of somewhat different kinds—cars, bicycles, horse-drawn carts, and ... pedestrians." Travel on streets and roads is regulated by a "traffic code," "a set of rules" allowing "vehicular units independent use" of the streets "for the purpose of moving from one point to another" safely, without "collision and mutual obstruction" (1971: 6).

Goffman's description of vehicular units as outer shells with inner, living pilots suggests conventional modern notions of the individual as a body-mind duality and also, as we shall see, the history of the politics of traffic in nineteenth- and twentieth-century North American cities. According to Goffman, vehicular units vary "according to the thickness of their skins":

> There are ships, submarines, trains, and armored cars, all of which have thick skins, being guided by men who are well hidden and in some ways well protected. There are buggies, open cars, sedan chairs, rickshaws, bicycles, and sporting devices such as skis, surfboards, toboggans, kayaks, skates, and skateboards, which leave the navigator relatively exposed. The more protective the shell, the more ... the unit is restricted to simple movements.... Viewed in this perspective, the individual himself, moving across roads and down streets—the individual as pedestrian—can be considered a pilot encased in a soft and exposing shell, namely his clothes and skin. (1971: 6–7; see also Lipset, Chapter 1 and Wayland, Chapter 3, this volume).

The relative thickness and rigidity of skins or shells has been an important factor in the twentieth-century history of traffic rules, since the development of mechanically powered hard-shelled vehicles threatened pedestrians in ways that even horses did not. And while it is perhaps disconcerting to think of human individuals with shells like those of submarines or cockroaches,[2] Goffman makes other, equally striking observations about the way human persons can be conceptualized in modern settings. Consider his remarks concerning some normative restrictions on individuals' use of their senses both to engage other people and to present themselves as normal individuals whom others can engage:

> In everyday thinking about the receiving senses, it is felt that ordinarily they are used in a "naked" or "direct" way. This apparently implies a restriction on boosting devices—mechanical, chemical, or electrical—except as these raise the faulty senses of a particular individual to average unassisted strength: glasses, for example, but not binoculars; hearing aids but not microphones. Electric lighting would have to be allowed as merely raising a room to day-time standards. (1963a: 14–15)

These examples invalidate commonsense arguments about the deterministic impact of technological and scientific innovation on social forms: in our society, to be a normal individual for purposes of routine interaction, one must abjure or renounce the use of available technical devices that can enhance natural powers. (Such devices are standard tools used by certain classes of deviants, like the criminals and spies Goffman so lushly documented [1969].) Later in *Behavior in Public Places,* Goffman makes a similar point concerning doors and windows, which are always more powerful as symbols than as physical barriers. People act *"as if"* a door or a window "had cut off more communication than it does." Thus, "children in our middle-class society [must be] ... taught that, while it is possible to address a friend by shouting through the walls ... it is none the less not permissible" (1963a: 152). As these examples show (and there are many others, like "banned substances" [steroids] in athletics), to be a normal, adult individual in our society requires adherence to convention with respect to the body's relationship to available techno-scientific devices. And those conventions are governed by a logic that is not "rational" or "maximally efficient" with respect to the technological possibilities that scientific culture affords.

Having described, in "The Individual as a Unit," the body as a self-guided vehicle, Goffman goes on to analyze automobile and pedestrian traffic rules. He assumes, probably correctly, that by mid-century, pedestrian traffic rules had been heavily influenced by auto traffic rules. He saw the latter as more formalized than the former, and more directly subject to police control. Road traffic is for the most part functionally specific ("the overriding purpose is to get from one point to another"), whereas foot traffic co-occurs with many other social purposes: "individuals who are vehicular units will often be functioning in other ways, too, for example, as shoppers, conversationalists, [and] diners" (1971: 8). In road traffic, collisions ("accidents," in native parlance) are much more consequential than they are in foot traffic, and autos are far less maneuverable than human bodies on foot. A key similarity of the two kinds of traffic, according to Goffman, is that both organize the "passings-by of unacquainted pilots" (1971: 7). And, of course, the two systems intersect—at crosswalks for law-abiding pedestrians, and in unpredictable spots, in the case of "jaywalkers."

The Car in the City

Goffman begins his discussion of vehicular units by quoting "the opening paragraph of a famous book" by the early-twentieth-century progressive sociologist and eugenicist Edward Alsworth Ross:

> A condition of order at the junction of crowded city thoroughfares implies primarily an absence of collisions between men or vehicles that interfere with one another. Order cannot be said to prevail among people going in the same direction at the same pace, because there is no interference. It does not exist when persons are constantly colliding one with another. But when all who meet or overtake one another in crowded ways take the time and pains needed to avoid collision, the throng is *orderly*. Now, at the bottom of the notion of social order lies the same idea. The members of an orderly community do not go out of their way to aggress upon one another. Moreover, whenever their pursuits interfere, they make the adjustment necessary to escape collision, and make it according to some conventional rule.[3]
> (Ross 1901: 1; Goffman 1971: 6)

This is perhaps the most interesting paragraph of Ross's book, which is a 450-page treatise—at once socio-evolutionary, conventionally racist, and progressive—on the rise and global spread of modernity. The ultimate message is a mainstay of progressive-era social reformers: modern society requires expert guidance to harness the strivings of aggressive white men for socially useful purposes. Over the course of social evolution, social control developed from familial and group ties, from religion, law, education, and art; but in the modern era (as Ross saw it in his time), too much control was exercised by big business and its subsidiary, the press (see Ross 1909: 83–136). Social "enlightenment" thus required a scientific elite to "awaken a sense of responsibility" on the part of "good citizens," teaching them about "the social consequences of conduct." Once the public came to understand a "rational theory of social relations," its conventional "utilitarianism" would give way to thinking based on "social science," which in turn would lead to the harmonious development of social resources (Ross 1901: 302).

It was in similar terms that city officials at the turn of the twentieth century were beginning to think about traffic control (Norton 2008: 105–8). In nineteenth- and early-twentieth-century North American cities, the maintenance of orderly streets required officials to consider the rights and claims of various constituencies, often defined and divided in terms of social class and gender. "Domesticating the street" (as the title of a monograph about Hartford, Connecticut, puts it) meant more than balancing the rights of pedestrians, carters, and horses and teamsters; it included as well more morally charged issues, like confining prostitutes to vice districts, regulating newsies and other child laborers and, ultimately, getting children out of the streets (whether they were working there or playing) altogether (Baldwin 1999). To deal with such issues was to manage rationally the most pressing urban social problems of the time: immigration, sanitation, vice, work, and, always, increasing population density in city centers linked to increasing suburbanization on the edges.

The arrival of the automobile presented a challenge to accepted versions of street order that took city officials several decades to answer. In nineteenth-century cities, horses were central to transportation, both for hauling freight and—with the advent of horse-drawn omnibuses (in 1829) and then of horse-drawn street railways (in 1852)—for hauling large numbers of people. To be sure, horses and horse-drawn vehicles were a dangerous presence for pedestrians, but people could maneuver away from or around horses more easily than they would be able to do around cars; and horses, though they might panic and kick, were nonetheless more maneuverable than cars would prove to be (McShane 1994: 41–56; Norton 2008: 49). More important for present purposes, despite the omnipresence of horses in late-nineteenth-century North American cities (McShane and Tarr 2007), the streets were still considered to be the domain of pedestrians. Urban residents worked, played, walked, chatted, marketed, and generally socialized in the streets. As Norton puts it, "before 1920 American pedestrians crossed streets wherever they wished, walked in them, and let their children play in them" (2008: 70; also McShane 1994: 62–65). It was this "customary" use of streets as public space, and the cultural understandings that supported it, that the auto would challenge.

The size, weight, and power of cars, and the hardness of their shells, made them deadly to pedestrians. And for the first three decades of the twentieth century, city dwellers battled motorists for control of the streets, a story that the historian of technology Peter Norton tells in fascinating detail. The key turning points in the battle (for purposes of this discussion) were the invention of the concept of the jaywalker (Norton 2008: 71–79; see also Norton 2007) and the reconceptualization of streets in terms of "a supply-and-demand model of street capacity" (Norton 2008: 174) as opposed to the older definition of streets as public spaces or utilities, to be regulated by government for the good of all users.

The automobile was at first seen (with good justification) as a "pleasure vehicle" for wealthy people. It followed, then, that pedestrians who were struck, injured, and sometimes killed by cars were victims:

> In the prevailing construction of the traffic safety problem before the mid 1920s ... frightened parents and pedestrians ... blamed automobiles and their drivers, regardless of the circumstances. City people were angry. Their anger is shown in mob attacks on reckless motorists, and in newspapers that played up the automobile accident stories when the victim was easy to represent as innocent (a child, a young woman, an old person), the victim of an unambiguous "villain" (the motorist who leaves the victim bleeding in the street, the "speed maniac," the fleeing criminal, the drunk). (Norton 2008: 25)

As Norton further observes, "driver and vehicle were not clearly distinguished, neither were responsible and irresponsible drivers" (27). Above all, convention held "that people on foot, including children at play, had a rightful claim to street space" (72).

In this context, motorists and the auto industry made efforts to "rebrand" cars, streets, and pedestrians. The term jaywalker was apparently first applied (in the first decade of the twentieth century) to pedestrians who failed to keep to the right, but it quickly came to be used by motorists to describe pedestrians who crossed streets in unpredictable ways. The term's semantic load derived from its reference to rural backwardness as opposed to city sophistication. To quote at length from Norton again:

> A "jay" was a hayseed, out of place in the city; a jaywalker was someone who did not know how to walk in a city.... According to one early (1913) definition, jaywalkers were "men so accustomed to cutting across fields and village lots that they zigzag across city streets, scorning to keep to the crossings, ignoring their own safety ... and impeding traffic." (2008: 72; the internal quotation is from the *Washington Post*, May 18, 1913)

In the war between drivers and pedestrians, the latter tried to fight back by coining the term "jay driver," but they failed to establish it in common usage. Pedestrians' defenders could gain rhetorical traction by painting accident victims as innocent, but they could not reverse the dominance of auto traffic over foot traffic on the scale that privileged modernity over tradition. As Norton puts it, "critics of motorists could call them cold-hearted, tyrannical, or selfish, but a motorcar's power, modernity, and worldly sophistication made its owner anything but a 'jay'" (78).

With respect to the supply-and-demand model of streets, its triumph must be understood in the context of engineering experts' inability to solve the problems of traffic (not only accidents but, increasingly, "congestion"), given the limited carrying capacity of city streets coupled with the demand of downtown business interests to maintain the unimpeded circulation of traveling customers—in ever increasing numbers. In the first decades of the twentieth century, engineers persisted in imagining streets as public utilities to be regulated by government. Moreover, many traffic experts thought that private cars were a far less efficient means of urban transportation than streetcars, trains, and subways. According to Norton, the rise of the gasoline tax (and secondarily, of the parking meter) changed the equation. Such taxes and fees were at first fought by both motorists and the auto industry, but these interests gradually realized that a model of streets as a free-market commodity paid for by users would work in their favor (Norton 2008: 197–206).

From the mid-1920s onward, motorists and auto interests (organized now as the American Automobile Association, the National Automobile Chamber of Commerce, the National Automobile Dealers Association, etc.) mounted a rhetorical counterattack. Not only did they begin to depict the street as a free-market commodity; they also promoted the car as a means of freedom for individual motorists, and the safety problem as one to be solved by the recognition of shared responsibilities. In this new model, motorists had as much right to the streets as pedestrians—perhaps even more right. Using Goffman's terms, we might say that both the car-driver pair and the individual pedestrian ("encased in a soft and exposing shell, namely his clothes and skin" [1971: 7]) were now to be considered equivalents as vehicular units. Motorists could be distinguished as responsible or "reckless" drivers, and it was the latter, not the former (that is, not the vast majority of drivers) who caused accidents. But, similarly, jaywalkers and other irresponsible pedestrians also caused accidents. In sum, not only were pedestrians going to have to share the streets with motorists; they were going to have to share responsibility for safety. The fact that cars had more power and harder shells than pedestrians had early on made this a practical necessity; the lobbying of the auto interests made it a moral necessity as well.

Through the Looking Glass: Drivers and Pedestrians in Mid-Century Drivers' Manuals

By mid century, when Goffman was writing, the model of a street to be shared by equally responsible drivers and pedestrians (all staying in their appropriate lanes and walkways and all cognizant of the same traffic rules) was well established. We can find it charted and formalized in the drivers' manuals of the time. Here I analyze a modest sample of manuals published between 1951 and 1962. I will focus on the prescriptions for conventional interactions between motorists and pedestrians and on the construction of the driver-car pair as a vehicular unit.

The manuals I have examined[4] cover the same topics (licensing of drivers; registration and inspection of vehicles; devices and features vehicles are required to be equipped with; traffic regulations or "rules of the road;" traffic signs, signals and pavement markings; accidents, legal liability, and insurance), although the order and treatment of topics varies. In the earliest manuals in my sample, the historic hostility between motorists and pedestrians is close to the surface, and the new model (in which it is recklessness that causes accidents) seems only tentatively established. In the New York manuals from 1951 through 1961, a brief initial section on licensing is followed by a one-paragraph section titled "How to Operate Your Vehicle Safely," which reads as follows:

> Most automobile accidents result from ignorance or carelessness. Operating an automobile is a full-time job; we must be careful and alert at all times. Few persons ever deliberately risk their lives by driving dangerously, but many injure themselves because they either do not know enough or do not try to keep out of tight situations.... We shall try to show you the reasons why people have accidents and what you can do to drive safely. (NY 1951: 6)

This emphasis on the causes of accidents, worthy of Zande philosophers as described by Evans-Pritchard (1937), is quite explicit in the New York manuals and implicit in all that I examined. The theory of causality these manuals suggest is an important part of the new model of the street as described by Norton. Causality can be parsed to highlight reckless drivers, careless pedestrians, faulty equipment, badly maintained cars (another type of malfeasance on the part of drivers), and bad "conditions" (whether due to weather or irresponsible road maintenance); but the historically prior model, in which pedestrians are always innocent and motorists always guilty, is gone.

Immediately following the one-paragraph section just quoted there is a longer section titled "Speed and Pedestrians" (NY 1952–1961). Speed is not dangerous as such (as it was in the prior model [Norton 2008: 30–31]), only in relation to conditions. And among the most dangerous conditions for drivers, apparently, is the presence of pedestrians (NY 1951: 7). "Pedestrians always have the right of way on highways in New York State," but more important, because cars can "kill or permanently cripple" pedestrians, "you [the driver] should keep as far away from them as possible." Indeed, pedestrians are presented as muddled and foolish—in short, as jays:

> Studies have shown that pedestrians who are killed are usually the ones who are unfamiliar with cars—children, old people, and those who have never driven. In driving, watch each pedestrian carefully and expect him to do something foolish.... Pedestrians do foolish things, and what is worse, they often do them at night when they have less chance of being seen. As an operator, you must realize that pedestrians may be unreasonable, but since they have so little chance to survive a collision with your destructive vehicle, you must protect them. (NY 1951: 9)

In the 1958 manual, there is an important change. Most of the language depicting pedestrians as wooly-minded rubes who are a menace to motorists has been removed. Instead, a more business-like section on "Rules Covering Pedestrians" specifies under which circumstances, and at which places, pedestrians may or may not cross traffic, when they must yield to drivers, and when drivers must yield to them. The implication seems clear: these rules of pedestrian-driver interactions reflect the underlying rules of legal liability for pedestrian-driver collisions. Drivers must be careful, but if they kill a jaywalker, they will probably not be held legally responsible. The other manuals I examined cover the topic in a similar, rule-oriented manner (Mattern and Mathes 1957: 42, 45; NJ 1960: 46–48, 56–62).

All the manuals list two categories of persons—children and the blind (both being stigmatized categories, in Goffman's terms [1963b])—who require special attention from motorists. Some of the manuals also pay special attention to old people and to people exiting streetcars (historically, an important issue, as Norton [2008: 33, 61, 188] makes clear).[5] The establishment (in the early twentieth century) of safety zones or streetcar and bus "landings" to protect pedestrians entering and exiting buses and streetcars seems related to the rules (explicitly detailed in the manuals) concerning school buses and school zones. By mid century, there is little mention of streetcar and bus passengers. By contrast, the explicit attention in all manuals to children and school buses indicates the continuing salience of what the historians have shown us to be a key issue in the battle for control of city streets: children, their innocence and irrationality, and the responsibilities of various adults (parents, drivers) for their safety.

While the manuals present children (and sometimes, as we have seen, pedestrians in general) as a category of persons who lack good sense, they admonish drivers to be careful and sensible at all times. Crucial here is the idea of attention or alertness. Unlike Goffman's pedestrians, who routinely and normally function simultaneously as vehicular units and participation units—disattending the rules of urban walking while they attend to conversations, store windows, or street scenes—drivers must focus their attention on their driving and not allow themselves to be distracted by other social engagements. In a section on "Inattention," the New Jersey manual asserts that safety depends on drivers "giving full attention to the road ahead and being constantly alert." "Well-known errors" in this regard include "permitting conversation or other activities among passengers to divert the driver's attention." Other factors similarly categorized are roadside sights and occurrences, fatigue, "highway hypnosis," impatience, anger, and alcohol (NJ 1960: 63–64). A related rule prohibits more than three people from riding together in the front seat (Mattern and Mathes 1957: 47). In sum, the responsible driver cannot by definition function simultaneously as a vehicular unit and a participation unit; during the time in which one designates oneself as a driver (to borrow the current term promoted by the makers of alcoholic beverages), one must renounce other social engagements.

If we turn from the alert, attentive pilot to his or her shell, the car, we find that all the manuals have explicit rules about the equipment required for safe operation. Following Goffman, we can think of this equipment as a toolkit of sense-boosting devices. (Indeed, 1940s animated cartoons come to mind in which cars are made to move like people, rearing up on their hind legs, or tires, and peering about with their enhanced eyes, their headlights.) All the manuals have similar requirements for headlights, which must "be strong enough to enable the driver to see a person or object 500 feet ahead" (Mattern and Mathes 1957: 26), and for taillights, reflectors, and the light that illuminates the rear license plate. Lights render ego's vehicle visible to other vehicles, and the headlights render other vehicles visible to ego. Rules about dimming lights when approaching oncoming vehicles create the conditions for a normal exchange between two otherwise unrelated cars passing in the night. Dimming one's beams "when you are following another vehicle" is also mentioned, as "a matter of courtesy and safety" (NY 1958: 11). As Goffman might have observed, it is in spy and crime movies that such practices as turning off one's lights for a stealthy approach are common. Other kinds of delinquency involving the willful renunciation of a car's sense-boosting devices are warned against in the manuals, as in an example of police going to "war against a teen-age dare game—driving a car while blindfolded" (Elkow et al. 1955: 2).

In addition to lights, windshield wipers and mirrors are required to enhance the vision of drivers. "Signs, posters, or stickers on the windshield" are prohibited, and already by the 1950s, states had passed laws prohibiting the installation of television screens "within view of the driver" (Mattern and Mathes 1957: 29). Requirements for both horns and mufflers control the type and loudness of the sounds the vehicle can make. The manuals state explicitly that horns are to be "audible for at least 200 feet under normal conditions," and used only as necessary, for safety: "nobody likes a loud-mouth, and a driver who constantly toots his horn is the loud-mouth of the road" (Mattern and Mathes 1957: 27; NY 1962: 41). The manuals do not prescribe a maximum loudness for horns, but they warn that drivers cannot equip their cars with "sirens, whistles or bells" that are for the exclusive use of "emergency vehicles" (NJ 1960: 38). Finally, the manuals of this period teach hand signals (for stopping and turning) while also mandating that new cars be equipped with electric directional signals as of January 1952 in New York and July 1954 in New Jersey. The 1951 New York manual explicitly recommends electric directional signals as an enhancement to those who "are short of arm and stature" (NY 1951: 24).

All the drivers' manuals I examined have lengthy sections to teach proper driving techniques: how to stay in lanes, make turns, overtake (pass) other vehicles, read road signs, attend to speed limits, and, as we have seen, how to interact with pedestrians. By mid century, the authors of these manuals had come to theorize safe driving behavior in terms quite similar to those Ross had used at the beginning of the twentieth century:

> Driving a motor vehicle is a simple operation in itself. But when a vehicle must be operated in proximity to many other vehicles and pedestrians on the streets and highways, driving becomes complex. As with any activity involving large numbers of individuals, a set of rules is required to avoid conflicts and confusion.
>
> The rules of the road are basic regulations designed to enable motorists and pedestrians to use the streets and highways freely, orderly [sic], and safely. These rules restrict any extreme action on the part of any individual and require all highway users to follow a uniform and consistent pattern of traffic behavior for the common good. (NJ 1960: 44)

When Ross was writing, the traffic problem had not been solved. By mid century, it had: streets were still conceived as public spaces, but they had largely been taken over by automobiles. The system encompassed both cars and pedestrians on apparently equal terms, "for the common good." But the common good had been redefined to privilege the most powerful and hardest-shelled vehicular units, which had won the right to buy as much street as they could pay for, and then some.

Other Roads, Other Loads

To explain these rules of the road and the associated vehicle equipment requirements solely in terms of rationality or self-interest is to forget the peculiar, culturally constructed features of modern personhood that Goffman taught us to see. The modern person is a mind or self inside a shell. All persons are in theory alike, and, as such, "normal." To be normal is to respond normally to others and to possess a shell, with its attached devices for monitoring the environment, which is similar to those of all other persons. Many persons, however, are stigmatized due to faulty shells or monitoring equipment, or inability to follow the rules of interaction. All normal persons, and all abnormal persons who can compensate for their defects, have the right to use common spaces like streets and roads, so long as they "follow a uniform and consistent pattern of traffic behavior for the common good" (NJ 1960: 44).

This basic model of persons and roads can be traced back into the European middle ages. In *Behavior in Public Places*, Goffman (1963a: 9 n.6) cited G. T. Salusbury's 1948 monograph, *Street Life in Medieval England*. There, Salusbury asserted his conception of what he understood to be the attitude of medieval town officials toward the street: "the street is mainly regarded as a channel which the local authorities strove to maintain in good condition in order that the flow of every kind of lawful traffic might be orderly and unimpeded" (1948: 10; see also Norton 2008: 327 n.97). Terms like "orderly" and "unimpeded" can be found (as we have seen) in twentieth-century drivers' manuals; and terms like "right-of-way" and an established rule for passing—keep to the left (in England)—can be found in medieval documents (in North America, of course, the rule is to keep to the right). But without engaging the difficult problem of separating the medieval from the modern in Euro-American civilization, we can guess that in places and times distinct from our tradition, our familiar rules about persons and roads would not obtain.

Take, for example, Papua New Guinea. Roy Wagner (1974) once asked, "Are there social groups in the New Guinea Highlands?" His answer was, no, not until colonial administrators and then social anthropologists invented them. In this paper, the social-anthropological twin to his book on the "invention of culture" (1975), Wagner argued that the Daribi people among whom he worked (in the 1960s) did not organize themselves as stable, continuously-existent groups clustered in villages lined up on roads. Rather, they relied on some key social distinctions (preeminently, male/female) to "elicit" contextually relevant "social collectivities" and "collective response[s]" for particular purposes (Wagner 1974: 108). Groups, as social scientists imagine them (as "social facts," as Durkheim said [1966], or as bounded entities which pre-exist and outlast the individuals who are born into or otherwise join them), simply were not part of Daribi ways of constructing their world:

> Even though one does not "start out" with groups, since these are never deliberately organized but only elicited through the use of names, one always ends up with specific bunches of people.... It is an "automatic society," one that suddenly appears in concrete form wherever the right distinctions are made. What we might want to call the "permanent" sociality exists as an associational context flowing from one such *ad hoc* occasion to another. (1974: 111)

This sounds quite a bit like Goffman's sociology of encounters, a sociology he had to invent precisely because the one he inherited could not easily see beyond "corporate" groups to examine what he called, in a classic four-page statement, "the neglected situation" (Goffman 1964). But more to the present argument: Wagner goes on to point out that not only did Westerners have to create groups in Papua New Guinea; they sought, for purposes of administrative control, to arrange them into villages living on straight roads: "people, who had been living in ... longhouses ... scattered among their shifting garden-sites, were obliged to abandon the traditional pattern and settle in nucleated villages" (Wagner 1974: 112). The shift had occurred several years before Wagner's fieldwork, and by the time he arrived, "the 'village' ... took the form of a straggling line of houses ... scattered for half a mile along a cleared track that is locally known as 'the big government car road'" (114–15). Thus in the Western imagination villages and roads go together and, in some ways, constitute one another.

But in a world where longhouses and roads do not go together, what do roads look like? Salusbury's discussion, which we reviewed briefly above, is resolutely particularistic, but it is apparently easy for us to forget that European conceptions of roads are not universal. For example, William Maltbie's treatise on "the law of the highway" (which Norton claims [2008: 289 n.8] is the best overview of the topic) begins with a narration of the rise of civilization in relation to travel, as this judge of the Superior Court of Connecticut understood it in 1924: from biblical times, to Rome, to the Crusades, to colonial New England, to the twentieth-century United States (Maltbie 1924: 32). In this grand sweep of what he understood to be all of travel history—"from the rude paths of the aboriginal people, carried in direct lines over the surface of the country, passable only by passengers or pack-horses, to the comparatively modern thoroughfare" (Angell and Durfee 1857: 3, quoted in Maltbie 1924: 33)—highways, roads, and "city streets" ("but not waterways") had one invariable feature: "this quality every true highway must have, that it shall afford a free passage for all who have occasion to use it" (Maltbie 1924: 33). From this fundamental premise all other regulations (in Anglo-American law, at least) flow: the rights and responsibilities of those whose property abuts the highway (see Salusbury 1948: 13–39), traffic rules (or "the Law of the Road") governing the interactions of co-present users and vehicles (Maltbie 1924: 36), and the oversight functions of governments, to keep roads open and unobstructed so that individuated users, acquainted or unacquainted, can have "free passage."

In New Guinea, roads have not worked this way at all. Thanks now to the historical research of Lise Dobrin and Ira Bashkow, we have an account of Reo Fortune's manuscript materials (held in the Alexander Turnbull Library in Wellington, New Zealand) concerning the concept of "road" among the Arapesh of the Sepik lowlands, with whom both he and his wife (at the time), Margaret Mead, worked. In an unpublished fragment titled "Pigs for Dance Songs," Fortune described his travels with local friends and consultants, experiences that taught him to see roads not as neutral public spaces, as we do, but as manifestations of localized socio-political relations. Fortune apparently organized a road trip to bring a contribution of pigs from Alitoa (where Mead was working) to Kobelen, a village several villages down the mountainside, where the people were orchestrating the purchase of a ceremonial complex from people on the coast (for a similar example, see Lipset 2009: 56–58).

From this trip, Fortune learned about what he called the "convention of the 'telescoping' safe road by repeated escort" (quoted in Dobrin and Bashkow 2010: 130):

> The carrying of pigs is a ritual business, and it is the gravest insult to carry pigs ourselves over neighbours' territory. We call on our neighbours and they carry our pigs on over their own territory. But first we sit down in the hamlet and our hosts give us coconuts to drink and food to eat ... and after the food there is some brief orating by the hosts. This is usually talk of the antiquity of the road, for the road that is open to the carrying of pigs today is the road that was open also in the old days of war.
>
> Once the oratory about the antiquity of the open road is done, our hosts take up the pigs and go off at a trot, while we follow behind. So we go up and down to the next hamlet on the coast-wards road....
>
> This is the manner of the open road. We A go to our friends B, who escort us to their friends C; then C escort us all to their friends D, who then take upon themselves the escorting of all of us to their friends E—and before escorting, feeding in each case. At least this is the manner of the open road when gifts of pigs are carried upon it. (quoted in Dobrin and Bashkow 2010: 130)

For our purposes, the important point is that an Arapesh road as described by Fortune was anything but open, in the sense of affording "free passage for all who have occasion to use it" (Maltbie 1924: 33). Instead, it was open to those who maintained the proper social alliances with friends and trading partners in adjacent villages along the road. This is just the sort of arrangement that struck colonial administrators as utterly irrational and, hence, as proof of savagery. Colonial development, and development to this very day, takes it as given that one of the first modern advances to bring to backward peoples is a system of well-maintained, open roads that function as the King's (or Queen's) highways (Maltbie 1924: 33), or a "big government car road" (Wagner 1974: 115).[6]

That such roads are open equally to all is, of course, our own fantasy, since once roads were conceptualized as commodities, as Norton argued, individuals with comparatively greater resources could afford to buy more road, or use roads more intensively, than other users could. In our day, we complain about tractor-trailers that tear up our roads, even though we try to regulate them by restricting the size and weight of their loads. (Salusbury [1948: 13–15] reported that carts with metal-rimmed wheels were the bane of medieval town officials, for the same reason.) In the Arapesh region of Papua New Guinea as described by Reo Fortune, it was not the traveler's status as a vehicular unit among other unacquainted units, nor the weight of the traveler's load, that counted; it was the traveler's connections to particular hosts in particular places that made travel as safe as it could be for the people of that world.

Returning, finally, to Erving Goffman, enduring insults in his Volkswagen: in our world, people inside car-shells gesture and gesticulate at one another, or they use their vehicles' horns and lights to communicate. And there are some neighborhood streets where custom still allows pedestrians to engage drivers in vehicles in conversations that interrupt auto traffic. But for the most part, our streets and roads are public spaces for fleeting encounters between anonymous, hard-shelled travelers. While the idea is open access and safe passage, these streets and roads are as dangerous as any roads in pre-colonial New Guinea; if anything, they are far more deadly given the volume of traffic, the speed of the vehicles, and the "rage" of some of the drivers. But the cultural basis of this deadly violence is of course modern rationality itself, which is a most peculiar mode of thought, as Goffman demonstrated.

NOTES

1. Lipset wrote, "when I was 16, my father gave me his car, a black beetle, which Goffman had sold him. I had no idea at the time who he was, of course.

But I remember that he always took off his shoes when he came in our house in Berkeley" (May 27, 2008).
2. Reviewing *Relations in Public*, Marshall Berman (1972) celebrated Goffman as a great writer, comparing him to Kafka, whose story, "The Metamorphosis," is a paradigmatic example of the modernist resonances of the metaphor of the shell. Another example, less well known to Anglophone readers, is Max Weber's lament at the end of *The Protestant Ethic and the "Spirit" of Capitalism*, concerning the hegemony of capitalist culture. Talcott Parsons famously translated Weber's phrase (*stahlhartes Gehäuse*) as "iron cage," but in a new translation, Peter Baehr and Gordon Wells prefer "a shell as hard as steel" (Weber 2002: 121). They argue that Weber chose the word steel, not iron, and, more to the present point, that the word *Gehäuse* should be translated not as "cage," but as "casing" or "shell." A shell, they write, "has an organic quality and symbolizes something that has not just been externally imposed but that has become integral to human existence" (Baehr and Wells 2002: lxx–lxxi), a description, we might note, applicable to automobiles in contemporary society.
3. Distinguishing social order from natural behavior and crowd-influenced behavior was an important task for turn-of-the-twentieth-century sociologists; compare Weber, writing a few years later: "Not every type of contact between human beings is of a social character, but only where the individual's conduct is meaningfully oriented toward that of others. Thus a collision of two cyclists is merely an isolated event comparable to a natural catastrophe. On the other hand, any attempt by any one of them to avoid hitting the other, with ensuing insults, a brawl or even a peaceful discussion, would constitute a form of 'social behavior'" (Weber 1962: 56).
4. *Driver's Manual: The Laws of the Forty-eight States*, by T. Mattern and A. Mathes, rev. ed. 1957; the 1960 revised edition of the New Jersey manual; manuals from New York State from 1951 to 1968; and *Driver Education: A Student's Manual and Workbook*, by J. D. Elkow et al., 1955.
5. There is some attention in Goffman's work to rules of interaction obtaining for pedestrians as passengers, waiting for or traveling on moving vehicles. For example, he wrote several paragraphs on "elevator behavior" (1963a: 158; 1971: 32, 131). Americans tend not to classify elevators and escalators as vehicles of mass transportation, although a moment's reflection suggests they are; thus Lewis Mumford (1938: 239–40) argued that elevators played an important role in twentieth-century urbanism, since they allowed cities to expand upwards. Perhaps it is difficult for us to recognize elevators as mass transportation because we think of buses and trains as traveling outdoors, whereas elevators are machines that travel inside buildings. As Goffman might have noted, our conceptual ambiguity concerning elevators is reflected in films that use them as settings for sexual encounters or as staging grounds for spectacular crimes. Contemporary artist Matthew Bakkom similarly called attention to the ambiguity of elevators by showing films

in them, an installation he called "the cinevator," featuring "engines inside engines" (Queens [NY] Museum of Art, May–August 2000).
6. While I was writing this, Ira Bashkow directed me to the then-current (June 2010) World Bank website (http://go.worldbank.org/Y8EU10J7H0), which reported on a Road Maintenance and Rehabilitation Project for "promoting an efficient, safe, and reliable roads system for the people of Papua New Guinea."

REFERENCES

Angell, Joseph, and Thomas Durfee. 1857. *A Treatise on the Law of Highways.* Boston: Little, Brown.

Baehr, Peter, and Gordon C. Wells. "Note on the Translation." In *The Protestant Ethic and the "Spirit" of Capitalism.* Translated by P. Baehr and G. C. Wells. New York: Penguin Books.

Baldwin, Peter C. 1999. *Domesticating the Street: The Reform of Public Space in Hartford, 1850–1930.* Columbus: Ohio State University Press.

Berman, Marshall. 1972. "Relations in Public." *New York Times Book Review*, Feb. 27, 1972.

Dobrin, Lise, and Ira Bashkow. 2010. "'Pigs for Dance Songs.' Reo Fortune's Empathetic Ethnography of the Arapesh Roads." *Histories of Anthropology Annual* 6:124–54.

Durkheim, Emile. 1966. *The Rules of Sociological Method.* Translated by Sarah Solovay and John Mueller. New York: Free Press.

Elkow, J. D., et al. 1955. *Driver Education: A Student's Manual and Workbook.* Englewood Cliffs, NJ: Prentice-Hall.

Evans-Pritchard, E. E. 1937. *Witchcraft, Oracles and Magic among the Azande.* Oxford: Clarendon Press.

Goffman, Erving. 1963a. *Behavior in Public Places.* New York: Free Press.

———. 1963b. *Stigma.* Englewood Cliffs, NJ: Prentice-Hall.

———. 1964. "The Neglected Situation." *American Anthropologist* 66 (Part II, Special Issue): 133–36.

———. 1969. *Strategic Interaction.* Philadelphia: University of Pennsylvania Press.

———. 1971. *Relations in Public.* New York: Basic Books.

Handler, Richard. 2009. "Erving Goffman and the Gestural Dynamics of Modern Selfhood." In *The Politics of Gesture: Historical Perspectives* (*Past and Present* supplement), edited by Michael J. Braddick, 280–300. Oxford: Oxford Journals.

Lipset, David. 2009. "A Melanesian Pygmalion: Masculine Creativity and Symbols of Castration in a Postcolonial Backwater." *Ethos* 37:50–77.

Maltbie, William. 1924. "The Law of the Highway." In *Proceedings of a Conference on Motor Vehicle Traffic,* edited by R. S. Kirby, 32–49. New Haven: Yale University Press.

Mattern, Theodore, and Anne Mathes. 1957. *Driver's Manual: The Laws of the Forty-eight States*. New York: Oceana Publications.

McShane, Clay. 1994. *Down the Asphalt Path: The Automobile and the American City*. New York: Columbia University Press.

McShane, Clay, and Joel Tarr. 2007. *The Horse in the City: Living Machines in the Nineteenth Century*. Baltimore: Johns Hopkins University Press.

Mumford, Lewis. 1938. *The Culture of Cities*. New York: Harcourt, Brace & World.

New Jersey [NJ]. 1960. *Driver's Manual*. Department of Law and Public Safety.

New York State [NY]. 1951–1962. *Driver's Manual*. Albany: Bureau/Department of Motor Vehicles.

Norton, Peter. 2007. "Street Rivals: Jaywalking and the Invention of the Motor Age Street." *Technology and Culture* 48:331–59.

———. 2008. *Fighting Traffic: The Dawn of the Motor Age in the American City*. Cambridge: MIT Press.

Ross, Edward Alsworth. 1901. *Social Control: A Survey of the Foundations of Order*. New York: Macmillan.

———. 1909. *Changing America: Studies in Contemporary Society*. New York: Century.

Salusbury, G. T. 1948. *Street Life in Medieval England*. Oxford: Pen-in-Hand.

Schegloff, Emanuel A. 1988. "Goffman and the Analysis of Conversation." In *Erving Goffman: Exploring the Interaction Order*, edited by P. Drew and A. Wootton, 89–135. Boston: Northeastern University Press.

Wagner, Roy. 1974. "Are There Social Groups in the New Guinea Highlands?" In *Frontiers of Anthropology*, edited by Murray Leaf, 95–122. New York: Van Nostrand.

———. 1975. *The Invention of Culture*. Englewood Cliffs, NJ: Prentice-Hall.

Weber, Max. 1962. *Basic Concepts in Sociology*. Translated by H. P. Secher. Seacaucus, NJ: Citadel Press.

———. 2002. *The Protestant Ethic and the "Spirit" of Capitalism*. Translated by P. Baehr and G. C. Wells. New York: Penguin Books.

PART II

Vehicles as Gendered Persons

CHAPTER 3

"It's Not an Airplane, It's My Baby"
Using a Gender Metaphor to Make Sense of Old Warplanes in North America

Kent Wayland

Fifi, *Goodtime Gal*, and *Miss Mitchell* are just three of the more than one hundred aircraft flown by the Commemorative Air Force, a World War II heritage group in the United States, yet those three names evince a distinctive feature of how the group's mechanics and pilots relate to the aircraft: the planes are female.[1] This metaphor is long-standing; it parallels the common gendering of automobiles and reflects centuries of gendering ships. Despite this deep tradition, the metaphor is not dead, or even sleeping. Indeed, borrowing meaning from the domain of women shapes both work on and with the aircraft and the broader understandings of the aircraft and the war in which they were used. At the same time, these pilots and mechanics use the metaphor in the opposite direction, borrowing from the domain of aircraft to assign meaning to women. In this chapter I will explore the cultural sense that this metaphor makes for a particular group of people who restore and fly World War II warplanes as a form of heritage. Put differently, I will trace how the metaphor serves to "concretize the inchoateness of" both airplanes and women by using them to make sense of each other (Fernandez 1974: 129).

Aircraft Names and "Nose Art"

The association of vehicles with women has a long history. The proper pronoun for a ship in English-speaking societies has been feminine for centuries (see Lipset's introduction to this volume). Sailors usually refer to their vessels as female, even when the name of the ship is ostensibly male (as with the USS George H. W. Bush). This has been true even though sailors' lore holds that women on a ship are bad luck (Rodgers 1984). Cars, too, have often received female nicknames and may be referred to using feminine pronouns. Like ships and automobiles, planes have long borne names, and during World War II U.S. Army Air Corps aircraft often, but not always, bore the names of women.

Even when an aircraft did not have a female name, its "nose art" often depicted a woman. Nose art is artwork painted on an aircraft, usually on the side of the forward fuselage, or "nose" of the aircraft, and it became most common—and most famous—during World War II. The artwork was unofficial, painted by the ground crew or the flight crew, and it could depict a wide range of images, most often a person, cartoon character, or animal (Ethell and Simonsen 2003). Despite its unofficial nature, nose art has become iconic for World War II and World War II aircraft (cf. Ethell and Simonsen 2003; Wood 1999).

The practice of naming aircraft and/or adding nose art to them has been continued by individuals and museum groups that restore and fly these old aircraft. Hundreds of these "warbirds," as the groups call them, fly today at airshows, civic ceremonies, and other events where the memory of World War II might be invoked. The largest, and one of the earliest, of these warbird groups is the Commemorative Air Force (CAF).[2] Headquartered in Texas, the CAF has units across the United States and in a few other countries. My research mostly took place with the Southern California Wing (located near Los Angeles) of the CAF.

The CAF, like other warbird owners and groups, is most centrally a cultural heritage organization, but rather than focus on preserving just the aircraft themselves as objects of heritage, they seek to preserve the experience of the war. The central cultural-heritage premise of the warbird movement is that an airplane has to operate in order to fully capture and communicate its memory, and, metonymically, through its memory, the memory of the war. People today should be able to see, hear, feel, and smell these vehicles in operation, this thinking goes, so that today's audiences can have the same phenomenological sensations of "the Good War" that its participants did (except for the associated violence).

Verisimilitude, therefore, is the central justification for the selection of names and the depictions of women on warbirds. One study showed that during the war slightly over 50 percent of nose art depicted women, though no data were available on names (Klare 2003). Bredau (1989: 67), however, found that the prevalence of female nose art varied by theater of war. In the European theater, only 43 percent of the nose art depicted women, while the number was 65 percent in the Pacific theater. This discrepancy, he argues, resulted from the Pacific aircrews' relative isolation from women, from high-ranking generals, and from disapproving allied populations. By my count, 65 percent of the Commemorative Air Force's (CAF) planes with names or nose art had either a female name or an image of a woman, so the CAF's practice fits with that of the Pacific theater. The remaining wartime planes with non-female representations fell into a few broad categories: cartoon characters, animals, and historical characters (Wood 1999). For the CAF planes, the categories are similar, with nose art depicting animals, cartoons or comical figures, and names celebrating military groups ("Tuskegee Airmen") or branches ("Semper Fi" for the Marines). It is significant that, in an extensive but not exhaustive search, I have seen no nose art, either on wartime planes or on warbirds, that depicts non-famous or non-cartoon male figures. There are no male pin-up images and no generic male names assigned to these aircraft.

The female names and nose art also serve as an index of restorers' seriousness about representing the past, their devotion to authenticity and heritage. If the restorer can establish that a particular airframe[3] was used in the war and bore a name, he[4] will often use that name and associated nose art, if any. Many of today's warbirds, however, were planes that were never shipped overseas to fight in the war, so they have no previous name on which to draw. In these cases the restorers either use the name of a plane that was used in the war or create their own name and nose art. If they use a name from the war, they sometimes draw on a personal favorite story, but they also often choose a famous pilot's aircraft. For example, two different owners restored airplanes to represent the plane of American fighter ace George Preddy.

In cases where owners do not use names and nose art from the war, they draw on wartime themes and styles (or their interpretation of them) to create the art. A frequent wartime motif in names was a pun that linked war to the pursuit of women. Hence, "Target for Tonight" is a famous wartime name-nose art combination in which the name of a 1941 movie about British bombing missions was matched with nose art depicting the "target" as four women sitting in a cocktail glass. Similarly, the CAF plane "Texas Raiders" suggests soldiers from Texas, but the nose art depicts an alluring cowgirl with a just-fired pistol, riding a bomb (Figure 3.1).[5] Neither this name nor this nose art is a copy of a wartime plane; the CAF unit that restored this plane created it (Gibson n.d.). Like the names, the visual style of warbird nose art mimics that of the wartime pinups of Alberto Vargas and George Petty, among others. The soft, idealized, and airbrushed style of these painters provided the template for most representations of women in World War II nose art, and this style has set the standard for warbird nose art, again in a quest for verisimilitude (Ethell

Figure 3.1. Texas Raiders. Photo: Kent Wayland.

and Simonsen 2003). For instance, another CAF warbird bears the name "Sentimental Journey" (after a famous wartime song) and one of the most famous pinup images of the war, of Betty Grable.[6]

Nose art, then, involves both a particular aesthetic and an assertion of a connection to a particular past, not unlike the deeper roots of "barriology" that Chappell describes (this volume). By adopting this thematic and visual style, contemporary warbird owners demonstrate their quest for authenticity; names and nose art therefore serve as indexes of this dedication to cultural heritage.

This devotion was evident at the CAF's SoCal Wing, where I did fieldwork. This particular CAF unit has several aircraft that it maintains and flies. The flagship of the wing is a big cargo plane named *China Doll*. The plane's name stems from the activity for which this particular type of plane (a Curtiss C-46) was most famous: flying supplies over the Himalayas into China. It was painted originally by a famous nose art artist from World War II—his last nose art, according to the wing historian—but it was reimagined years later by a wing member's wife (Fleishman n.d.;

Sica 2010). The name itself might suggest a child's plaything, but the "nose art" for the aircraft (Figure 3.2) makes clear that the "doll" in question is an alluring Asian woman. The art on *China Doll* itself mimics the wartime airbrushed-pinup style, though in choosing an Asian woman as its eroticized subject it departs somewhat from wartime practice because the objects of desire painted on aircraft were more commonly white, representing women "back home" (Kakoudaki 2004). Asian women were represented in nose art, but the representation usually echoed the ste-

Figure 3.2. China Doll. Photo: Kent Wayland.

reotype of the "Dragon Lady," an Asian woman who threatens control of Euro-American men through her wiliness and sexual potency (Shah 2003).[7] Despite this shift in focus, the erotic nature of China Doll's nose art echoes much wartime nose art.

Eroticism, Power, and Gendered Spheres

With only a few exceptions, warbirds that depict women bear alluring, erotic representations of women, like many of the wartime aircraft before them did. Aside from *China Doll* and the planes mentioned above, the CAF has, as a representative sample of planes depicting women, *The Yellow Rose of Texas*, on which the name is currently paired with a barely dressed cowgirl (Figure 3.3), and the aforementioned *Miss Mitchell*, which depicts a shapely woman flying through the air.

This aggressively erotic style of representation has both a basis in historical practice and a contemporary political resonance. As should be clear, much of the wartime nose art, especially on planes based in the Pacific, far from high officials, included such erotic depictions of women (cf. O'Dwyer 2004). Commentators seeking to explain the acceptance of these erotic images have argued that they both boosted morale and "reminded the boys what they're fighting for" (Klare 2003). The ideology operative

Figure 3.3. Yellow Rose, Today. Photo: Kent Wayland.

at the time connected heterosexual desire and aggression (Gaines 1980). For warbird painters, however, these explanations do not apply. They are not fighting in a war. They explain, rather, that their designs simply reflect the past, and that they are authentic and should therefore be preserved as a form of heritage. Yet, the images are still meant to titillate, to attract the gaze of heterosexual male desire, as casual conversation around and about them —whether in the hangar or at an airshow—demonstrated. Indeed, one prominent restorer put his wife's face onto a racy nose art portrait, even though he lost a *concours d'elegance* competition for altering the original nose art. He spent millions of dollars restoring the plane as authentically as he could, and yet he choose to have a racy picture of his wife on the plane (whether for private reasons or to display her as a kind of trophy is not clear). As this event suggests, reproducing such nose art in the present—even granting the quest for verisimilitude—participates in current cultural discourses and politics of gender.

Erotic nose art also has political resonance as an anti-feminist assertion of heteronormative masculinity. With an increasing number of women in the military, military and civilian officials have decided to ban from military airshows any aircraft bearing nose art that depicts nude women. This policy has had a significant impact on warbird groups because military airshows are the most common event where the planes are shown (and an important source of income). Indeed, the previous nose art for "Yellow Rose" had a bare-breasted figure. In interviews and casual conversation, warbirders objected vociferously to this ban as a form of "political correctness" that has gone too far. This argument sometimes falls back on a heritage argument: we do it because they did. For example, one warbird museum official explained to me why he wanted to keep nose art with nude women: "we're not going to rewrite history." At other times resistance to the criticism of erotic nose art reflects a conservative critique of feminist complaints that such images objectify women: the warbirders argue that such representations are a natural and healthy expression of male sexuality. Further, they delight in resisting this "political correctness." A SoCal Wing member and aviation writer gave a response that captures this anti-feminist sentiment: "The other issue [for which they get criticism for not being politically correct] is the lady on the nose of our C-46, and as far as I'm concerned, may she live forever. We all get a kick out of the occasional outrage at airshows" (Deakin 2001).

Not all wartime planes or warbirds bore erotic images. Some have either a non-sexualized image of a woman or simply a woman's name. Among the CAF planes, *Fifi* is the most famous. That plane, a B-29 bomber, is both the largest CAF plane and the flagship of its fleet. It was named after the wife of the sponsor of its initial recovery and restoration (Anonymous 1975). The plane has no nose art depicting Fifi herself, but it has borne the name ever since the CAF restored it in 1974. The mention or chaste depiction of wives was an occasional practice during World War II as well. In addition to non-suggestive names, a range of aircraft during the war had non-erotic images of women, usually wives or mothers. Dick Bong, the American pilot who shot down the most enemy planes, named his fighter plane *Marge*, after his wife, and he had a chaste depiction of only her head on the plane. No CAF plane bears a similarly chaste portrait, although many bear nose art that does not depict women. Non-erotic images of wives or even mothers seem to have been more common then than now. No CAF plane bears such an image, and only a few without nose art bear non-suggestive female names.

The depiction of women on warbirds and the use of female names, then, stem from both heritage-based concerns for authenticity and a certain form of masculine pleasure derived from suggestive pictures of women (and from the way that those depictions raise the ire of feminists). Critics of the practice have objected not so much on heritage grounds, but more on the grounds of how erotic images of women are experienced and interpreted when they appear in public places like airshows and military bases. Both the heritage and the anti-feminist advocacy of nose art, however, are political. The gender politics are clear, but the representation of the past always has a political dimension, and the heritage practices of the warbird movement are explicitly political (Wayland 2006).

Even given the political tenor of these representations, however, the use of female names and images is only the beginning of a cultural practice that metaphorically links women and airplanes. While many aircraft bear these names and images, not all of them do, yet even those that have no overt linkage to women on their fuselage still become women in everyday interaction around the warbird hangar.

The Metaphor as Gender Politics

The metaphor "airplanes are women" taps into a long Euro-American history of gendering vehicles and machines, and we have to see this gendering as reflecting also an equally long-standing gendered division of the workplace in general and of work with technology in particular. By linking the aircraft with objects of sexual desire (through nose art), the planes become the province of (heterosexual) men. By making the object of labor female, within the dominant gender binary, the work itself becomes masculine. Human activity is thereby divided into gendered productive spheres, with the higher-ranked, technological sphere assigned to men (Cockburn 1981; Oldenziel 1999). It both makes men the relevant actors in the process *and* assigns them a particular agency in this work. Gender therefore brings with it a hierarchy that establishes male control over technologies like these vehicles.

This hierarchy was felt by several women I met during my fieldwork, who wanted in some way to work on the aircraft but found themselves subtly excluded.[8] Women remain marginal in warbirding more broadly, even if a few have prominence in the movement. One way to elicit this is to imagine replacing the female nose art on a warbird with a male erotic figure, paired with a generically masculine name (especially if it could have some *double entendre*). Such a figure not only would not fit with the themes established during the war, thereby violating the mandate for verisimilitude, but it also would be unthinkable because it would transgress the established gender spheres.

Some might object that the role that women played in World War II has gained greater visibility in recent decades, even in the warbird movement, which has embraced the Women's Air Service Pilots (WASPs) as aviation heroines of the war. These women were skilled pilots who did a lot of non-combat flying for the Army Air Corps during the war, most centrally ferrying aircraft around the country. Most warbird museums do indeed have a side exhibit about the WASPs, usually noting how skilled those pilots were. Such inclusion is praiseworthy, but in the end it highlights how WASPs were marginal figures during the war because the exhibits are always minor parts of an entire display demonstrating male prowess with technology.

One part of the metaphor's work, then, is the social work of reinforcing and policing gendered spheres, a political activity with wider resonance. For example, similar political implications stem from the gendering of ships, which were female entities even when human females were not welcome aboard because they were thought to be bad luck (Rodgers 1984). This history has led to political debates within maritime museums. The usage of the feminine pronoun to refer to ships in museum exhibits has recently sparked controversy for curators and journalists, who have debated whether to adopt the feminine pronoun because it reflects traditional usage or to avoid it because the language implicitly suggests male domination of women (Mellefont 2000). This gendering of technological development and labor on machines stems from cultural and historical forces much more powerful than this metaphorical construction of meaning, but the metaphor resonates with those forces.

The Metaphor Creates a Relationship

This political analysis of the metaphor, while an important critique, does not exhaust the metaphor's workings. In warbirders' everyday interaction with the aircraft, the nose art and names go beyond merely naming the aircraft and titillating the viewer to establish paradigmatic links between the separate domains of aircraft and women. The female names given to the aircraft come to entitle them, so that a plane does not simply have a name or an image of a woman on its side; it becomes a female entity with whom they interact (cf. Crocker 1977b).

Putting female names and nose art on the aircraft provides an initial association that gets much further elaborated in everyday practice, starting with the ways that people refer to the aircraft. The names become gendered nicknames that express a personal familiarity with the airplane. People will talk about what is happening with "China Doll" or "the Doll." "Yellow Rose" may suffice or even just "Rose." It is common practice to find some naming shorthand to identify and register familiarity with the plane, even if it does not have nose art or an official name. At the SoCal Wing, I heard people use "290" to refer to a military trainer—using its tail number—and "the Bear" to refer to the F8F "Bearcat."[9] The use of a gendered name or nickname is therefore not the exclusive form of registering familiarity with the aircraft, but gendered language as a register of familiarity goes well beyond names and nicknames. The common usage of the feminine pronoun to refer to the aircraft is explicitly gendered. If pilots or mechanics do not use the name, they will sometimes say "she." These pronoun references carry an undertone of affection, and they carry the resonance from the metaphor that the aircraft is a person with whom they interact (see also Živković and Notar, this volume).

The commonsense and scholarly explications of nose art, on the other hand, delve more into their psychoanalytic workings than the metaphorical connection between the plane itself and women. The popular notions, as noted above, focus mainly on the raciness of the nose art as either an expression of or an attempt to relieve the male sexual tension of serving in the military (Klare 2003). The symbolic power of the pinup as an icon of Americana was clearly important (cf. Kakoudaki 2004) but does not hinge on seeing the planes themselves as female. Giving the plane a name and nose art has also been seen as an important index of the flight crew's group identity, enhancing unit cohesion because it singularizes the aircraft amidst dozens or even hundreds of similar ones (Bredau 1989). A third psychoanalytic argument holds that the images served to channel sexual desire into aggression against the enemy. These arguments are worth considering but they take us away from the workings of the metaphor.

Another kind of psychological argument might posit that personifying the aircraft as a woman served to relieve the anxiety of war. Making the plane into a woman would elicit the sense that "she"—as a nurturing female—would protect the crew. Seeing the aircraft as a woman—and especially treating it as such—would protect the crew from the arbitrariness of wartime violence. This psychological analysis is echoed in similar work on automobiles. Wetmore (n.d.) argues that this shift serves to relieve the anxiety associated with operating a complex, not-fully-understood machine. In effect, his argument is that the metaphor redefines the interaction as an intersubjective one in which proper cultivation of the subjectivity of the other will bring about the desired end of safety, proper performance, etc. Similar explanations have been offered for the gendering of ships, as the sailors' dependence on the ship becomes, by metaphorical extension, a relationship with the ship (Mellefont 2000).

In each of these cases, the metaphor the-machine-is-a-woman frames the interaction as one of a relationship that must be cultivated. My analysis builds on these arguments, extending them beyond their psychological functioning to examine how they structure the field of meanings emergent from interaction with the aircraft. Among other things, metaphors render the inchoate choate, and thereby they help "make sense" of the world in a way that both gives meaning to experience and guides action. Like Crocker's discussion of Bororo men whose insistence that they are red macaws provides a way to make sense of their difficult social situation, the frequent metaphorical linkage of airplanes and women provides a way to make sense of their interaction with the aircraft (Crocker 1977a). In this case, gender is both a model of and a model for their connection to the aircraft (Geertz 1973: 93–94). The model that gender brings is that of a relationship.

Making the Interaction a Matter of Relationship

Using the metaphor of gender, the men borrow a diversity of elements from the domain of "female" to interpret different dimensions of the aircraft. This metaphor goes beyond simply interpreting behavior/events (a model *of* the interaction); they also extend the metaphor metonymically to model the kind of connection or relationship (a model *for* the interaction) they should have with the plane, including especially the way they should behave toward the aircraft. In this metonymic extension of the metaphor, the female aircraft is understood as a person, and it has a person-like (and heteronormative) relationship with them, the men.

When warbird mechanics and pilots identify the aircraft as a woman, they can understand the actions of the airplane in terms of their models of women's behavior. Women become models of aircraft, expressed in two major types of usage: those that express affection for and intimacy with the aircraft and those that articulate the difficulty of dealing with the aircraft. These models become explicit once the pilots and mechanics who interact with the plane start talking about them. One pilot, whom I will call Aidan, said, "It's not an airplane, it's my baby," transforming the aircraft not simply into a woman, but into his girlfriend or wife (via the additional metaphor that a female sexual partner is like an infant), which indicates the level of affect. Aidan went on to talk about the nature of his connection to the aircraft, while drawing a parallel to the experiences of World War II veterans:

> It makes certain noises when you're doing good and other noises when you're doing bad. You talk to her. During the war, with the [bomber] crews, it was their airplane, so they were with it day after day. Some would say they had the feeling that when they came out on the ramp, the airplane would kind of sit up a little higher on her struts.

He models his connection to the plane on his understanding of what the wartime pilots felt, which was a responsive relationship with the airplane. In this passage, the initial "it" quickly becomes a "she." "She" tells the pilot—in a not unsuggestive way—when he is doing something right or wrong, and "she's" glad to see him. The plane, then, is a female person who has the ability to respond to the pilot and reward his attention with proper functioning and even happiness. We can see why, then, a different mechanic, "Anthony," talked about his connection to an airplane as one of "intimacy." He had developed a deeply felt connection to the aircraft, not unlike the connection to the Fića that Živković describes (this volume).

Another person, a pilot who was quoted in a magazine, demonstrated a form of the metaphor that I have not seen elsewhere: "'This aircraft is freshly painted, so try to avoid banging it up,' Shorty said. 'Think of it as an old woman: It's very fragile, and it needs a kiss once in a while'" (Schulze 2008). While he refers to the airplane as "it" in this passage, he also draws on a different form of the feminine to express his connection to the aircraft. Rather than the erotic partner, the plane is a fragile elderly woman. Yet another pilot used a weaker, but still resonant, simile to connect airplanes to women. "I can't tell you why I like it in particular. That's somewhat similar to why one man thinks a woman is beautiful while another man wouldn't think she was." This insistence that a man's taste in airplanes is like his taste in women again connects women and aircraft (although the relation is a metonymic one, in that both are extensions of a man's tastes). These different usages share a sense of intimacy and affection for the aircraft, modeled on different kinds of connections to women.

Paired with this expression of affection is a set of usages that describes the difficulty of interacting with the aircraft. Again, these usages build upon their conception of the female domain. One restorer, Pierre, described airplanes as having menstrual "periods," by which he meant certain times when several things went wrong at once, especially after a long period of no problems. He also frequently referred to aircraft as "bitches" as a way to point out how difficult they could be. William, an experienced warbird pilot and instructor, argued that airplanes were women precisely because they are difficult: "[A]n airplane is like a woman because some of them are temperamental, and you have to know how to treat 'em, or else they'll bite you. So that's why men call airplanes, they're all female. They're all female." The sense that aircraft will "bite you" plays off of a conception that women are difficult and capricious. The planes are difficult not only because they are powerful, but also because they are not very stable in flight, a result of their design for quick combat maneuvering. They are capricious vehicles because parts can fail, especially given their age, and because they are complex technologies that can develop problems whose solutions are elusive. Later, William compared an extensively restored aircraft to a trophy wife: "I guess that's like having a racehorse for a woman, you know? Most of those racehorses are very high maintenance, cost a lot of money, but it's worth it to the guys." In this form of the metaphor (which has the added metaphor of wife as trophy-winning racehorse), the planes are both demanding and expensive, but "worth it" for the sense of status they bring.

These two patterns of usage, affective and difficult, both draw on meanings attributed to women, and specifically to relationships with women. The presumption here is of connection, a heteronormative assumption that men always have women as partners, and because of that "natural" connection, these pilots' and mechanics' involvement with the aircraft is both pleasurable and painful, yet unavoidable.

The planes therefore can be affectionate, alluring, moody, difficult, capricious, or demanding. Anthony spoke glowingly of his "intimacy" with the aircraft, while William spoke warily of how aircraft could be so demanding and difficult. This metaphor therefore shifts the aircraft from a machine into an entity that fosters affect, both positive and negative. Indeed, the positive dimensions of the relationship, the intimacy and affection, become explanations for why the pilot or mechanic tolerates the negative dimensions, the caprice and difficulty. Gender therefore becomes a positive means to make sense of what the aircraft does.

At the same time that the metaphor provides a model of the aircraft and their interaction with it, it also offers a model for interacting with it. The suggestion from the affective coloring of the metaphor is that the aircraft *requires* devotion in a way modeled after an intimate male-female relationship. Hence, Anthony's "intimacy" with the aircraft leads to demands for a great deal of attention to any problems it may have. At one point he spoke of a problem with oil leaks keeping him up at night. Even the coloring of the metaphor in which airplanes/women are difficult leads them to conclude that this "relationship" requires care and attention, in addition to wariness. William's insistence that airplanes were difficult and could "bite" him did not lead him to stay away from aircraft. On the contrary, he paid ever-closer attention so that the plane/woman would respond to his attention and fly properly. In this way the metaphor converges with a kind of ethic of care, and even craftsmanship, that the experienced warbird pilots and mechanics I met voiced. Good mechanics and pilots, in their view, were those who paid full, careful, and embodied attention to their aircraft. This advice, not surprisingly, also serves as a model for relationships with women.

Using Airplanes to Understand Women

Since metaphors are bi-directional, the metaphor "airplanes are women" colors the meaning of women as well (Sapir 1977). The experience of parts failing unexpectedly, of planes requiring careful attention, lest they suddenly veer off in an unexpected direction, and of the basic complexity of a machine colored their understanding of women. This graphic (Figure 3.4), for example, sums up the notion that women are like complex machines. I downloaded it after a warbird pilot told me about it. It models the difference between women and men as being a difference in degree of complexity. This complexity, it implies, lies especially in the difficulty of stimulating a woman's sexual desire (although one could understand the picture merely as a commentary on temperament). After describing this picture to me, he went on to make the comment noted above that warbirds are temperamental and will bite you.

In fact, we can read all of the metaphors "backward" if you will, to see what the picture of proper connection to a woman might be. This is a kind of borrowing back of the initial associations, except the re-directed metaphor is colored by (cf. Sapir 1977) the discontinuous elements of

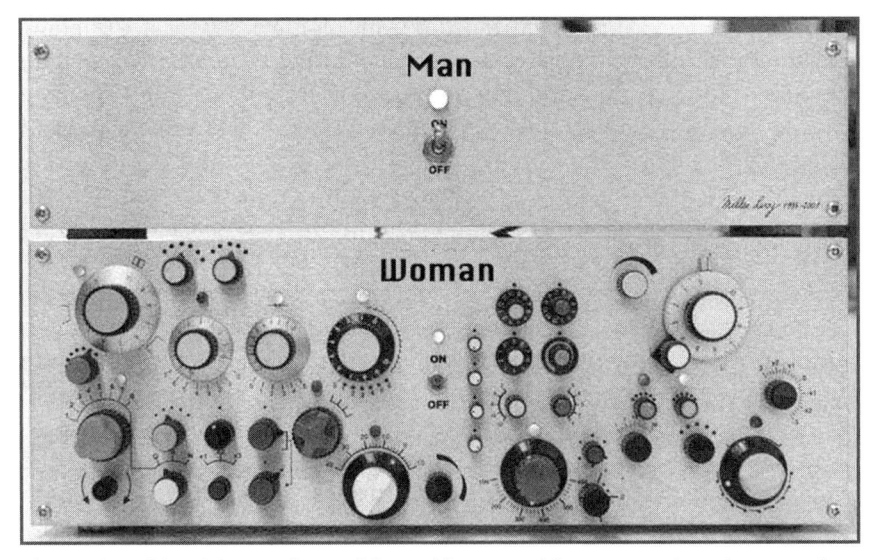

Figure 3.4. Man-Woman Control Box. *All reasonable attempts have been made to contact the copyright holder.*

airplane-ness—the elements of airplanes that are not immediately similar between them—such as parts failing out of the blue, mysterious engine behavior, and so on. These discontinuous elements give a material dimension to capriciousness and difficulty that provides the basis for understanding the actions of women (and perhaps a model for handling the disruptions they cause).

Further, these men's conception of male-female relations arguably becomes modeled on the connection they have with vehicles. While the vehicles are powerful, beautiful, and charismatic, they ultimately require the care, attention, and even the control, of men. The metonymic extension of the metaphor leads them to think of being a husband/boyfriend (again, in this heteronormative framework) in terms of being a pilot or mechanic for an airplane. They therefore need to attend carefully to the signals the women send, looking for any sign of trouble before it can get out of hand. This kind of understanding came out most frequently when the men spoke of their wives, who often required extra time and attention so that the men could spend the time they did at the hangar, working on the airplanes. Indeed, an occasional topic of conversation around the hangar was the problem of spending enough time at home so that they could come to the hangar.

During the war, putting nose art on the planes and referring to the planes as gendered at the very least evoked the involuntary absence of women. The warbird hangar, however, serves as a retreat from women, a place of "work" apart from the domestic, female space of the home (Kerber 1988), even, or perhaps especially, for the retirees who made up the bulk of the weekly workforce. As a retreat from women, it became a place to think about women. While women were rarely physically present in the maintenance hangar, they were also rarely absent from conversation. Occasional discussions of sexual adventures (usually in Southeast Asia, given the age of the mechanics and pilots) took place, but a lot of conversation focused on wives and the complexity of women. Indeed, the "Man-Woman Control Box" fits this discussion well. For example, one mechanic insisted that men were simple creatures, wanting only to "eat, screw, and play with their toys." Another told a joke in which the punchline was that it would be easier to build a bridge to Hawaii than to understand women. Such discussions illustrate the fluidity with which these men shifted from airplanes to gender relations and back, all the while sustaining both the love for, and wariness of, women and aircraft. This careful positioning gives a great deal of power to the women (and airplanes), to whom the men must attend, but ultimately, as this discussion has shown, it reinforces hierarchy of gendered spheres, with the masculine sphere predominating.

Conclusion

Despite the long history of gendering vehicles and the insistence that the practice is merely a matter of heritage-based verisimilitude, the metaphor remains a lively way to perform a lot of cultural work. To combine Levi-Strauss's famous dictum with the work of Sandra Harding (1986), gender and vehicles are good to think with. If we attend to the cultural world of the warbird hangar, the metaphorical linkage of women and World War II warplanes proves to be a productive way to understand both what the aircraft are and how people should interact with them. The notion that men can and should have a *relationship* with an aircraft makes that interaction alluring, especially when the potential object of affection carries such cultural fame. This meaning making carries a great deal of political weight, as well. Classifying the object of work (and pleasure) as female reinforces longstanding relationships of power. Masculine mastery and control of technology has long been key to male power. Making the airplanes female implicitly extends that mastery and control to men.

The gender metaphor also does two other forms of work, the extent of which I can only suggest here. Metaphors not only influence the meaning of an event or practice, but they also frame which aspects of a phenomenon are salient and which are unimportant. The gender metaphor frames the meaning of warbirds around gender politics and gender relationships, and this framing lends itself to two quite different readings of the violence of war.

First, the connection of women with the tools of war allows a psychoanalytic reading that connects violence and sex. Indeed, making the aircraft into a woman who performs the violent act can heighten the desire to have a "relationship" with the aircraft. The nose art for Texas Raiders (Figure 3.1) makes this connection, with the cowgirl depicted as having just fired her gun.

The second reading of this emphasis on relationship, in contrast, is that gendering the aircraft obviates the violence they performed during the war. The more the airplane becomes an entity with which one has a relationship, the less salient its role as destroyer of bodies and buildings becomes. This reframing is clearest, if ultimately unsuccessful, in the case of the plane named after Paul Tibbets's mother, the *Enola Gay*. The warbirders' long-term, quotidian interaction with the aircraft, aided by the model of a male-female relationship, produces affection for the plane. This affection then gets metonymically extended, through the aircraft itself, to the aircraft of wartime, making the story of the war itself in some ways the story of the relationship between the aircrews and their "women." The foregrounding of this relationship helps overcome the potential stigma of war's violence, which recedes into the background. These heroines of the "Good War" make fantastic intimate companions, whatever they may have done in their previous life.

NOTES

1. This research was supported in part by a grant from the History and Philosophy of Science, Engineering and Technology program of the National Science Foundation, #SES-0094536.
2. The organization's name was the Confederate Air Force for most of its history. The change from "Confederate" to "Commemorative" came in 2001, when objections to the Confederate name led to fundraising problems for the organization. The change was highly controversial within the organization, and to this day CAF members decry the "political correctness" that led to the name change. I will address the role of the Confederacy and whiteness in the organization's history in future work.
3. The term "airframe" here refers to the actual plane that flew during the war, in contrast to a plane that stayed in the United States but is painted to represent a plane that saw combat.
4. I use the masculine pronoun intentionally. I know of no female warbird restorers.

5. I note that this could be interpreted two ways. The first could be that the woman is the aircraft itself, firing at the enemy. The second is that the woman is the object pursued, the reward for fighting.
6. This name/nose art combination demonstrates, like most warbird images, the reflexive nature of their memory of the "Good War." The very name of the aircraft evokes the nostalgia at work in warbirders' representation of the past, and the pairing of an iconic song and image from the war further cements the depiction not as a moment-in-time during the war, but as an after-the-fact assembly of an idealized image of the past (Handler and Saxton 1988).
7. Another alternate reading of the image could be that it echoes the wartime feminization of the Chinese allies.
8. It is true that a few prominent women exist in the warbird movement, but even their visibility, in my experience, did not affect the daily roles of women in warbird hangars.
9. The name Bearcat is the official nickname given to the type of aircraft, and most military aircraft have some official name. The naming system for these planes deserves further exploration in another context.

REFERENCES

Anonymous. 1974. *The Ghost Squadron of the Confederate Air Force: A Pictorial History of the Preservation of the World's Greatest Combat Aircraft of World War II*. Dallas, TX: Taylor Publishing Co.

Bredau, Robert N. 1989. "The Meaning of Nose Art: An Anthropological Perspective." Master's thesis, California State University, Sacramento.

Cockburn, Cynthia. 1981. "The Material of Male Power." *Feminist Review* 9 (Autumn): 41–58.

Crocker, J. Christopher. 1977a. "My Brother the Parrot." In *The Social Use of Metaphor: Essays on the Anthropology of Rhetoric*, edited by J. David Sapir and J. Christopher Crocker, 164–92. Philadelphia: University of Pennsylvania Press.

———. 1977b. "The Social Functions of Rhetorical Forms." In *The Social Use of Metaphor: Essays on the Anthropology of Rhetoric*, edited by J. David Sapir and J. Christopher Crocker, 33–66. Philadelphia: University of Pennsylvania Press.

Deakin, John. 2001. "Pelican's Perch #47: The Old Commando." http://www.avweb.com/news/columns/182136-1.html, accessed October 15, 2003.

Ethell, Jeffrey, and Clarence Simonsen. 2003. *Aircraft Nose Art: From World War I to Today*. Detroit: Motorbooks International.

Fernandez, James. 1974. "The Mission of Metaphor in Expressive Culture." *Current Anthropology* 15, no. 2: 119–45.

Fleishman, Ron. N.d. "Curtiss C-46: A Four-Engined Airplane With Two Engines." http://www.orgsites.com/ca/caf-socal/C46History.htm, accessed March 12, 2005.

Gaines, Jane. 1980. "The Showgirl and the Wolf." *Cinema Journal* 20, no. 1: 53–67.
Geertz, Clifford. 1973. *The Interpretation of Cultures*. New York: Basic Books.
Gibson, Jr., Col. Everett K. N.d. "About 'Texas Raiders' B-17G." http://www.gulfcoastwing.org/GCW/AboutUs.htm, accessed July 31, 2010.
Handler, Richard, and William Saxton. 1988. "Dyssimulation: Reflexivity, Narrative, and the Quest for Authenticity in 'Living History.'" *Cultural Anthropology* 3, no. 3: 242–60.
Harding, Sandra G. 1986. *The Science Question In Feminism*. Ithaca: Cornell University Press.
Kakoudaki, Despina. 2004. "Pinup: The American Secret Weapon in World War II." In *Porn Studies*, edited by Linda Williams, 335–69. Durham, NC: Duke University Press.
Kerber, L. K. 1988. "Separate Spheres, Female Worlds, Woman's Place: The Rhetoric of Women's History." *The Journal of American History* 75, no. 1: 9–39.
Klare, George R. 2003. "Why Nose Art? A Psychologist's View." In *Aircraft Nose Art: From World War I to Today*, edited by J. Ethell and C. Simonsen, 11–16. Detroit: Motorbooks International.
Mellefont, Jeffrey. 2000. "Heirlooms and Tea Towels: Views of Ships' Gender in the Modern Maritime Museum." *The Great Circle, Journal of the Australian Association for Maritime History* 22, no. 1: 5–16.
O'Dwyer, Carolyn. 2004. "Tropic Knights and Hula Belles: War and Tourism in the South Pacific." *Journal for Cultural Research* 8, no. 1: 33–50.
Oldenziel, Ruth. 1999. *Making Technology Masculine: Men, Women and Modern Machines in America, 1870–1945*. Amsterdam: Amsterdam University Press.
Rodgers, Silvia. 1984. "Feminine Power at Sea." *Royal Anthropological Institute News* no. 64: 1–4.
Sapir, J. David. 1977. "The Anatomy of Metaphor." In *The Social Use of Metaphor: Essays on the Anthropology of Rhetoric*, edited by J. David Sapir and J. Christopher Crocker, 1–32. Philadelphia: University of Pennsylvania Press.
Schulze, Michael. 2008. "Wings & Water: Ghost Story." *Robb Report*. Available at http://www.robbreport.com/Wings—Water-Ghost-Story.aspx, accessed June 29, 2010.
Shah, Hemant. 2003. "'Asian Culture' And Asian American Identities in the Television and Film Industries of the United States." *Studies in Media & Information Literacy Education* 3, no. 3: 1–16.
Sica, Patricia. 2010. Personal communication.
Wayland, Kent A. 2006. "A Better Past through Technology: World War II Warplanes as Cultural Heritage." PhD dissertation, University of Virginia, Charlottesville.
Wetmore, Jameson. N.d. "Moving Relationships: Befriending the Automobile to Relieve Anxiety." http://www.drdriving.org/misc/anthropomorph.html, accessed July 13, 2010.
Wood, J. P. 1999. *Nose Art: 80 Years of Aviation Artwork*. New York: Barnes & Noble.

CHAPTER 4

Is Female to Male as Lightweight Cars Are to Sports Cars?
Gender Metaphors and Cognitive Schemas in Recessionary Japan

Joshua Hotaka Roth

Gendered Driving

As a young adult, Koji dropped out of Japan's most prestigious engineering program to work as a mechanic for the Mazda racing team. The team was a perpetual underdog in the Le Mans 24-hour endurance race but, in 1991, came from behind to beat the favorite Mercedes Benz team. Just one year later, however, Mazda's team was disbanded, a casualty of the recession that hit Japanese automobile manufacturers in the early 1990s and rule changes at Le Mans limiting the power of Mazda's rotary engine. Koji has gone on to have a successful career as a software programmer, but he still regrets how short-lived was his pit crew career. His dreams of professional racing in part fuel his late night excursions in his black Mazda RX-8 on the highways around Tokyo and Yokohama. One of his favorite routes is the narrow and winding Tokyo loop highway (*shuto kōsoku*, 首都高速), where he speeds past other cars, accelerating into sharp turns, his tires losing their grip for a fraction of a second as they pass over metal strips, giving the sensation that the car might fly over the railing onto the buildings below. On the long straight stretches of the newer bayside section (*wangan kōsoku*, 湾岸高速) he floors the accelerator and the car reaches 200 km/hr.

Koji's cousin, Daisuke, says Koji is crazy, pointing out that Koji's license has been revoked three times in the past ten years.

Neither Koji's wife, nor Daisuke's, enjoys driving. Koji's wife says that he and Daisuke both drive very aggressively (*gatsu gatsu unten*), and that they would certainly get into an altercation if they ever encountered each other on the road. In response, Daisuke suggests that women pose a greater danger puttering about in their miniature *kei* cars (軽自動車 *kei-jidōsha*, literally, lightweight cars, hereafter abbreviated "K"), driving in a sluggish manner (*noro noro unten*), disrupting the flow of traffic.

The gendered quality of driving expresses itself both in descriptions of how men and women drive and also in the kinds of vehicles that they drive. A range is available for both men and women, but I will focus here on two kinds—the sports car and the lightweight K-car—that exemplify and reinforce gender differences. Men are to women, as sports cars are to K-cars. We may represent the relationship thus:

>   men   : women
> sports cars : K-cars

It is more commonplace for driving to be experienced by men such as Koji as something that frees them, even if just temporarily, from the constraints of their daily lives. This liberating possibility is embodied in the form of the Mazda RX-8 or other sports cars, which are impractical for daily use but which give material form to the ideals of speed and power. In contrast to the sports car, the lightweight car embodies practicality. Women are the primary drivers of privately owned Ks. These tiny, fuel-efficient vehicles are ideal for daily shopping or ferrying children to and from school. Rather than providing a release from the daily routines, these vehicles yoke women ever more closely to their domestic duties. This suggests other paired oppositions:

>   freedom   : domesticity
> transcendent : quotidian

Sports cars may serve as metaphors for masculinity not just because men drive them more than do women, but also because they express an underlying association of men with power and speed. Likewise K-cars serve as metaphors for femininity not only because women drive them more, but also because the latter vehicles express an underlying association of women with family and nurturance. As we will see, there are entire discourses on speed and on safety that have coexisted for decades in Japan without much sense of contradiction because they have been effectively compartmentalized according to gender.[1] At the same time that safety is held up as an ideal for all, there is the implicit understanding that men speed, and that women drive safely and with consideration for others.

Lakoff and Johnson (1980) suggest that metaphors constitute the basic building blocks of thought, and that certain conceptual metaphors organize other metaphors. Strauss and Quinn (1997) critique Lakoff and Johnson's focus on metaphors and prefer to think in terms of "cognitive schema"—patterns of associations built up over time that correspond to neural pathways. They argue that particular metaphors can come and go, without really affecting the underlying cognitive schema, which will find other metaphors and other means to express itself. Despite the differences between these approaches, they both posit a multilayered cognitive organization in which relatively stable layers undergird more fluid ones.

In fact, however, metaphors can actively sustain underlying cognitive schemas, not just passively express them. For example, the physical characteristics of the K-car vehicle allow us to add other paired oppositions to our set:

> sports cars : K-cars
> speed and power : economy

And, as Fernandez (1977, 1986) suggests, metaphors may further motivate performance, as men race their cars and women give way. This, plus the physical qualities of the K-car allow us to add more paired oppositions:

> flow : stop and go
> aggressive (*gatsu gatsu*) : lethargic (*noro noro*)
> danger : safety, consideration

By examining K-cars and sports cars as gendered vehicles, we may gain certain insights about how these conceptual levels relate to one another. Certain metaphors may help organize others, and it may not be so easy to replace an important metaphor with another. As we will see, a shift in vehicle-metaphors may signal larger-scale shifts in socioeconomic contexts. In this chapter, I explore these topics by drawing on ethnographic data, popular culture representations, as well as the Japanese online social networking site Mixi.

Harmonizing Cars and Humans in the Era of Mass Motorization

Automobiles arrived in Japan in the early twentieth century, but for the first several decades they were insignificant in comparison to the cultural and physical transformation wrought by the expanding rail systems (Freedman 2010; Fujii 1999). In the 1930s, streetcars started to face competition in the form of buses. Buses and trucks dominated the streets through the mid 1960s, but the number of private cars rapidly increased at this time. In 1966, the number of vehicles in use in Japan surpassed the 10 million mark, 3.8 million of which were private cars, leading some commentators to mark this year as the start of the "mai-ka" (literally, "my car") era (Plath 1992: 230; JAMA 2008: 3). Rising wages and lower costs made personal cars affordable for many people who could only dream of owning one prior to the 1960s (Plath 1992). Although the cars that people could afford were very economical, they allowed a sense of participation in a consumer-based modernity. By 2006, there were almost 76 million vehicles on Japan's roads, of which 57.5 million were cars (JAMA 2008: 3). The novelty of driving in Japan in the 1960s, and the excitement of so many embarking on a newly motorized lifestyle, resembles descriptions of Chinese car culture in the first decade of this century (Hessler 2010; Notar 2012).

The newly developing car in Japan also had a dark side, one characterized by congestion and chaos. Traffic fatalities increased steadily until they hit their high of 16,765 in 1970, for a rate of 16.2 deaths per 100,000 people. Literary critic Jeffrey Schnapp (1999) writes that in the European context, at the start of the automotive era, artists, filmmakers, and other cultural elites embraced not just speed but crashes too as central aspects of the modern experience. Indeed, we may think of cars and their crashes as metaphoric vehicles for other dimensions of modern experience, for example, the speed of financial flows and cyclical financial crashes, or the speed of scientific development and the terror of modern warfare (Virilio [1977] 1986). As we will see later in the section on speed and masculinity, cars in Japan too have served as metaphors for the enormous complexity of modern society, built upon human labor and ingenuity, spinning out of human control.

Yet from the point of view of urban planners, other administrators, as well as the broader public, concern about the grim toll of traffic accidents in the 1960s and 1970s led to extensive discussion in Japanese automotive magazines about how to ensure greater safety. Some advocated for the "harmonization of cars and humans" (*kuruma to hito no chōwa*) (Kuruma no techo 1970; Roth 2011). The very high numbers of fatalities involving children who had used the streets as playgrounds until the 1950s and 1960s led planners to construct more dedicated play areas in Japanese urban environments, one step toward "harmonization." School children were trained to walk on designated routes between home and school (*tsūgakuro*).

In 2007, elementary schools in Kawagoe (Saitama Prefecture) and other cities had children make neighborhood maps that indicated all kinds of danger, many focusing on car traffic. The map below (Figure 4.1) reads:

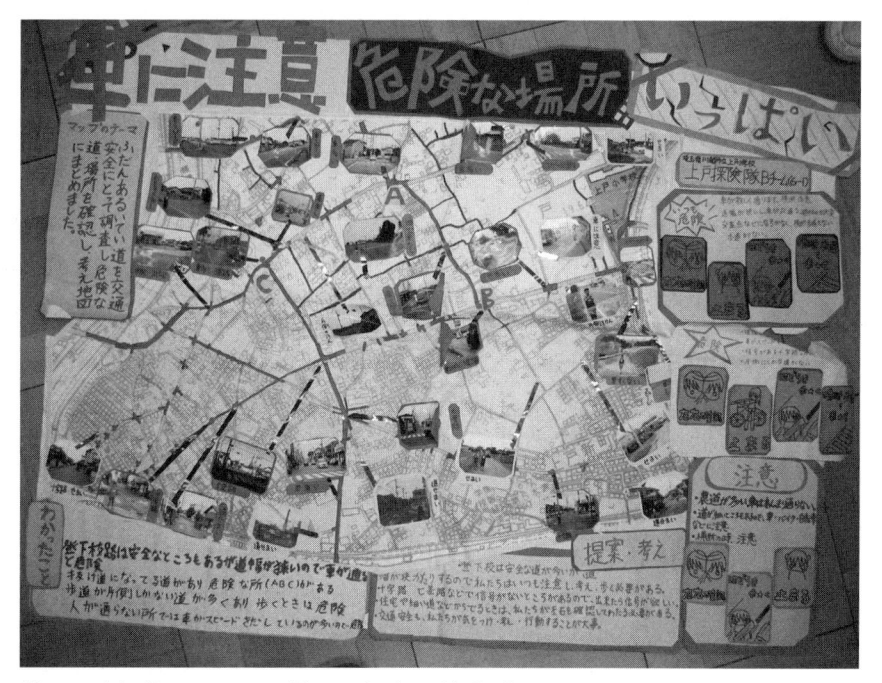

Figure 4.1. Danger map. Photo: Joshua N. Roth.

"Be careful of cars! Dangerous places are all around!" Competitions are held in which school children make traffic safety posters, many of which are displayed in city halls or police stations all over the country.

In urban centers, sidewalks have been gradually installed to replace the standard painted lines along the edges of roads, providing much-needed separation of pedestrian and automobile traffic. But many Japanese streets in the 2000s still lacked sidewalks, even in major cities, as shown in the image of Kawagoe below (Figure 4.2), and even as the overall number of fatalities has dropped, pedestrian and bicycle fatalities were still almost 50 percent of traffic-related deaths in 2009 (National Police Agency 2009: 128).

A discourse on driving manners emerged in the 1960s at the start of Japan's era of mass motorization. At that time, Japanese car magazines provided a forum for an emerging manners discourse which highlighted the term "*yuzuri-ai*" (譲り合い yielding, or mutual giving way) (Roth 2012). Giving way involves the consideration of others through the deliberate halting of one's own progress. One author writes that well-mannered drivers give way to each other (*tagaini yuzuriau manā ga ari* 互いに譲り合うマナーがあり), and drive in a way that avoids creating a nuisance (JAF 1968). At a time when driving still was not accessible to the entire

Figure 4.2. No sidewalks in the 2000s. Photo: Joshua N. Roth

population, one author criticized Japanese drivers' misplaced sense of special privilege, which, when combined with the qualities of impatience (*sekkachi* せっかち) and competitiveness, leads to terrible driving manners (*doraibu manā no warusa* ドラブマナーの悪さ) (JAF 1967). A 1970 letter from a reader of one magazine frames the hurried quality of Japanese driving explicitly in terms of manners, admonishing Japanese drivers to slow down and "respect manners" (*manā o sonpu* マナーを遵守) (JAF 1970). Slogans continue to adorn the roads throughout the country, with many sprouting regularly with every traffic campaign, while others linger on throughout the year.

The manners campaign and the project to "harmonize" cars and humans acknowledge the fact that heavy metal objects propelled at high velocities had the potential to do great damage to human flesh. The trick was to find a way to allow them to co-exist without undue harm to humans. Ultimately, harmonization involved the normalization of the system of automobility and the acceptance of some level of injury as inevitable for drivers, passengers, and bystanders (Roth 2011; Jain 2004; Handler, this volume). Perhaps the acceptable level of injury remained somewhat higher than it could have been because harmonization was feminized, and seemed most clearly to embrace drivers of K-cars.

K-Cars, Manners, Femininity

No more than 11.15-feet long and 4.86-feet wide, and with a 660 cc engine, K-cars are the smallest class of vehicles in Japan. These specifications have increased somewhat since the category of the K was first established in 1950, reflecting the increase in size and power of cars in general. In that year, the Transportation Ministry specified K-cars as those not exceeding 9 feet, 84 inches in length and 4 feet 32 inches width, with a tiny 300cc engine (Ozeki 2007:13). The next year the limit on engine size was increased to 360cc. But it was not until 1955 when Ks started to be taxed at a substantial discount compared to larger cars that manufacturers began making them in substantial numbers. Since then, the number of Ks has increased rapidly.

Initially, most cars were of limited power and the category of Ks was not particularly feminized. Cars became more and more distinct from each other over the same period of time that the number of women drivers was rapidly increasing beginning in the early 1970s, and as the ideal of the female homemaker took hold in Japan. In 1969 women comprised just 17 percent of all license holders. Their share had risen to 29 percent by 1980, and 42 percent by 2004 (National Police Agency 2005). This is the period during which Ks became feminized. In some two-car families, there may be a larger sedan that the husband will drive, and a K (marked by the yellow license plate) for the wife (Figure 4.3). In one entry in the Mixi interest group with over 1,000 members called "Do not make fun of K-cars!" (軽自動車をバカにするな!), a woman writes that she's very happy with her K, that it gets great mileage, and feels roomy on the inside. The one drawback, "compared to her husband's sedan, is that other cars on the road do not give way to her K" (だんな様のセダンに比べ…道譲ってくれない('•_•')(笑)).

Ks represent practicality and economy. They do not represent the exciting potential of other kinds of cars. Their speed is limited. They generally cannot go on highways. They are perfect for puttering about city streets to go shopping, or taking kids to and from music or English lessons or play-dates with schoolmates. While many mothers may take their preschoolers to school on the backs of their bicycles, and older kids generally walk to school, cars are important for many child-centered activities, especially in suburban areas such as in Hamamatsu City, Shizuoka Prefecture, where I did my dissertation research in the mid 1990s, as well as in Kawagoe City, Saitama Prefecture, where I did car-related research in 2007. One mother on a Mixi site wrote that she had logged more than 27,000 kilometers in the last two and a half years going back and forth to the preschool and that the K was serving as "the legs of the family in

Figure 4.3. A husband and a wife. The yellow license plate indicates a K-car. Photo: Joshua N. Roth.

place of the bicycle" (通勤でもなく保育園の送り迎え…後はチャリンコがわり … 家族のアッシー等等 …).

The association of Ks with women drivers is evident in the numerous posts on Mixi about how women view men who drive Ks. In addition, there is an entire interest group with over 800 members called "What's the problem with men driving Ks?" (男が軽自動車に乗って何が悪い?). Some posts express anxiety about whether driving a K makes one an undesirable marriage prospect. While other posts reject the inclination to judge a person by his car, they acknowledge that many people continue to do so.

The K's diminutive size and lack of speed make it an ideal vehicle for the performance of domestic duties and create the association of Ks with women. These qualities also make drivers of Ks more attentive to other vehicles on the road. We might think of the style of driving associated with Ks as premised on what Goffman calls the "participation unit" (1971, cited in Handler, this volume), in which traffic is understood as a social order that demands all drivers be attentive to each other. Goffman contrasts the participation unit with the "vehicular unit" which prioritizes the relationship between driver and the car, a focus that reduces other vehicles on the road to the status of mere obstacles (1971). The attentiveness to other drivers and pedestrians that is characteristic of women driving Ks allows them to exemplify the driving manners of the safety campaigns from the 1960s to the present day.

On its surface, the discourse on driving manners appears to be gender neutral. Yet several factors suggest that driving manners can be construed as distinctly effeminate. Not only do drivers of K-cars exemplify driving manners; these manners have to be understood within the larger framework of manners discourses in Japan, which focuses much more on women than men (Bardsley and Miller 2011). Hundreds of manners books line the shelves of most bookstores. There is a sub-genre of business manners that is directed as much to men as to women, but the overwhelming majority of writing on manners is focused on women. Representative titles include *How to Behave Like a Lady* (美人の作法), *Manners Book for Women* (女性のためのマナーBOOK), *Women's Beautiful Manners Encyclopedia* (女性の美しいマナー事典).[2]

While manners books and advice columns were very popular in the United States in the early and mid twentieth century, there is a sense now that manners are a thing of an earlier time, that they are elitist, and that they suppress a more authentic expression of self. In the United States, popular advice columns discuss issues related to manners, but more emphasis is given to self-realization, even when the topic involves relationships. Children's books now are the genre most likely to deal explicitly with manners in the United States, with titles such as *Dude, That's Rude, Get Some Manners*, and *How Do Dinosaurs Eat Their Food?*. By contrast, manners continue to pervade many social contexts in Japan, and can be thought to be consonant with self-realization rather than contradictory to it (Roth 2012: 183–85).

The public spaces of mass transit in Japan are one site in which manners discourse is particularly pronounced. The Tokyo Subway has had frequent public service campaigns that advocate for and against a variety of behavior since at least the 1970s (Eidan 1983; Eidan 1991). In 1975, a caption on one poster of two fashionably dressed women seated with crossed legs in a subway car read, "Glamour is glamour, a nuisance is a nuisance, to say nothing of ill-mannered men" (魅力は魅力、邪魔は邪魔、まして男性の 無作法なんて *miryoku wa miryoku, jama wa jama*) (Eidan 1983: 18). This was just one of many posters that criticized women whose crossed legs inconsiderately jutted out among the standing passengers crowded around her. The caption for another poster from 1983 reads, "Princess! You are too spread out!" criticizing women for spreading out too much laterally (Eidan 1991: 22). There are posters that criticize ill-mannered men, but women are generally held to a higher standard.

When they violate convention, it seems to undermine their status in a way that similar infractions committed by men do not.

The gendered association of apparently gender-neutral manners discourse also emerges in the distinctly masculine speed discourse. If the key term in popular-culture discourse on manners, *yuzuri-ai,* or mutually giving way, involves the deliberate halting of one's own progress, the discourse on speed emphasizes flow, and the courting of danger rather than its avoidance (Sato 1991: 3–36). The social relationship in this case is more competitive, with each driver attempting to pass the next, rather than give way. While manners are about safety, speed is about danger. Two widely read *manga* series from the 1990s—"Initial D" and "Wangan Midnight"—exemplify the speed discourse. It is precisely the greater sense of danger and possibility of death that attracts the protagonists of these series to cars and street racing.

Sports Cars, Speed, Masculinity

It was in the early and mid 1990s when the *manga* "Wangan Midnight" and "Initial D" documented the culture of street racing that had developed in the liminal time-space of the late-night mountains encircling Tokyo and on urban highways. These long-running *manga* spun off *anime* series, video games, and live-action films, and are a part of a much broader "automotive cultural industry" (Fuller 2005: 10) that arose with widespread motorization in Japan in the 1960s. The main protagonist in each is a lower-middle-class high-school boy, one living in his own apartment after his parents divorced, another growing up with his father. Each is immersed in a schedule of school, part-time work, and a home life lacking in emotional warmth. They are *hashiriya,* good kids who achieve an emotional high through speed, as opposed to *bōsōzoku,* who specialize in loud roars, ostentatious modifications, and harassment of other drivers and entire neighborhoods for their own sake. The main protagonists of "Initial D" and "Wangan Midnight" are slender, introspective types, who evoke a style of masculinity that has had a long history in the Japanese literary tradition (see Morris 1975). In both series, the masculinity of the protagonists is defined in terms of a profound involvement with cars, rather than with female characters. The protagonists' intimate understanding of their cars' potential and limits in every situation, whether going uphill or downhill, around turns or on straightaways, in good weather and bad, allows them to meld with the machine in a way unattainable by others and gives them the edge when racing.

The main protagonist of "Initial D," Takumi, lives with his father. His mother is completely absent from the story. Takumi drives his father's old Toyota Sprinter Trueno (a Corolla model introduced in 1983) and has honed his driving skills on the mountain roads around his town making deliveries for his father's tofu shop. Slowly, it becomes clear that Takumi's quiet father is skilled at tuning the old Trueno and that he has had racing experience in the past. The father's aura and that of the car seem to propel Takumi toward racing as a means toward self-understanding.

In "Wangan Midnight," the high school-aged protagonist Akio lives by himself. Akio drives an original model Nissan S30Z (a model first introduced in 1969) that he salvaged from a scrap yard. It is revealed that the old S30Z was actually the notorious "Devil Z," the fastest and most dangerous car that had raced on Tokyo's streets in the 1970s, several of whose previous owners had died in fiery crashes. Akio eventually tracks down the mechanic who had tuned the Devil Z and is now running a small bicycle shop, and convinces him to help revive this car. We learn that this mechanic had been one of the top tuners in the country, and eventually he fills the role of father figure for Akio. While the father in "Initial D" and the father figure in "Wangan Midnight" have given up racing themselves, they serve to inspire the young protagonists to continue where they left off.

If father figures motivate racing, female characters generally impede it. The young male protagonists never develop romantic relationships with female admirers, fixated as they are on their cars. The lesser characters that appear in this series show how female companionship gets in the way of racing. In "Wangan Midnight," one married mechanic's passion for racing has waned, but is rekindled upon encountering the Devil Z on the highways around Tokyo. When he blows his savings on a new Nissan GT-R in order to take up racing again, his pregnant wife leaves him and moves back in with her parents in the countryside. They are reunited only when he gives up racing once and for all. Another mechanic rebuffs an old girlfriend's marriage proposal, explaining that he cannot make her happy. She finally wins him over when she makes clear that she loves him for the intense passion he has for his work with cars. In the world of street racing depicted in these works, women and cars seem incompatible, unless women are willing to take a 'back seat.'

There are several female characters in these dramas, however, who defy the gender norms. In "Initial D," a pair of women form an impressive racing team. Although they compete well with some of the lesser male characters, they cannot defeat Takumi and his Trueno. In "Wangan Midnight" one of the main racers is a woman. Much like the male characters, however, she is single, and driven to race for reasons she does not fully comprehend. Ultimately, her character does not challenge the inverse relationship between driving and familial or romantic relationships. The high school-aged daughter of a successful middle-aged mechanic becomes a successful mechanic in her own right. But once again, doing so confers upon her masculine characteristics more than it undermines gender norms. Her ultimate validation comes in the last sequence of episodes in the animated series when Akio brings the Devil Z to her to tune. Her parents comment that she has become like the son they never had, and that she has the ability to carry on the family business.

The masculine ideal of the almost exclusive relationship between driver and car comes across in the quasi-spiritual bond between Takumi and his Trueno in "Initial D," and between Akio and the Devil Z in "Wangan Midnight." While Takumi's Trueno is not nearly as powerful as more modern cars, it handles the mountain roads extremely well, and Takumi is able to perfect an uncanny technique of drifting around sharp curves. In the furious downhill races, he interacts with his car at a completely unconscious level, allowing him to drift within inches of guard rails and find the most efficient line around the curves, and to overcome overwhelming odds against more modern and powerful cars, recalling Japanese fantasies of overcoming a much more powerful yet spiritually lacking adversary during World War II.

In "Wangan Midnight," the Devil Z enchants Akio from the time he first spots it in a scrap yard. It should be noted, however, that the relationship is not just between human and inanimate object. The car itself takes on an animate quality. Throughout the series, the Z is depicted as having its own volition, crashing in ways to hurt or save the driver, in effect choosing its driver. Unlike other drivers who know when to exit from racing, Akio resolves to drive his Z "until the end." Akio respects the Z for what it is, nurturing it, tuning it, but only in such a way as to preserve its character, refusing to install computer systems that could make it more efficient and powerful. By contrast, his primary rival, Shima, adds whatever technology is available to his Porsche 911, but eventually recognizes in Akio's relationship to the Z the possibility of a deeper kind of relationship with vehicles. In the final episode, as Akio speeds past his rivals, Shima notes that Akio and the Z have "overcome the barrier between human and machine."

The racing genre explores the blurring of boundaries between humans and vehicles, much as does the *mecha* genre of Japanese *manga* and animation, although with certain noteworthy differences. In the *mecha* genre, when human pilots fuse with an armored suit that provides superhuman strength, it simultaneously leaves them feeling drained and alienated, and bereft of romantic relationships (Napier 2001: 85–102). By contrast, the merging of pilots and cars in "Initial D" and "Wangan Midnight" does not seem quite as dark, for even while racing takes certain protagonists away from human relationships, this merging of humans and vehicle in the street racing series is depicted as a kind of consummation of a spiritually pure relationship.

In "Wangan Midnight," the racers seem to experience moments of greatest meaning precisely when darting around and past the lifeless, almost motionless traffic around them. There are frequent scenes of racers zipping through narrow openings between trucks, and we rarely get a sense of any volition or sentience in these other vehicles and their drivers. Those who drive at normal speeds appear to lack interiority; they are drones, part of the machine that is Japanese society. Both "Initial D" and "Wangan Midnight" convey the beauty and excitement of street racing, and the alienation of racers from broader Japanese society. The drivers appear to gain meaning in life by masterful control when driving at high speeds, but these series give no sense of the risk that they pose to others.

The emotional clarity about social relationships that some of the other drivers achieve never affects the hero of the series, Akio, whose relationship with the Devil Z remains undiluted. In the end, this series celebrates the transcendental experience of speed, and the driver's relationship to a quasi-sentient vehicle, all the while denying the agency of the everyday drivers on public roads. In these 1990s street racing *manga*, speed is premised on what Goffman calls the "vehicular unit" and is considered a masculine trait (see Handler, this volume). Masculinity is defined in terms of the human-vehicle relationship of the speed discourse in contrast to femininity, which is defined by the human-human relationship of manners discourse.

Driving in *Uchi* and *Soto* Spaces

Masculine styles of driving are associated not only with male drivers of sports cars, but with specific locales—highways or mountain roads. Likewise, feminine styles of driving are associated not only with female drivers of K-cars, but with neighborhood spaces that may be considered extensions of domestic space. Numerous scholars of Japan have noted the cognitive structuring of space in the paired terms *uchi* (inner) and *soto* (outer), with different degrees of formality of interactions expected in each (Bachnik 1992; Kondo 1987; Doi 1973; Nakane 1970). Thus we may add a couple more paired oppositions to our set:

highways and mountain roads	:	neighborhood spaces
soto (outer) spaces	:	*uchi* (inner) spaces

Women's use of K-cars for shopping and for transporting children around town associate it with domesticity, and one might think of the neighborhood within which the K navigates as an extension of the *uchi* (inner) space, a kind of domestic space that allows for greater informality of self-presentation (Ashikari 2003). Certainly, it is a very different kind of space from the mountain roads and highways that are the province of late-night street racing. And yet men navigate these same neighborhood roads on their way between neighborhoods. For them, Ks may appear like women walking around in *soto* spaces with their aprons on.

Perhaps this interpretation also informed the views of my informants, Koji and Daisuke, who commented to me that Ks drive in a sluggish manner (*noro noro unten*), disrupting the flow of traffic, and should be taken off the road. There is much opportunity for men and women to contest the status of neighborhood spaces—women defining them as extensions of *uchi* space and men defining them as *soto* space. It is in this contest that men may berate women just for being on the public roads as if these roads were their own private spaces. For their part, women may criticize men for their aggressive attitudes that violate both the expectation of decorum in *soto* spaces and the human feeling expected in *uchi* spaces.

Some women noted a stark difference on the road when they drove Ks by contrast to when they drove full-sized cars. One woman I knew in her mid-thirties mentioned that when she drove a K she was tailgated much more frequently (*yoku aorareru*) than when she drove a larger car. Another complained that men assume that larger cars have priority over Ks. She described one instance when she turned off a main road onto a smaller alley, one of many in Japan open to traffic in both directions but wide enough for just one car to pass. There, she had a stand-off with an oncoming taxi about who should back up. The male taxi driver invoked a common stereotype that women did not know how to back up. In this case, however, the woman would have had to back up into a busy street. More than anything else, the taxi driver's attitude galled this woman, who took down his license plate number and phoned in a complaint.

Male aggression toward women drivers takes its most extreme form when criminal gangs target them. One woman described an experience with an *atariya* (当たり屋 accident faker) where one car tailgated her, and another car in front stopped short on purpose. She was able to stop without hitting the car in front. Nevertheless, a "scary looking" guy got out of one car and accused her of hitting him and demanded compensation. When she threatened to call the police the other cars drove off, but she said that other women could easily be intimidated into handing over money.

Some women are clearly able to resist male aggression directed toward themselves and their Ks on neighborhood roads. Yet in other instances, the compartmentalization of space and types of cars may help sustain the differentiation of masculine and feminine driving styles.

Driving in Drag

When we consider the ways in which gender structures the domain of automobility, we need to recognize that not all Japanese women drive in a stop-and-go manner. Some love to drive fast and are perfectly able to weave through traffic at high speeds with the best of the guys, as was the case of one of my neighbors in Kawagoe. In college, she enjoyed taking car trips with friends and fondly recalled the accolades she received for her quick reflexes and good sense for mountain roads. Later, she redirected her love of speed toward a mastery of road networks in various delivery jobs, a formerly male-dominated occupation into which women have entered in substantial numbers since the 1980s. In the *manga* "Initial D" and "Wangan Midnight," there are several female racers. We noted, however, that they are all single young women unattached to families, and we may consider them to play masculine roles in contrast to the majority of female characters whose role is to care for, wait for, worry about, or fall in love with the male drivers. On the one hand, these female racers present the possibility that women can define themselves apart from the domestic ideal. On the other hand, they can end up reinforcing the gender ideology by fulfilling a recognized gender ideal, albeit a masculine one that is not normally associated with women, rather than fashioning a more radical alternative.

The multiple interpretive possibilities in the case of female street racers are in some ways similar to that of the female actors who specialize in male roles in the all-female Takarazuka Theater. In her study of Takarazuka, Jennifer Robertson (1998) highlights this ambiguity. At one level, these female specialists in male roles (*otokoyaku*) do not challenge the heterosexual gender norm in which romance is only possible between masculine and feminine gendered characters. Indeed, many in the audience find a fulfilling representation of their heteronormative romantic fantasies in Takarazuka (Nakamura and Matsuo 2003). And yet at another level, the audience is quite aware that the *otokoyaku* are women, and that these actors are able to create male roles that are somehow different from and more desirable than men in the real world. To some degree, this has led to a lesbian fan subculture centered around the dashing and romantic *otokoyaku* (Robertson 1998).

Yet the comparison between *otokoyaku* and female street racers only holds to a certain point. Women who drive in drag—women who reject Ks for other kinds of cars that allow for much more masculine styles of driving—may end up reinforcing gender stereotypes in a less ambiguous way than do the Takarazuka theater's *otokoyaku*. After all, cars encase and obscure drivers, rendering their sex irrelevant in a way that is not the case with Takarazuka, where the knowledge of drag facilitates an interpretation that potentially directly conflicts with official gender ideology. The relative anonymity of confident and aggressive women drivers dampens, if not precludes, such an effect.

People could more significantly undermine official ideology if they were to drive large and powerful cars in a more polite and less aggressive manner. Likewise, they could drive Ks in a more aggressive manner. This would represent a radically different stance on the part of a vehicle that serves as metaphor for female drivers, in a way that an unseen woman driving a masculine gendered car in an aggressive fashion cannot express. The economic circumstances of the past several years make this kind of subversion of gender more likely.

Gender Schema and Driving Metaphors in Recessionary Japan

Sales of K-cars have exploded with the onset of the long-lasting recession in Japan. The K's proportion of total car ownership has increased from a low in 1980 of 17 percent to a high in 2010 of 35 percent, with the rapid increase in market share occurring since 1990 (Ozeki 2007: 156). Not only do Ks cost substantially less than do other cars, but they continue to enjoy a lower tax status, they are often exempt from the rule that requires purchasers of cars to show proof of having a parking space (*shako shōmei*) when registering the car, and their fuel economy has become a greater advantage in this era of high gas prices. While many Ks are trucks and minivans used for business purposes and are not gendered in the same way as K sedans, the proportion of K sedans has risen from just 11.22 percent of the K market in 1990 (Ozeki 2007: 156) to 65.59 percent in 2010 (Zenkeiren 2010).

The increased number of Ks in itself may not have been sufficient to transform their gender associations, but they lay the groundwork. Increased engine size and efficiency have complemented the increased numbers. Engines have expanded from just 300cc in 1950 to 660cc in

1990. Greater efficiency also means that substantially more power is harnessed even from a modest increase in combustion. Today, Ks have a lot more pep than they used to, allowing people to drive them much more aggressively than before. In the past, people thought it would be too dangerous to drive Ks on highways. Now, even without modifications they can more than keep up with high-speed traffic.

Many posts on several K-car related Mixi social media groups record the surprise of the drivers of normal sedans when their Ks are able to shake tailgaters or pass other cars. One recounts driving home from work stuck behind a slow-moving car: "When I moved into the other lane to pass I found that there was a line of ten or so cars, but it would not look good to return and I could not if I wanted to, so I just floored it and passed the entire line ... The drivers I passed must have thought what, a K?!" One woman writes that she drove a 13-year-old MOVE: "Although it is a K, I'm an idiot who tailgates normal cars."

We notice the breakdown of compartmentalizing analogy of sports cars : K-cars :: men : women. Modified, turbo-charged K-cars now speed about. A monthly magazine, *Hot-K*, was launched in November 2009; it competes with other recent K magazines such as *K Refine*, which appeared in 2007; *K Style*, which came out in 2010; as well as the more venerable *K Car Special* which started back in the late 1980s. Japan's long recession has affected street racers as much as anyone, and some have switched to racing K-cars that are much cheaper to maintain. In addition to the lower sticker price and taxes, many parts for Ks cost significantly less than parts for other cars. Those who practice drifting on the mountain roads, spinning their wheels as they go around tight turns, generally have to replace their tires every week. K tires cost half as much as standard sized tires, a savings that quickly adds up.

The transformation of Ks may mean that at least this dimension of automobility will no longer offer the same metaphorical and analogical support for official gender ideology. Of course, the transformation of K's metaphorical function will not in itself transform gender in Japan. In fact, Naomi Quinn argues that people use most metaphors opportunistically to express ideas that are already shaped by underlying cultural schemas (1997: 141–61). She argues against Lakoff and Johnson's claim that metaphors shape thought itself (Lakoff and Johnson 1980), noting that people use a wide range of metaphors, often mixing metaphors in order to get across what they want to say. From her perspective, Ks never supported gender ideology so much as they expressed it. Thus, if this vehicle's metaphorical function was no longer available, Quinn would argue that the underlying gender schema would easily find alternative means of expressing itself.

There is evidence, however, that the large-scale economic transformations which have given new prominence to Ks and contributed to the shift in their metaphorical value are simultaneously putting pressure on the underlying gender schema. As in many other countries, more and more jobs in Japan have been outsourced to part-time labor forces or sent overseas. If the gender schema was based in part on differentiated labor conditions, with men working in full-time, permanent jobs, and women in part-time jobs and in the home, more and more of the jobs in the new economy are precarious, like those that have traditionally been associated with women. Fewer men than before are able to fulfill the ideal of working for prestigious and stable companies. And fewer women than before are interested in the old ideal of marrying and having children.

It would be mistaken to assume that economic shifts ultimately determine metaphor, cognitive schemas, and all other cultural ephemera. The recession could easily lead to a retrenchment, as well as to a reformulated gender system. But we do know that economic restructuring may be forcing more men to drive Ks, and Ks themselves have been transformed into more powerful and speedy vehicles. Quinn and Strauss would argue that the gender schema expresses itself in the domain of automobility in terms of a series of oppositions. I would argue, however, that within this domain, the opposition of the two vehicles, Ks and sports cars, has played an especially prominent role in organizing these oppositions. Once the properties and uses of Ks are transformed, partly as a result of economic contingencies, partly because of technological changes, and other reasons, the other oppositions all become somewhat less stable. I would suggest that this could have the effect of putting further pressure back on the gender schema. It may not be so easy for the schema to continue unaffected and find other means of expressing itself. A shift in gender schemas may lead to more conscious linkages of the conflicting discourses of speed versus manners, breaking down their cognitive compartmentalization, and forcing some resolution. In the changing meanings of these vehicles, we may be witnessing in Japan a shift from a somewhat integrated and durable cultural system to one characterized by uncertainty and change.

NOTES

1. See Claudia Strauss (1997) on compartmentalization.
2. Even titles that seem to include a broader audience, such as "How to Behave Like an Adult" (大人の作法), "Manner Essentials for Adults" (大人の絶対マナー), "Manners for those 21 and Older" (２１歳からのマナーBOOK), "Man-

ner Notebook for Fast Learning" (マナー速習帖), "Manners Practice Book" (マナー練習帳), "Happy Manner Book" (ハッピーマナーブック), "School for Manner Beauties" (まなー美人塾) and "Manners for Kimono and Japanese Customs" (和ときもののマナー), are primarily directed toward women, with depictions of elegant women adorning their covers.

REFERENCES

Ashikari, Mikiko. 2003. "Urban Middle-Class Japanese Women and Their White Faces: Gender, Ideology, and Representation." *Ethos* 31, no. 1: 3–37.

Bachnik, Jane. 1992. "The Two 'Faces' of Self and Society in Japan." *Ethos* 20, no. 1: 3–32.

Bardsley, Jan, and Laura Miller, eds. 2011. *Manners and Mischief: Gender, Power, and Etiquette in Japan.* Berkeley: University of California Press.

Doi, Takeo. 1973. *The Anatomy of Dependence.* Tokyo: Kōdansha.

Eidan (Teito kosokudo kotsu eidan). 1983. *Mana- Posuta- 100* (Manner Poster 100). Tokyo: Teito kosokudo kotsu eidan.

———. 1991. *Mana- Posuta- 200* (Manner Poster 200). Tokyo: Teito kosokudo kotsu eidan.

Fernandez, James W. 1977. "The Performance of Ritual Metaphors." In *The Social Use of Metaphor: Essays on the Anthropology of Rhetoric,* edited by J. David Sapir and J. Christopher Crocker, 100–31. Philadelphia: University of Pennsylvania Press.

———. 1986. *Persuasions and Performances: The Play of Tropes in Cultures.* Bloomington: Indiana University Press.

Freedman, Alisa. 2010. *Tokyo in Transit: Japanese Culture on the Rails and the Road.* Stanford, CA: Stanford University Press.

Fujii, James. 1999. "Intimate Alienation: Japanese Urban Rail and the Commodification of Urban Subjects." *Differences: A journal of Feminist Cultural Studies* 11, no. 2: 106–33.

Fuller, Greg. 2005. "The XXX Test." *Philament: An Online Journal of the Arts and Culture* 7:9–21.

Goffman, Erving. 1971. *Relations in Public.* New York: Basic Books.

Hessler, Peter. 2010. *Country Driving: A Journey through China from Farm to Factory.* New York: Harper.

Jain, Sarah L. 2004. "Dangerous Instrumentality: The Bystander as Subject in Automobility." *Cultural Anthropology* 19, no. 1: 61–94.

JAF (Japan Automotive Federation). 1967. "Rojo no kyoui o nozoku mono"(Things that will abolish menaces on the road) 5, no. 11: 8–9.

———. 1968. "Watashi no anzen unten tora no maku" (My safe driving crib notes) 6, no. 5: 36–37.

———. 1970. "Hiroba: Doraibu mana- ni tsuite" (Forum: On Driving Manners) 9, nos. 1–2: 72.

JAMA (Japan Automotive Manufacturers Association). 2008. "Motor Vehicle Statistics of Japan." Tokyo: Japan Automotive Manufacturers Association, Inc. http://jama.org/library/pdf/MVStatisticsofJapan2008.pdf, accessed August 14, 2010.

Kondo, Dorinne K. 1987. "Creating an Ideal Self: Theories of Selfhood and Pedagogy at a Japanese Ethics Retreat." *Ethos* 15, no. 3: 241–72.

Kuruma no techo. 1970. "Kuruma to hito no chowa" (harmonization of cars and humans) November, no. 83, pp. 37–40.

Kusunoki Michiharu. 1993. "Wangan Midnight." Vol. 1. Tokyo: Kodansha.

Lakoff, George, and Mark Johnson. 1980. *Metaphors We Live By.* Chicago: Chicago University Press.

Morris, Ivan. 1975. *The Nobility of Failure: Tragic Heroes in the History of Japan.* New York: Holt, Rinehart, Winston.

Nakamura, Karen, and Hisako Matsuo. 2003. "Female Masculinity and Fantasy Spaces: Transcending Genders in the Takarazuka Theater and Japanese Popular Culture." In *Men and Masculinities in Contemporary Japan: Dislocating the Salaryman Doxa,* edited by James Roberson and Nobue Suzuki, 59–76. London: RoutledgeCurzon.

Nakane, Chie. 1970. *Japanese Society.* Berkeley: University of California Press.

Napier, Susan. 2001. *Anime from Akira to Princess Mononoke: Experiencing Contemporary Japanese Animation.* New York: Palgrave.

National Police Agency (Keisatsuchō). 2005. "Hyō 1-13, Menkyo hoyu jinkō no suii, 1955–2004 (Figure 1-13, License holders 1955–2004). *Keisatsu hakusho* (Police Agency White Paper). http://www.npa.go.jp/hakusyo/h17/hakusho/h17/figindex.html, accessed August 14, 2010.

———. 2009. Keisatsu hakusho (Police White Paper). http://www.npa.go.jp/hakusho/h22/honbun/pdf/22p03000.pdf, accessed July 11, 2011.

Notar, Beth E. 2012. "'Coming Out' to 'Hit the Road': Temporal, Spatial and Affective Mobilities of Taxi Drivers and Day Trippers in Kunming, China." *City and Society* 24, no. 3: 281–301.

Ozeki, Kazuo. 2007. *Nihon no kei jidōsha* [Japan's lightweight cars]. Tokyo: Miki Shobō.

Plath, David. 1992. "My-Car-isma: Motorizing the Showa Self." In *Showa: The Japan of Hirohito,* edited by Carol Gluck and Stephen R. Graubard, 229–44. New York: Norton.

Quinn, Naomi. 1997. "Research on Shared Task Solutions." In *A Cognitive Theory of Cultural Meaning,* edited by Claudia Strauss and Naomi Quinn, 137–48. Cambridge: Cambridge University Press.

Robertson, Jennifer. 1998. *Takarazuka: Sexual Politics and Popular Culture in Modern Japan.* Berkeley: University of California Press.

Roth, Joshua Hotaka. 2011. "Harmonizing Cars and Humans in Japan's Era of Mass Automobility." *The Asia Pacific Journal* 9, no. 45: 3. http://japanfocus.org/-Joshua-Roth/3643.

———. 2012. "Heartfelt Driving: Discourses on Manners, Safety, and Emotions in the Era of Mass Motorization in Japan." *Journal of Asian Studies* 71, no. 1: 171–92.

Sato, Ikuya. 1991. *Kamikaze Biker: Parody and Anomy in Affluent Japan.* Chicago: University of Chicago Press.

Schnapp, Jeffrey. 1999. "Crash (Speed as Engine of Individuation)," *Modernism/modernity* 6, no. 1: 1–49.

Shigeno Shuichi. 1995. "Initial D." Vol. 1. Tokyo: Kodansha.

Strauss, Claudia. 1997. "Research on Cultural Discontinuities." In *A Cognitive Theory of Cultural Meaning,* edited by Claudia Strauss and Naomi Quinn, 210–51. Cambridge: Cambridge University Press.

Strauss, Claudia, and Naomi Quinn. 1997. *A Cognitive Theory of Cultural Meaning.* Cambridge: Cambridge Univ. Press.

Virilio, Paul. [1977] 1986. *Speed and Politics: An Essay on Dromology.* Translated by Mark Polizzotti. New York: Semiotext(e).

Zenkeiren (Zenkoku keijidosha kyokai rengokai, National Association for K Cars). 2010. "Kei san/yon rin sha oyobi zen jidosha hoyu daisu no nen betsu shu betsu sui'i" [Changes in the numbers of 3- and 4-wheel K-cars by year and type]. http://www.zenkeijikyo.or.jp/statistics/, accessed August 17, 2010.

PART III

Equivocal Vehicles

CHAPTER 5

Little Cars that Make Us Cry
Yugoslav Fića as a Vehicle for Social Commentary and Ritual Restoration of Innocence

Marko Živković

> To love a Fića is to know what is love, and those who don't know how to suffer don't know how to love.
> —Motto of a Fića Forum member

On a hot summer's day in Valencia, a few years after General Franco's death, the eponymous hero of Graham Greene's novel, *Monsignor Quixote* (1982) worries about the fate of his old Seat 600. He prays to God that the little car may survive him and hopes that unlike many of his unanswered prayers this one does get "logged in the Eternal ear." He cannot bear the thought that his Rocinante, as he calls the car in memory of his 'ancestor,' Don Quixote, will rust on a scrap heap: "He had sometimes thought of buying a small plot of land and leaving it as an inheritance to one of his parishioners on condition that a sheltered corner be reserved for his car to rest in, but there was not one parishioner whom he could trust to carry out his wish, and in any case a slow death by rust could not be avoided and perhaps a crusher at a scrapyard would be a more merciful end" (Greene 1982: 3–4). When, at the end of the novel, the car is shot at by the Spanish Guardia Civil and crashes into a church wall, the first thing that Monsignor Quixote asks his Communist ex-mayor friend when he comes to consciousness is whether Rocinante is all right. He dies shortly after, not knowing that Rocinante got completely crushed.

Rocinante was the Spanish version of Italian Fiat 600D (itself a descendant of Topolino), the immediate ancestor of the Yugoslav Fiat 750 popularly known as Fića.[1] Monsignor Quixote loved the little car, but to say that he anthropomorphized it is not entirely precise. He loved it, rather, with the kind of love we reserve for animals.

Sometime rather early into the Yugoslav wars of 1990s, I watched a TV report from a recently devastated city (it might have been Vukovar). The camera briefly passed over a completely burnt out Fića. By then, I had seen plenty of devastation, but it was only when I saw a destroyed Fića that I felt a lump in my throat for the first time. I don't know if I actually cried, but I remember that the sight of a destroyed Fića hit me much harder than any images of dead humans or burned-down buildings. This feeling corresponds quite well with what one of the Yugoslav national bards, singer and composer Djordje Balašević, expressed in ballad called a "Warrior with a Peasant Heart" (*"Ratnik paorskog srca"*), in which he recounts the horrors of the Great War, and says how sorry he was—not for the people or the villages, but for the horses (*"Rat je krvav da znate. Al'nije mi žao ni ljudi ni sela. Ej žao mi konja"*). It seems that the death of little cars, just like the death of horses, may touch us very deeply.

The immediate occasion for writing about Fića was a panel in honor of Daphne Berdahl at the American Anthropological Association Annual Meeting in 2008. Anyone familiar with life in socialism would be able to come up very quickly with a wealth of jokes and urban legends, sentiments of pride and resentment, or practices central to everyday life that revolved around vehicles—tram cars and trolley-busses, metro trains and private cars. In a word, a lot of (ethnographic) mileage is to be gotten out of vehicles. I know of no better example of this than Daphne Berdahl's article on GDR's icon—the Trabi (2001). I first heard Berdahl talk about Trabi at the panel in honor of James Fernandez at the 1999 Anthropology meetings. She presented a spluttering two-stroke car as figuring quite prominently in the arguments of images attending the German reunification. I started photographing Trabi on the streets of Belgrade and collecting the Trabi lore after Berdahl's account enchanted the little car for me. The last photos I sent her before her death in October 2007 were of a Trabi made into an extended wedding limo that adorns the main square of Emir Kusturica's wooden city of Drvengrad on Mokra Gora (Figure 5.1).

I don't know if she ever got to see them. My favorites, however, are a series of photos I took on a Belgrade street in the fall of 2003—of a rundown, abandoned Trabi side by side with the equally dilapidated Fića (Figure 5.2).

When I first presented the argument developed in this chapter in 2008, I choked at the end; I couldn't finish. It was only in part on account of Daphne Berdahl, who was a dear friend. It had a lot to do with Fića himself. After all, it was really about the power of little cars to make us cry. Or to use our metaphor of metaphors—how they succeed in *moving* us.

LITTLE CARS THAT MAKE US CRY 113

Figure 5.1. Trabi as an extended wedding limo in Kusturica's Drvengrad on Mokra Gora, Serbia, 2007. Photo: Marko Živković.

Both metaphors and cars move us, but unlike physical vehicles, metaphors do so instantaneously. They are teleporting machines rather than sputtering cars. It is only when we have a series of metaphors (or tropes), a whole "argument of images," as Fernandez would say, that we can be taken for a ride (see Fernandez 1982, 1986). This is, for instance,

Figure 5.2. Trabi and Fića on a Belgrade street, 2003. Photo: Marko Živković.

the kinesthetic experience I have when Fernandez guides me through a Bwiti sermon with its many, sometimes incommensurable metaphorical domains. It is like poetry itself, that William K. Wimsatt said in his *The Verbal Icon*, is "the vehicle of a metaphor which one boards heedless of where it runs, whether cross-town or downtown—just for the ride" (1954: 76).[2] And when the piled-up metaphors are mixed, as Dale Pesmen (1991) taught us, that ride could be like a roller-coaster and provoke serious motion sickness.

A ride in Fića could be nauseating in many senses of the word. My concern, however, is with what such a "ride" can tell us about the power of small cars to carry enormous emotional loads, transport us into other worlds, and move us to tears. Such efficacy, when it exists, may well be seen as a kind of figurative density or thickness that inanimate things accrue in their social life. Unpacking of Fića's appeal may then illuminate something about vehicles as metaphors and metaphors as vehicles.

I will first position Fića in the Yugoslav car system, and will then explore it as a family time-binder, a peg in social frameworks of memory, and a link in the "economies of favor." I will finally analyze a keyword I translate as jury-rigging, and try to show how Fića, as a canonical object of jury-rigging, works as a trope for a jury-rigged social universe, and how, by lovingly restoring it to its "factory condition," this jury-riggedness could be ritually undone.

Fića in the Yugoslav Car System

Just as in the photo, the Trabi was indeed close to the Fića in the ex-Yugoslav car system. It was a part of an inner circle of Eastern Bloc-produced cars and thus felt more intimate than the outer circle of cars produced in Western Europe, the United States or Japan. That circle included Soviet Ladas, Moskwitches, and Volgas; Czech Škodas; Polish Fiats; and Romanian Dacias, in addition to East German Trabants and Wartburgs.

As about 10 percent of Yugoslav population had worked abroad in Germany, Switzerland, Italy, France, and other Western countries since the 1960s, there was always a plentitude of mostly used Western European cars as well. Most familiar were probably the German ones—starting from VW Bugs, Passats, and Sciroccos, through Audis and BMWs to Mercedes. To these should be added very popular French Renaults, Citroens, and Peugeots, Italian Alpha-Romeos and Lancias, Swedish Volvos, and to lesser extent Saabs and Dafs, even British Austins and Mini-Morrises, with an occasional Sunbeam, Rover, and Land Rover. Japanese cars were mostly represented by Mazdas and Hondas. Opel was always big, and so was the European-produced Ford. In a word, this was a much more varied car universe than could be found anywhere in the Eastern Bloc.

In the innermost circle of familiarity, or "ournessness" were the cars produced in Yugoslavia. At various points in time, VW Golfs were assembled in Sarajevo, Citroens and Renaults in Slovenia, and Opels in Vojvodina. The Zastava factory in Kragujevac, however, despite relying on a Fiat license, was in a different position. It was the only factory that actually produced the cars rather than just assembling them from imported parts. Moreover, the cars they produced, while owing a lot in their design to Fiats, were actually different from their Italian models, and bore their own, domestic names. Zastava cars belonged to the innermost circle and were felt, with a predictable mix of pride and embarrassment, as the most ours of ours. Fića was at the very center of this innermost circle—there was no car that ever felt more completely "ours." It was the first of the domestically produced cars, and the pride in socialist production success was with Fića thus at its freshest. It was, moreover, the first car to become affordable for a relatively wide segment of the population which quickly made it a true "people's car." It was small and hardy, easy to take apart and maintain, and it could pull astounding loads. Fića soon began appearing in movies and film news, and became a mainstay of the so-called National Class category in car racing that started producing its own popular heroes. Finally, Fića achieved a kind of apotheosis in one of the most popular Yugoslav movies, *The National Class* (Marković 1979).

Fića stories, I found, are very easy to elicit in Serbia and pretty much anywhere else in the former Yugoslavia, especially among people older than about twenty. So widespread was it and such an important role did it play in daily life, that it would be hard to find an ex-Yugoslav who didn't have some personal experience with it. If nothing else, many driving schools used it until late 1980s; and driving lessons being obligatory, most of those who became licensed before 1990s did so in a Fića.

An association of Fića devotees ("*Udruženje ljubitelja fiće*") appropriately named the "National Class" after the movie, was established in 2002. And as of June 30, 2013, its internet forum (http://forum.nacionalnaklasa.net) boasted 2,119 members and contained no less than 171,579 messages distributed in 6,745 topics. On my visit to Belgrade in September 2008, I managed to attend one of their Fićiads (*Fićijada*) in the Serbian town of Šabac. It turned out that the forum represented a precious mine of precisely the kind of stories I was looking for. When, for instance, a member asked in September of 2007, "What [does] Fića mean to you?", he elicited answers that by June 2010 spanned 6 web pages.[3]

Fića as Person and Family Time-Binder

As might be expected, Fića is often explicitly referred to as a living being, a person. A tall young Belgrade engineering student, who somehow fit into the front passenger seat of a Fića we drove in to the Fićiad in Šabac, said so in an emotion-filled voice. Numerous forum members agreed. "For me, the little blue one is alive," one of them wrote,

> I imagine her[4] and understand her as a living being who is a member of the family.... I know exactly when something bothers her, when she is not feeling well.... I grew up with her.... Even my dad drove me up and down the street in her as a baby so I would fall asleep. ... I am listening to the stories about her my whole life.... My little blue one is a part of the family and whatever happens to her I will not renounce her not even if she just stayed broken and rotted or in whatever shape in the garage.... I simply love her and no other Fića will ever replace her!!!

Here, we have several motifs that crop up again and again in the online forum. Fića is a person, a family member, and finally the motif of being put to sleep as a baby by being driven up and down the street. Here is the image of ultimate intimacy—Fića as a cradle and nurse, its engine's sound and characteristic vibrations as a lullaby.[5]

As often as not, either grandparents or parents own the first Fića in the family, and the present drivers, whether teenagers, or 40-year-olds, should they happen to inherit the original one, usually do so after some sort of gap. Typically, the family Fića survives some sort of period of dormancy and neglect before being resurrected. Those who own, or owned, the original one are often fiercely proud of the fact and swear they would never renounce it. If the current family Fića is not the original one, its predecessor tends to be remembered with special affection.

There is a strong sense in these accounts that Fića threads itself throughout domestic time (*"taj se fića jednostavno provlači kroz moj ceo život"*), and this is often the first response given to the question of what does Fića mean to you? That a family Fića is resuscitated, or another one is acquired, often elicits special approval and even tears from the parents and grandparents, and among older generations in general. In a word, Fića is a master time-binder, a memento, that recalls family history. "It reminds me of some of the most beautiful moments of my growing up," said *Vlada* in a message on September 9, 2007. "Since ... whenever I sit in it, I remember some event from the past and immediately feel better," wrote *Tamcic* on October 24, 2007.

> I think I was conceived in my dad's white *fikus* (old folks always grin when I ask them). First vacation trip (and almost all the others). First

driving at 12. First girl at 16 (nothing immoral). A bit of racing experience at 18 (crashed terribly). Escaping military service in brakeless Fića on weekends. The love of my life in a pink *fiki*. Always as a family member or a part of the décor, Fića has been present (and still is) in my life.

At the same time as it is personified and carries domestic, life-cycle related memory, Fića has come to stand for a whole way of life in the former Yugoslavia and has indeed become one of the major icons of Yugonostalgia, just as Trabi has become perhaps the most potent single icon of Ostalgie. "Some have discovered a medicine for sorrow and nostalgia toward old Yuga (Yugoslavia) in this little, bug-eyed machine," wrote *Neba* on the forum on September 3, 2007. And *Djenka 018* added on May 26, 2008:

> Majority of us here has a Fićko not because they have nothing better to drive at the moment but out of pure love for the times that have passed but not forever. To have/drive a Fićko is the same as possessing a part of the past ... practically.... A picture on the wall only reminds of past times but a Fićko in front of your house is an excursion into memories.

Fića thus links the family past and the past of the wider community. Its trajectory through the family can very handily organize social frameworks of memory by providing a chronological marker. Fića was typically the first car acquired by a family, and it formed the first link in what was a canonical sequence of family cars in Yugoslavia—Fića followed by Zastava 1300, then Zastava 101, and then finally a Yugo. Just like many cars elsewhere, this little vehicle has in that way acquired the power to date both family history and the *zeitgeist* of an era.

Fića in the "Economy of Favours"

Halfway between family memories and Yugonostalgia, Fića also figures in an informal "economy of favours" (see Ledeneva 1988). "You always remembered the Trabi repairman's birthday, and we usually tried to bring him homemade sausage," one woman told Daphne Berdahl (2001: 132). Fića participated in a similar exchange network in its heyday, but now, almost thirty years since the last Fića rolled off the production line, resurrecting it involves a kind of exchange that dealing with more modern cars does not. It may involve, for instance, painstakingly warming yourself into the good graces of an extremely grumpy old man who keeps around one hundred Fićas in his backyard. The quest for parts is never-ending, and masters of Fića maintenance are hard to find. To be a Fića owner today is to be forced to network, and the fact that Fića gets enmeshed in such exchange of favors may be, in part, what endows it with "soul."

To summarize, due to its unique position in the ex-Yugoslav car universe and in a canonical sequence of car ownership, Fića acquired great metaphoric potency as both an icon of Yugonostalgia and a marker of familial frameworks of memory. The vehicle tended to be enmeshed in a typical socialist economy of favors, and was, moreover, ubiquitously and explicitly treated as a family member. An object of pride,[6] its sound a lullaby for sleepless babies, a mule that helped build the family *dacha* by hauling brick and mortar carload by carload, a hero of family vacations and epic trips to the seaside, a racing car and a way to pick up girls, even a haven for backseat sex. It was cute and buggy, and when suitably souped up, a superb source of that particular kick one gets by leaving bigger and more expensive cars in the dust.[7]

In its role as a time-binder for families and larger imagined communities such as ex-Yugoslavia, however, Fića embodies a hiatus. It usually spends years forgotten in a garage before revived by the third generation, and when it is resurrected it faces the world in which it cannot function as a mere practical vehicle but always also as a relic bearing of all kinds of ironies. It thus binds various pasts, familial or collective, but it also indexes a gap and a loss.[8]

Fića as a Canonical Object of Jury-Rigging

Just like Trabi, Fića was an object of endless modifications and enhancements, over and above the huge expenditure of time, effort, and *blat*-capital required merely to keep it running. Just like other Eastern Bloc cars, the Fića was the major locus of a certain kind of practice that is perhaps best conveyed by the term *budženje*, and the whole family of expressions derived from it. Budženje could be glossed as jury-rigging (or jerry-building, or bodgery) in English, but it has other, different connotations. I would like to argue here that budženje is a keyword well worthy of careful unpacking, and that Fića has been its major avatar. To examine budženje is a good way to attend to the way Fića functions as a metaphor.

Budžiti has a sense of augmentation in Serbia, not just rigging something up in a makeshift, slipshod, or improvised manner, but also in a way that makes the thing bigger, more awkward and ungainly. It does have a Turkish loanword sound to it, and thus an aura of rough intimacy, vulgarity, and lower register as words felt as Turkish often do (see Kazazis 1972).[9] As a verb, it is often used with a few prefixes. Thus *zbudžiti*, and an even more powerful *skarabudžiti*, has a stronger connotation of making something in a hurry and in a slipshod manner—just so it would hold together for a minimum amount of time. *Nabudžiti*, on the other hand, emphasizes the quality of augmentation, or making something bigger and stronger but in a rough manner. *Prebudžiti* has an additional sense of transforming something into something else by rough rigging. The noun *budževina* is used very often and is sometimes modified with the prefix *kara-* as in *karabudževina*. *Kara* is "black" in Turkish, but in the folk sense it also serves to augment words it precedes and in a particularly rough manner. Karabudževina could therefore, but only imperfectly, be rendered as "mega-jury-rigging."

Cars present the original and most important locus for budženje, perhaps rivaled only by houses.[10] When it comes to cars, specifically, the concept has two basic meanings that can shift according to the context. One is to soup up the car by enhancing the engine and other parts. The alternative and more precise word is *frizirati* (the same word used for hair styling). In that sense, a rigged car (*budžena, nabudžena,* or even *prebudžena mašina*) is a souped-up car, although, unlike with *frizirati,* there is still a lingering sense of rough and improvised work. Yet, the word in that latter usage usually conveys a kind of approval and even admiration. The other sense is more negative and means jury-rigging or jerry-building that may or may not include enhancements and souping up. At the Fićiad in Šabac I heard the word quite often in both senses, as well as in a way that left it unclear what was meant.[11]

Budženje hovers between Levy-Straussian *bricolage* and engineering, sometimes emphasizing one, sometimes the other, and, in the most delightful and powerful uses, suspended between the two. What is interesting here is that this family of expressions very easily and richly lends itself to all kinds of metaphorical extensions. Its original home may be in car and house rigging, and its locus might have now shifted to computers (notoriously rigged in this piracy-ridden computing environment), but it is quite readily also extended to society as a whole. If Americans can joke that the whole universe is held by the duct tape, ex-Yugoslavs could be quite seriously depressed by a profound sense that their whole social existence is jury-rigged—one huge, ugly *karabudževina*.

A brilliant example of just such a usage was expressed by Milosav Marinović in the radio show *Peščanik,* broadcast on the Radio B92 on March 2, 2006.[12] He defined *karabudževina* as "a particularly serious, strong and thoroughly performed *budževina*," and claimed that "we live in a society that is one big *karabudževina*."[13] Other societies, especially the poor ones, need to patch and mend things, but keep it to things, objects while "with us, this is a part of psychology and consciousness."

> It's this strange need to take all this garbage we keep in the basements of our reality and build it into the fine machinery that we call

society. It is this *karabudževina,* that is to say, we all see that this is a country where closets are made out of balconies, basements out of closets, rooms out of basements, living rooms out of kitchens, and a study or a business out of the living room. We make public interest out of private matters, fathers of the nation out of populist ideas and demagoguery, dogma out of stupidity, a saint out of a racist and some other things, history out of leftovers, wisdom out of ignorance, victory out of defeat. In a word, we discard nothing, we are constantly jury-rigging something up (*"budžimo nešto"*) just so it could continue to serve some impossible and useless, and in any case, some wrong purpose.... For instance, Milošević, he is one of our crucial *budževinas* of the twentieth century and modern era, because this was a process whereby out of a bit of a communist, a bit of a dictator, and a bit of a nationalist—well, we made a statesman out of all this. I don't think just anyone could have succeeded in something like this.

Here, the society is seen as a fine mechanism that has been jury-rigged over and over again to the point of hopelessness.[14] Things are made to serve purposes that were not intended for them, and most importantly, all kind of past debris is jerry-built into the present making it hopelessly confused, makeshift, crooked, improvised, shoddy, unreliable, irrational, ill-formed, and ungainly. The author points out a kind of pride his countrymen, in his opinion quite wrongly, have in the resourcefulness and ingenuity that goes into all this rigging-up of things—from cars and living spaces (he does use cars at the very beginning of his tirade) to politics and society in general. Instead of celebrating the everyday improvisations and bricolage, as for instance de Certeau (1988) famously does, he laments them. This genre of laments strongly projects and implies, even when not explicitly stating it, a kind of ideal state of things: an ordered universe, a society as a finely-tuned machine in this case, a world of systematicity, precision, and predictability where everything has its right place, and where nothing gets mixed up. Moreover, this kind of lament projects an idealized Europe as a gloss for idealized civil society, rule of law and ordered economy. These lamenters, and there is a great number of them, are the truest followers of the European idea as an ideal of a perfectly rational social order.

To return to the world of vehicles. The car-related jury-rigging could be seen as prototype, the metaphoric template for the whole family of jury-rigging-like practices and by metaphoric, metonymic and other figurative extensions, the very jury-rigged nature of the social world.

Of course, the laments about the make-shift, crooked, improvised, shoddy, unreliable, irrational, ill-formed, confused, etc. nature of the social world are relational and situational. One's world is such in comparison to other worlds. And here I would take another car that is a central figurative device—the jury-rigged Dyana of the Belgrade Roma.

The opposite of the jury-rigged world of *karabudževina* is usually seen to be some idealized version of Europe, and within Europe, the Northerners, the Swiss, the Swedes, and perhaps most commonly, the Germans.[15] In the GDR, the immediate other were the Wessies, whose major symbol was their gleaming Mercedes. In Serbia, as well, the Germans were and continue to serve as a major image of rational, orderly life. But there is a sense too that, as in all other things, Serbians are actually not the opposite of some sort of Western civilized order, but in fact stand somewhere in between, with the polar extreme being Gypsies. They are the true masters of mega-jury-rigging! It is true that Roma tend to live in dwellings that are often the epitome of slipshod, jury-rigged, makeshift architecture, but it is again a vehicle that crystallizes the role jury-rigging plays in their way of life.

A wonderful 2003 documentary, *Pretty Dyana: A Gypsy Recycling Saga*, shows Roma refugees from Kosovo now dwelling in Belgrade lovingly rebuilding Dyanas, the successors to the legendary Citroen CV2s, sometimes equipping them with radios, cigarette lighters, even miniature TVs, and rigging carts up to them (Mitić 2003). As a contemplation of jury-rigging, the movie is both fun and desolate, demeaning and empowering (Figure 5.3). *Pretty Dyana* is delightfully suspended among these valences

Figure 5.3. A rigged-up cart on a Belgrade street, 2013. Photo Marko Živković.

and succeeds like no other Gypsy movie made in Serbia at avoiding the pitfalls of condescension, romanticization, and exploitation. All this *budženje* of Dyanas is surely a trope for something, but what? This open-endedness makes the film particularly delightful.[16]

If in Roma hands, Dyanas present an extreme image of mega jury-rigging, and if Trabi conveys the conundrums and ironies of German reunification as perhaps no other single thing, then what does Fića do for those who have it at their disposal?

Restoring Fića as Revitalization Ritual

Fića is a vehicle for Yugonostalgia, for family memories, and for the pride and ruefulness associated with a jury-rigged world. Resurrecting a Fića, as a process, however, may also act as a ritual revitalization. I have written elsewhere about a widespread sense people in Serbia had in the 1990s and still feel that their reality has been "warped" in a compounded way—warps on top of warps that have made life became messy beyond reckoning. I explored figurative devices people use in order to express this sense, such as dream-like states, as well as "amorphous substances" (Živković 2001, 2011). We can discern the same anguished sense of compounded, agglutinated, agglomerated "warpings" in the lament about the whole Serbian society as a *karabudževina*. It is all so hopelessly rigged over and over again that one ceases to see how it could be straightened and made right again. And here, I learned, Fića can appear as a device for ritual revitalization. This was suggested to me by the Fića enthusiast who drove me to the Fićiad in Šabac.

Rather morose and grumpy otherwise, he became quite animated when he started explaining to me how to restore Fića to its "factory condition." There are basically two recognized categories of Fića-work and two aesthetics I noticed among Fića buffs. One is to restore the vehicle to factory condition, and the other is to soup it up as a racing or sports car where all kinds of extravagances are allowed and even admired (Figure 5.4). Getting a Fića back to factory condition is actually more difficult and expensive than souping it up, my driver explained.[17] And then he launched, transformed by his own enthusiasm, into a detailed account of how it is done, which more or less went as follows.

The body should be inspected and all damaged, or rusted parts replaced. It should then be sanded thoroughly and professionally painted in an absolutely dust-fee chamber that allows for constant 40-degree Celsius heat. This process requires several coats, but the result could outshine the original paint job. The engine should be completely taken apart,

Figure 5.4. Lined-up Fićas of the of Fića Lovers Association at the 2008 Fićiad in Šabac. Note both the souped-up cars and those more or less faithfully restored to their "factory condition." Photo: Marko Živković.

and all wornout parts replaced. All the hoses must be replaced too, since they rot. A very good electrician should replace all the original wiring, since it was no good to start with. And then, "the final test," said my driver, now almost enraptured, should be to place a glass full of water on top of the engine, and should it have been rebuilt correctly, not a drop of water will be spilled when the engine is idling. Only then, he went on, may the Fića be said to have been properly restored to "factory condition." Then he paused and, almost as if surprised by his own revelation, said, "In fact, you bear it again." He used the word *roditi* that means only one thing—giving birth to a human baby (*"Ti ga zapravo rodiš"*)

The very next day, I visited the utterly dilapidated Museum of Science and Technology in Belgrade where the automotive curator, himself an engineer, told me when I recounted the story, that no chain transmission engines like the Fića's could ever run so smoothly as to pass the full glass test. It was a fantasy, he said, and I finally understood what this account of Fića rehabilitation reminded me of. It was a process that involved a decomposition, taking the vehicle apart, and then putting it back together again. The aim was nominally to restore a car to its factory condition, but in fact, the Fića that was supposed to result from this painstaking, expensive, and long process (he said it takes about a year) was much improved over anything that ever had left the Zastava assembly lines new. This was now a vehicle that was born again, in a form more faithful to the original than the original ever was, more shiny, more reliable—more itself.

I heard a kind of religious tone in the story. It rehearsed a process of renewal resembling shamanic initiation visions where a shaman is completely dismembered and then put together again (Eliade 2004). What I had heard, that is to say, was more akin to an incantation of a rejuvenation or restoration ritual than to an account of car repair. And like alchemists projecting their psychic transformations into the transformations of matter, so here was imagined a revitalization of society from its hopelessly jury-rigged state to a pristine, un-rigged state projected into and enacted through a car restoration project.

When Milosav Marinović spun his theory of Serbia on the radio as "mega jury-rigged," he first used the word in reference to Zastava cars. For him, Zastava cars were hopelessly jury-rigged and so citizens had to be persuaded to buy them for patriotic reasons. He applied it to other metaphoric realms, before finally extending the word to all of Serbian social and political life. It made sense to return to the first Zastava cars, probably manufactured in a slipshod manner, and start rebuilding them. Society as a whole, after all, cannot be manipulated, but a vehicle can.

> Indeed, it seems possible that much symbolic action that has as its proximal aim action upon some specific physical situation or object has distal aims that refer to the sociopolitical sphere ... symbolic action achieves its ends through its capacity to create expressive-iconic models within which the restructuring of a situation can take place (Munn 1973: 597).

Perhaps Fića could be seen as such an "expressive-iconic model," upon which operations of restructuring are performed that aim at restoring a dilapidated vehicle to its factory condition, while they simultaneously enact personal and sociopolitical rejuvenations or revitalizations. Ex-Yugoslavs who lovingly restore their Fićas are often quite explicitly conscious that they are thereby enacting some sort of ritual return to the idealized past of a country that had some weight, some order, and some self-respect. This is precisely what the street vendor exclaimed when I excitedly pointed to the glass bottle Fića he just laid down on his cardboard box (Figure 5.5). "Yes," he declared, "this is when we had a state!"[18]

Restoring a Fića is a labor of love. The Fića devotees I met in Belgrade and in Šabac never tired of pointing this out. As the motto of an online forum member's puts it: "To love a Fića is to know what is love, and those

Figure 5.5. The Fića-shaped glass bottle for brandy displayed prominently in a Yugo-nostalgia exhibition in Belgrade, 2013. Photo: Rea Mucović.

who don't know how to suffer don't know how to love." It was as if a Fića could not be properly restored to its factory condition without this crucial kind of sentimental attachment. Otherwise, it was implied, the magic will not work and the Fića will not be born again.

Conclusion: Thickening and Dilution of an Image

I would like to respond to an interesting and possibly useful criticism I once received on an earlier draft of this chapter by way of developing some concluding remarks about the power of vehicles to move us. The commentator claimed to have "lost count as to how many different attributes Fića could represent: from living being, family member, master family time-binder, memento, way of life, icon, medicine, object of pride, lullaby, mule, racer, hero," to being endowed with a "soul." All of which, he or she complained, served to dilute rather than strengthen the power of the image. Disciplinary wisdom, at least since Victor Turner, would have us believe that the power, or thickness of "dominant symbols" derives in part from the variety of meanings they evoke in different domains of everyday or ritual contexts. Accordingly, Fića should be a thick image ("intertextually thick," to use a different idiom), that is to say, potent and powerful. Obviously, for me Fića is indeed just such a thick image, so thick, that it regularly produces a lump in my own throat. Perhaps my exposition of the multivalence of the vehicle has simply been inept. This is a plausible explanation, but it is not theoretically interesting. The theoretically interesting question is rather this: under what circumstances would the power of this little car as a trope be diluted rather than thickened *because* it evokes so many things to so many people in so many different contexts.

Indeed, if the many associations that Fića provokes in different domains of Serbian life may seem incompatible with each other, then, by refusing to coalesce into a coherently imaginable entity, Fića may be producing something like the "motion sickness" Dale Pesmen (1991) noted as a typical response of rhetoricians to mixing metaphors. Instead of augmenting each other across many domains of life, the discrepancy of all these associations would diminish the power of this vehicle as a trope just as two sound waves out of phase can produce unpleasant interference effects or even cancel each other. This is how I think my critics may have explained the diminution of the image they got from my account. I actually don't think that Fića is incoherent to people in Serbia (and former Yugoslavia). People don't ordinarily take such a synoptic view of the various domains of their life so as to discern logical discrepancies among them. It is academics who have both the leisure and the training to do such things. The repugnance toward mixedness is directly related to the disposition to take a systematic view of one's lived reality. This is why it is the social critics (i.e., Marinović above), as professional surveyors of Serbian reality, who are the main lamenters of Serbian disorder.[19] In short, it is certain "ideological norms of consistency and parsimony" in both arts and sciences that provoke visceral disgust with mixed metaphors and jury-rigging in general (Pesmen 1991: 228). Mixing metaphors, that is to say, tends to be allowed by rhetoricians if the aim is to formally evoke the disorder of life on which the mixed metaphor is predicated (235). Fića could thus be seen as a trope in the Serbian "poetics of incongruity"—evoking the experienced inchoateness of life precisely because it is an awkward vehicle driven in and out of discordant or incommensurable worlds.

The power of Fića to move me, just as it obviously moves so many others, does perhaps come partly from the disjointedness, the mixedness of metaphoric domains through which it is driven. Sometimes, ungainly, awkward things move us more than perfectly formed ones.[20] And perhaps the metaphoric fit between the vehicle and life in the former Yugoslavia consisted of just this: both are somewhat ungainly, disjointed, and inchoate.

Taking certain poetic liberties, Alfred Gell compared Malangans, a type of memorial carving from Papua New Guinea, to charged batteries. The purpose of a Malangan, according to Gell,

> is to provide a "body," or more precisely, a "skin" for a recently deceased person of importance. On death, the agency of such a person is in a dispersed state ... indexes of their agency abound, but are not concentrated anywhere in particular ... all the dispersed 'social effectiveness' of the deceased, the difference they made to how things were, gradually becomes an objectifiable quantity, something to which a single material index may be attached, and from which this accumulated effectiveness may be abducted. This is what the Malangan is; a kind of body which accumulates, like a charged battery, the potential energy of the deceased dispersed in the life-world. (Gell 1992: 225)

Like a Malangan Fića accumulates the dispersed agency not only of a deceased person, but of a dead state, a way of life, now gone, that continues to be lodged in memories and decaying reminders. Fića was typically the first car grandparents drove, thus a part of their extended persons, but it was simultaneously a material embodiment of a socialist state with its modernizing rhetoric, non-aligned politics, and self-management. It is an object from which the agency of that state can be abducted. In fact, Fića seems to encourage such abductions—what else could the street vendor's exclamation, "We had a state then!" possibly mean? Therefore, to restore Fića to its factory condition is to magically gather the dispersed agency of a dead state, a dream and a desire to retrieve that which may never be recovered.

As David Lipset noted in the Introduction to this volume, "metaphors expose lacunae of one intangible sort or another in society in response to which something figural is done to relationships that are missing." In its social life, in stories it spawned, and figurative uses it inspired, Fića was perhaps felt as a vehicle that traverses, and thus binds together these "intangible lacunae." As the opposite of the mythical infallible, gleaming Mercedes, it did so in its unreliable, sputtering and jury-rigged ways, intimating as a kind of meta-commentary the hopes and ultimate failures attendant on such figural responses to an unresolvable reality. In this sense, even though much smaller, Fića suggests itself a strange counterpart to the 1977 Lincoln Town Car used in the lynching reenactment analyzed by Auslander in this volume. Both hover between being an ordinary sight on the road and true vintage cars, and both are notoriously unreliable. Perhaps, most importantly, both are time-binders that stitch together pasts that some would like to forget with the present. In Auslander's case, it is the unreliable, run-down car, driven by a known bricoleur always miraculously able to patch it up and bring it to life again that is felt as the best vehicle by those who want to precariously bind the past to the present.

As a rigged-up vehicle in the rigged-up life of the former Yugoslavia, the Fića has now become such a precarious time-binder. It has become Malangan-like, gathering together the agency of a deceased state, but its electrical wiring was notoriously shoddy and those who drove it had to be bricoleurs to maintain the vehicle and keep it running. And that is perhaps why this little rigged-up car may pluck at the strings of our souls better than a well-engineered one.

NOTES

1. The first Fiat 600Ds were made in the Zastava factory in Kragujevac in 1955. The first real Fića was made in 1972 as Zastava 750. Italians stopped making it in 1970, while Zastava continued to develop and produce Fićas until 1985. The engine grew from 633cc of the Fiat 600D to 843cc of the latest Zastava 850 models. To say that it could do 120 km/h—the maximum speed notched on its speedometer—as many owners would claim, always hovered on the brink of the believable.
2. In fact, I get a little nauseous with Wimsatt's metaphor here. Poetry, which is made of metaphors is a vehicle of a metaphor that is a vehicle taking us for a ride?!
3. When checking the forum in June of 2013, it turned out that the thread started by this question was erased during a server crash several months before. One of the original contributors started it again, and if it is recovered it may be returned to the site. The URL for the new thread is: http://forum.nacionalnaklasa.net/viewthread.php?tid=10701.
4. My own sense is that Fića is definitely a he, but lots of people feel Fića is a female just as this forum member does. The forum offers some interesting discussions on the topic.
5. Notar (this volume) observes how middle-class, middle-aged car owners she interviewed in China in 2008 "spoke about their new car as if it were a second child." One of my Fića fans actually said that restoring it to "factory condition" is to "give birth to it." I found this a startling pronouncement, since most of the nurturing metaphors I encountered among the Fića fans were exactly the reverse—showing Fica as a nurturing parent or a lullaby-singing nanny. Fića was also very often felt as a "family member," but this usually meant a sibling, rather than a child, and an elder one at that, since family Fićas could quite easily be older than the typical Fića forum member.
6. I have to temper my obvious Yugonostalgia here with observations Miljenko Jergović made in his essay on Fića in *Jutarnji list* (May 24, 2007) titled, "Fićo: A Good, Endearing and Loyal Little Car" (*"Fićo: dobar, drag i odan autić"*). Jergović warns that the tenderness we may feel today toward Fića is ret-

rospective. Rather than being an object of excitement and status pride, he argues, Fića was, especially in the 1970s, "a kind of existential minimum" of an ordinary family: "In school you lied to the kids that your dad drives a Ford Taunnus, the Citroen Frog (DS), or an Opel until they see him in his Fića."

7. The souped-up Carl, the "small car with a big heart," gives the three comrades in Erich Maria Remarque's 1936 novel *Drei Kameraden* (Remarque 1998) this kind of thrill when it leaves much more powerful cars in the dust. Carl is indeed the fourth comrade and a kin to Greene's Rocinante.

8. Sure, many still say they drive it because they cannot afford anything else, but to drive a Fića now is inescapably to make a statement, whether intended or not. Fića now provokes certain kinds of reactions that it didn't while it was still a normal vehicle. It makes people cry, or at least amusedly take cellphone photos, and for some of the forum members act as "filter for sluts." To admire somebody's Fića is obviously not to admire his or her status and wealth (although some Fićas have lots of money invested in them). Whoever admires it admires it not as a status symbol but for something else. Fića is simple and humble and so are by inference people who admire it on the street. Thus, it can act as a litmus test for girls, too. If they don't like it they must be after money and are thus "sponsored girls." Sponsored girls (*sponzoruše*), who appeared in the mid 1990s, were reputed to readily accept public humiliation and even physical abuse from their sponsors in return for expensive clothes and "high-life," Belgrade style. Forum members had a lively discussion on this type of girl and largely concurred in proclaiming Fića a superb "filter" for them. Those who like their Fićas, of course, are the right kind of girl.

9. In his *Dictionary of Turkish Loanwords*, Škaljic doesn't list *budžiti* at all, and the words that share the "budž" part don't seem like *budženje* has been derived from them. It may not therefore be derived from a Turkish loanword, even though to a native it does have the flavor (Škaljic 1989). According to Victor Friedman (personal communication), it might have this Turkish feel to it because of the sound "dzh" that occurs mainly in words of Turkish origin. "The sound does not occur natively in Slavic, and the few native words with native dzh are the result of specific phonetic processes," he says. "There is a Romani word 'budzho' which means 'bundle' or 'pack' or 'rag' but also 'scam.' Etymology obscure." It is interesting that its derivation might be from the Romani since, as we will see, it is the Gypsies who are the recognized masters of *budženje*.

10. Here is my favorite example of house-related *budženje*. An acquaintance told me that he has seen and remembered a personal advertisement, written with a marker on a wooden plank nailed to a tree at the corner of the Belgrade's Boulevard of Revolution (now Boulevard of King Alexander) and King Milutin street in 1998 that said: "Budžim po kućama"—"I rig at your home," or "I will jerry-build at homes." What is delightful about this is its apparent ironylessness and universality of application. Normally a part of an intimate repertoire of resourceful improvisation, *budženje* is here presented as a straight-faced,

open business proposition. My acquaintance thought the ad was addressed to people who had no money for a proper plumber, painter, or contractor but desperately needed stuff fixed somehow at home and would settle for a presumably cheaper jury-rigger who could rig up something so it holds, if only just so.
11. It was used, for instance, to refer to ingenious solutions to the amazing feat of converting Fića to the much cheaper propane. When I later mentioned that to a Belgrade taxi driver, he admiringly exclaimed, "Man, that's mathematics!" I took "mathematics" to be the exact opposite to *budženje*, and yet there is a sense in which even *budženje* could be done with "mathematical" precision.
12. *Peščanik* (Hour-glass) is a weekly talk show broadcast through the popular Belgrade B92 radio station that provides a community of commiseration for the marginalized anti-nationalist, anti-war intelligentsia of the Serbian capital city.
13. He further defines *budževina* as when "out of two ruined, broken or toppling things you try to build a third one to somehow serve for something," and where "that third thing contains elements of both of these dead things, has some sort of reminder of a true use or some other kind of value transferred from these dead things, but it is of course not the sum total of qualities but rather just an aggregate of shortcomings." The examples include to "make an aquarium out of a burnt out TV set, a tool cabinet out of a laundry machine, a closet shelf out of books, etc."
14. This is a typical lament coming from a particular type of intellectual elite in Serbia. Dale Pesmen (2000) and Nancy Ries (1997), for instance, have provided brilliant analyses of Russian laments, and I have analyzed Serbian "Jeremiads" in Živković 2001 and 2011.
15. The opposite to jury-rigging is embodied also in the perfectly aligned screw head slots a friend of mine swore once, with awe in his voice, to have seen with his own eyes on a Saab engine.
16. The entire film could be seen online at http://kosovoroma.wordpress.com/2008/01/10/pretty-diana-a-gypsy-recycling-saga/ (accessed June 30, 2013).
17. This confirmed my sense at the Fićiad that factory condition is felt as somehow superior since most admiration seemed reserved for the Fićas that looked pristinely original from the outside, but had a more powerful engine. The best example was the Fića of the organizer with a gleaming Abarth 70 horsepower engine small enough to allow the hood to close normally. This was the most powerful Fića there and yet it didn't look *nabudženo* (the second to the left Fića in [Figure 5.4]).
18. At the conference on post-Yugoslav anthropology held at the University of Chicago in 2008, Stef Jansen (2008) and Marina Simić (2008) talked about a similar use of "state" by former Yugoslavs to stand for a whole cluster of rather inchoate but strongly felt notions of order, grid, and functioning system in society.

19. For a more detailed analysis of how relative elevation over, as opposed to immersion in the everyday life relates to experiences of its incongruities in Serbia during the 1990s and what I termed the Serbian "poetics of opacity" see Živković 2011, especially chapter 9.
20. In fact, probably most of the really cult cars are cars with extraordinary faults. They may be hard to fix, unreliable in operation, or notorious for certain quirks.

REFERENCES

Berdahl, Daphne. 2001. "'Go, Trabi, Go!': Reflections on a Car and Its Symbolization over Time." *Anthropology and Humanism* 25, no. 2: 131–41.
de Certeau, Michel. 1988. *The Practice of Everyday Life*. Berkeley: University of California Press.
Eliade, Mircea. 2004. *Shamanism: Archaic Techniques of Ecstasy*. Princeton, NJ: Princeton University Press.
Fernandez, James W. 1982. *Bwiti: An Ethnography of the Religious Imagination in Africa*. Princeton, NJ: Princeton University Press.
———. 1986. *Persuasions and Performances: The Play of Tropes in Culture*. Bloomington: Indiana University Press.
Gell, Alfred. 1998. *Art and Agency: An Anthropological Theory*. Oxford: Clarendon Press.
Greene, Graham. 1982. *Monsignor Quixote*. Toronto: Lester & Orpen Dennys.
Jansen, Stef. 2008. "Looking for a Bus: How Certain Schemes to Improve the Suburban Condition Have Been Hailed." Paper presented at the *Critical Spaces of Hope: Locating Postsocialism and the Future in Post-Yugoslav Anthropology*, University of Chicago, Chicago.
Kazazis, Kostas. 1972. "The Status of Turkisms in the Present-Day Balkan Languages." In *Aspects of the Balkans: Continuity and Change: Contributions of the International Balkan Conference Held at UCLA, October 23–28, 1969*, edited by H. Birnbaum, 87–116. The Hague and Paris: Mouton.
Ledeneva, Alena V. 1988. *Russia's Economy of Favours: Blat, Networking, and Informal Exchange*. Cambridge: Cambridge University Press.
Marković, Goran, dir. 1979. *Nacionalna klasa*. 105 min. Centar film. Yugoslavia.
Mitić, Boris, dir. 2003. *Pretty Dyana: A Gypsy Recycling Saga*. 45 min. Dribbling Pictures. Serbia.
Munn, Nancy. 1973. "Symbolism in a Ritual Context: Aspects of Symbolic Action." In *Handbook of Social and Cultural Anthropology*, edited by J. J. Honigmann, 579–612. Chicago: Rand McNally.
Pesmen, Dale. 1991. "Reasonable and Unreasonable Worlds: Some Expectations of Coherence in Culture Implied by the Prohibition of Mixed Metaphor." In *Beyond Metaphor: The Theory of Tropes in Anthropology*, edited by J. W. Fernandez, 213–43. Stanford, CA: Stanford University Press.

Remarque, Erich Maria. 1998. *Three Comrades.* Translated by A. W. Wheen. New York: Ballantine Books.
Ries, Nancy. 1997. *Russian Talk: Culture and Conversation during Perestroika.* Ithaca, NY and London: Cornell University Press.
Simić, Marina. 2008. "Travel and State after the 'Fall' in Serbia." Paper presented at the *Critical Spaces of Hope: Locating Postsocialism and the Future in post-Yugoslav Anthropology,* University of Chicago, Chicago.
Škaljić, Abdulah. 1989. *Turcizmi u srpskohrvatskom jeziku.* Sarajevo: Svetlost.
Wimsatt, W. K., Jr. 1954. *The Verbal Icon: Studies in the Meaning of Poetry.* Lexington, KY: University of Kentucky Press.
Živković, Marko. 2001. "Jelly, Slush and Red Mists: Poetics of Amorphous Substances in Serbian Jeremiads of the 1990s." *Anthropology and Humanism* 25, no. 2: 168–82.
———. 2011. *Serbian Dreambook: National Imaginary in the Time of Milošević.* Bloomington and Indianapolis: Indiana University Press.

CHAPTER 6

"Let's Go F.B.!"
Metaphors of Cars and Corruption in China

Beth E. Notar

In the spring of 2008, while doing research in the southwestern city of Kunming, I met a young Chinese man in his twenties called "John" (an English name he had chosen for himself). I struck up a conversation with him about his car—a silver sports coupe that he had parked on the street near my apartment. His car had been modified (*gaizhuang guo*) with a front hood cover, fancy hubcaps, and various decals, and he was polishing it lovingly while he waited for his girlfriend to get off work. Over the next months I had the opportunity to interview John on several different occasions about his car, as well as to go to a new stretch of road not yet open to traffic where he and some of his friends (illegally) drag raced.

During one of our interviews, I asked John how, in addition to going drag racing, he used his car. He liked to take road trips, he answered, with friends to scenic towns around Kunming.

> John: For example, I will text message my friends and say, "Let's go to Dali to be corrupt!" (咱们去大理腐败吧 *Zamen qv Dali fubai ba*!)
>
> Beth: What? "Go be corrupt"?
>
> John: (laughing) Yes, "go be corrupt." That's how we say, "Let's go play" (*qv war*). Or we might shorten it in our text and say, "Let's go F.B.!" (去 F.B.! *qv F.B.!*)

Here, the "F.B." mentioned in John's text message stands for the first two letters of the *pinyin* Romanization of the spoken Mandarin *Fu Bai*. In contemporary China, the term *fubai* refers to corruption or corrupt practices, broadly defined.[1]

If corruption in China has been condemned as "an evil in itself" (Kinkley 2007: 171) that "gets people angry" (Kinkley 2007: 189), and can even lead to criminal sentences of execution (Barboza 2008), how can we make sense of John and his friends' playful use of "going to go be corrupt"? In order to understand this idiom, I suggest that we need to understand the metaphorical connection between cars and corruption in China.[2] This chapter therefore examines that connection from the 1940s to the present, with particular attention to critiques expressed in popular sayings and cartoons (car-toons), and very briefly, in films and novels.[3]

I discuss cars in contexts where they are both material and symbolic "multivocal" vehicles, conveying beings and things through space and across semantic domains. Whereas Victor Turner (1967) and James Fernandez (1977) have emphasized the polysemy of symbols in ritual contexts, this chapter focuses on cars in quotidian contexts—on the streets and in everyday speech and images. My analysis is akin to that of Pierre Lemonnier who examines seemingly mundane but meaningful objects that are made and used outside of ritual contexts. These objects, which Lemonnier terms "strategic objects" (2012: 167), convey *"key values or fundamental characteristics of particular social relations"* (2012: 12; italics in original). These "strategic objects," as I suggest cars in China are, remind us that "some things and thoughts and hierarchies and histories and gestures have to be thought together" (Lemonnier 2012: 120). From the perspective of this section of the present volume, we find not only that vehicles are precisely one of the redolent things and ideas that facilitate developing this kind of a holistic, composite image, but also that vehicles facilitate equally rich expressions of moral ambivalence.

Similarly, as Marko Živković points out about the Fića in the former Yugoslavia, we should not attempt to reduce the metaphoric significance of particular things to one domain, and in fact, part of the power of the Fića, or perhaps cars and vehicles in general, "does perhaps come partly from the disjointedness, the mixedness of metaphoric domains" (see Živković, Chapter 5, this volume). And as Diana Young has written about in South Australia: "The car, then, is a thing of many potentials. It is a social body, an anthropomorphized vehicle, and operates in various modes of spatial negotiation" (Young 2001: 54).

Cars have long held a special symbolic valence in China, not only as symbols of modernity, progress, and the future, but also as symbols of official status, power, and inequality. Recently, however, with a new entrepreneurial elite (see Goodman 2008) and emerging middle-class (Li 2008, 2010) who can afford to purchase their own private cars, both cars and corruption have begun to take on different metaphorical valences.

In China, cars fall under what Lakoff and Turner have termed "the general *machines are people* metaphor" (Lakoff and Turner 1989: 58), or the more general "things are people metaphor." In other words, cars are anthropomorphized to comment on the human condition. Of course, this can also be switched around, to the *people are machines,* or *people are vehicles* metaphor. In other words, people are mechanized or vehicularized, to comment on the relationship not only between people and things, but also on the relationships between different groups of people.

As we see in this volume, cars may be anthropomorphized. Among the Anagu of South Australia, to cite another case, cars are considered social bodies (Young 2001). Americans also view cars as extensions of their bodies (Katz 2000). Taking this metaphor a step further, Tim Dant has argued that we should consider the "driver-car" as an "assemblage": "neither a thing nor a person; it is a composite social vehicle-being that takes on properties of both and cannot exist without both" (2005: 74).

Yet, as Naomi Quinn has cautioned in her essay "The Cultural Basis of Metaphor," we must not assume that metaphors themselves structure our understanding of the world. Instead, she argues: "particular metaphors are selected by speakers, and are favored by these speakers, … because they provide satisfying mappings onto already existing cultural understandings" (Quinn 1991: 65; see also Quinn 1997). But what if these "cultural understandings" are in flux? In reform-era China, the Chinese Communist Party rules over the fastest growing, what some might call the most hypercapitalist, economy in the world. Is this "late socialism?" "Post-socialism?" "Neoliberalism?" How does one understand moral valuations of "public" and "private," for example, when government bureaus run private businesses (see Hsing 2008)? And when ideology and practice conflict, how does one define what constitutes "good," "proper," or "moral" action, or what constitutes a "good society" (Kinkley 2007: 177; Zhang 2008, 2010)?

While I strongly concur with Quinn's argument that we need to analyze the use of metaphor in context (1991, 1997), I am particularly interested in the use of metaphor in contexts of social change. Where and when do old metaphors work to help us make sense of new situations and where and when do they fall short?[4] When is there room for innovation, creativity and irony in metaphor? Metaphor often draws on familiar understandings but does so in order to take us to a conceptually different place. Or at least through the use of something familiar, we can envision some thing or some situation more clearly.[5]

In this chapter, I will argue that because cars, and more generally vehicles (*che*) in China have long been associated with those in power, they have been both symbols of power and targets for those who wish to critique abuses of power. However, I will also show that as access to cars has become more widespread during China's current reform era, cars in *general* are no longer symbols of corruption, and instead *particular* (mis)uses of cars and particular kinds of cars become marked as "corrupt" (*fubai*). In this context of market reform, "transgression" by officials works to reinforce power, and the meanings of "public" and "private" are shifting. Along the way, I will also suggest that ideas about metaphor, and the ways in which metaphor works, are not the same across languages and cultures, and there is something particular about the way metaphor works in ideographic written languages.

Che: Chariots, Cars, Power

In China, there has long been a symbolic connection between vehicles, whether in the form of chariots or cars, and power. Originally, emperors, officials, and their drivers were the only ones who had access to chariots. When an emperor or official died, these chariots, their drivers (*che ren*, literally "chariot people"), and their horses would be buried (sometimes alive) alongside each other (Zhongguo Shehui 1988; Bagley 1999).

The word "car" in Chinese, *qiche*, literally "vapor vehicle," comes from *che*, "chariot." One of the earliest textual references to *che* refers to an emperor's chariot. The reference states that the legendary Yellow Emperor, thought to have ruled in the twenty-seventh century BC had seven main officials; among them, Xizhong was the one who made the chariots.[6] Eventually, the legendary Yellow Emperor came to be known by his chariot: to refer to the emperor one could call him Xuanyuan, literally "official chariot" (Liang 1972: 1078). In other words, the chariot itself came to represent the emperor.

Written Chinese is an ideographic language, so that the character for chariot, and later, more generally, "vehicle," *che*, visually represents a chariot as seen from above (without its horses to the right):

車

Most Chinese characters are compounds, with one side, called the "radical," carrying the meaning, and the other side providing the sound. So *che*, "chariot" or "vehicle," as a radical appears in over hundreds of words—for example in the word *Xuanyuan*, "official chariot," there are the two characters:

軒   轅
Chariot + sound "Xuan"   Chariot + sound "Yuan"

Chariot-cart-vehicle-related words, come, by extension to have metaphorical meaning over time. For example: 軌 (*gui*) literally, the space between the right and the left wheels of a vehicle, comes to mean rut, track, path, and then by extension, rule or regulation (see Liang 1972: 1075–82).

An ideographic written language allows for another layer of symbolic significance that phonetic languages do not have. If, for example we are to use Charles Sanders Peirce's analysis of signs where there is:

- an object
- a sign vehicle, and
- the interpretant (the understanding of the sign vehicle-object relation)

in an ideographic language there are two sign vehicles—the spoken sound and the written symbol. When reading an ideographic language, metaphoric associations are symbolically reinforced in a way that they are not with phonetic writing systems.[7]

The Chinese terms for metaphor, 隱喻 (*yinyu*), literally "hidden, meaning," and "hidden comparison," 隱比 (*yinbi*), suggest that metaphor is not a vehicle transporting and conveying meaning across semantic domains, but rather it is implied to hide an element of moral equivocality. Like Cuna ideas of metaphor (Howe 1977: 137), the idea of metaphor in Chinese has a dark side. Interestingly, the Chinese idea of metaphor as something hidden below the surface contrasts with the obvious metaphorical connections that are apparent in the written ideographic language. Much more could be said here; suffice it to say that ideas about metaphor, and the ways in which metaphor works vary across languages and cultures. In the cartoons that I will discuss below, there is another level of metaphoric play available to the Chinese cartoonist and reader/viewer than there is to a cartoonist and reader/viewer of a phonetic language.[8]

Cars and Corruption

While the relationship between vehicles, status, wealth, and power can be traced back to the legendary Yellow Emperor, it is unclear when *che* as chariots, vehicles, or cars first became associated with corruption in China. However, at least by the 1940s, the connection between cars and corruption is clear.

China in the 1940s might be thought of analogously to contemporary Afghanistan: a weak national government tried to establish control over a country destabilized by war, contested by opium-dealing warlords, and challenged by insurgents or rebels (depending on your perspective), then, the Chinese Communists. The Communists, in their efforts to mobilize the population against the ruling Nationalists, employed images of cars to critique the corruption of the Nationalists and foreign "imperialists."

For example, in a 1946 woodcut cartoon by Ding Cong which appeared on the cover of the *Weekly News* (*Zhoubao*), a heavy, extravagantly dressed couple rides on the back of an emaciated, naked man (Figure 6.1). The body of this man is vehicularized—he becomes the car that conveys the couple. The caption on the cartoon reads: "Public Servant" (*gong pu*).

Figure 6.1. "Public Servant." Woodcut by Ding Cong, *Zhoubao* 23 (February 9, 1946).

The critique here is that the so-called "Public Servant"—the official (and his wife or mistress) who should be serving the people, is instead having the people serve him. In this cartoon the powerful "ride" (i.e., exploit) the poor and powerless.

In a 1948 cartoon (Figure 6.2), the popular cartoon character Sanmao (literally, "three hairs" because he has only three strands of hair on the top of his head), an orphan boy who lives on the streets of Shanghai, picks up a piece of coal from a nearby basket to throw at the driver of a large, black, shiny sedan. Sanmao is frustrated because he and his friend, another boy, marked as better off by his clothes and schoolbag, are trying to cross the street to see a show that is about to start, but cannot cross due to the traffic. Seeing a policeman and his twitching baton, the other boy tries to dissuade Sanmao from throwing the coal, but Sanmao seems determined. The cartoon, titled "Impatience" (*Ji bu ke nai* 急不可耐), captures a sense of popular moral outrage against the economic inequality of pre-liberation Shanghai as marked by the contrast between the driver of the new sedan and the orphan boy in particular, and drivers of cars and pedestrians in general. Moreover, not only does the policeman not attempt to help the young boys cross the street; he is preparing to beat

Figure 6.2. "Impatience" (*Ji bu ke nai* 急不可耐). Cartoon by Zhang Leping, *Sanmao the Vagabond*, vol. 1 (1948).

Sanmao for posing a threat (or at least a nuisance) to the established hierarchy and authority.[9]

In another example from the period, in the 1949 leftist film *Crows and Sparrows* (*Wuya yu maque*), made in secret on the eve of Communist victory, the corrupt and lecherous Nationalist Party official Mr. Hou (a pun for "monkey") is the only one in the film who has access to a car. His lechery manifests itself when he attempts to entice the wife of a schoolteacher, Mrs. Hua, whose husband will soon be arrested by the Nationalist secret police, into his chauffeured black sedan.[10]

The Mao Era

The Chinese Communists came to power because they were able to mobilize the "masses," in part by using images of cars in their critique of Nationalist and imperialist corruption. Ironically, in Mao's China (1949–1976), only high-ranking Communist Party cadres and government officials had access to cars.[11] Communist officials were supposed to be pure, beyond reproach, and their use of cars was not to be associated with the earlier, corrupt Nationalist officials' use of cars. Still, because virtually *only* officials had access to cars, the association between cars, officialdom, or more broadly, cars, power, and privilege continued.[12]

During the Mao years, there were large billboards in every city and town, written in Mao Zedong's calligraphy, with the slogan: "All under heaven belongs to/is for the Public" (*tian xia wei gong* 天下為公). But cars were certainly not for the public. For example, in her English-language memoir *Wild Swans*, Chinese writer Jung Chang [Rong Zhang] tells a story about her father, a Communist Party official in the 1950s. Her father would ride slowly in his chauffeur-driven official car (a jeep), while his pregnant wife (Jung Chang's mother) walked alongside. Jung Chang's father did this to illustrate that he was an upright comrade—not even his pregnant wife could share his car—but the story no less disclosed the privileges to which government and party officials had access and the public did not.[13]

Where cars are allocated by the state, primarily for use by officials, they more explicitly serve as symbols of state power. This link between cars and the state has been overlooked by analysts who have focused on capitalist contexts. For example, David Gartman has written of the "three ages of the automobile," based on different eras of production and consumption—the early age of "class distinction," the middle age of "mass individuality," and the recent age of postmodernism and Post-Fordism, where cars can serve as expressions of "subcultural difference" (Gartman 2005; see also Gartman 1994). However, these three ages assume an American and Western European context. In China and the former Soviet Union, for many decades, cars were not available for individual purchase—they were allocated by the state. In the Soviet Union, it was not until the 1970s that cars started to be available for individual consumption (see Siegelbaum 2008), and in China it was not until the mid 1990s that individuals could begin to purchase cars.[14] We cannot assume that ages of production, distribution, consumption and meaning-making apply across capitalist, socialist, and now China's communist-capitalist contexts (see Živković, Chapter 5, this volume).

The Reform Era

China has undergone radical changes since the death of Mao in 1976 and the start of the era of "reform and opening" (*gaige kaifang*)—reform of the economy and opening up to the world—in 1978. Over the past three decades, China has disbanded agricultural communes, downsized and privatized or semi-privatized state industries, attracted foreign investment in manufacturing, and encouraged domestic consumption. During this time, China has become the world's fastest growing and second largest economy. Yet, despite these vast social and economic changes (or perhaps because of allowing them), the Chinese Communist Party has remained firmly in power. In this new economic and social context, the privilege of "public cars" continues for government and party officials.

In contemporary China, official cars are called "public service cars," (*gongwu yongche* 公务用车), or literally, "public cars," (*gongche* 公車) for short, The *gong* of *gongche,* means "public" in the sense that the cars are state-owned. In practice, there is nothing "public" about "public cars." Public cars are allocated by official rank and are intended for the exclusive use of an official on his or her (usually his) official business. Popular critiques of official corruption poke fun at officials and their so-called "public" cars through common phrases, novels and cartoons.[15]

Popular sayings from the mid 1990s on have poked fun at officials' access to cars. For example: "Regardless of their rank, they all take to Audis" (*buguan shenme ji, dou lai zuo Aodi*). And, "Even when the [state-run] business is broke, the bosses flaunt their Hondas" (*Qiye kuile qian, zhaoyang wan Bentian*) (cited in Barmé 2002: 189, 383). As Kinkley (2007) has pointed out, some Chinese novelists in the 1990s critiqued official access to "public" cars as a symptom of corruption.[16] In his 1995 novel *Heaven Above* (*Cangtian zaishang*), Lu Tianming depicted corruption at the Wanfang Automotive Works (a fictional Sino-American joint venture) where officials misappropriate funds and knowingly use sub-standard parts. Like the legendary Yellow Emperor, the officials in the story come to be known by their vehicles, vehicles that are clearly ranked according to the officials' status. "The provincial leaders have Audis; the mayor, a Santana (and later ... an Audi); the lower level officials have a Mazda and a compact Ford Tempo" (Kinkley 2007: 45). In some critiques of corruption, it is not the officials themselves, but their family members who have access to cars. For example, in Chen Fang's novel *Heaven's Wrath* (Tiannu, 1997), the son of a high-ranking municipal official arrives at a luxury hotel in a fleet of black Mercedes 560s (Kinkley 2007: 60).

In Qiu Xiaolong's recent detective novel, *A Case of Two Cities* (2006), Chief Inspector Chen of the Shanghai Police Bureau sets out to investigate the case of Xing, a county-level party secretary in Fujian province who has built an elaborate smuggling operation in cars, alcohol, drugs, and women. "No one had taken advantage of the labyrinthine system in a more skillful and more surprisingly simple way—corruption upon corruption" (Qiu 2006: 26). The most potent symbol of Xing's success was a Red Flag limousine that had apparently been built for Chairman Mao himself.

Between 2003 and 2005, Minglu Chen (2008) conducted interviews with fifty-six wealthy women entrepreneurs in the town of Mianyang, Sichuan province, a new center for light industry. She found that as the women's wealth increased, so did their political connections and participation in local politics. Chen also found that while cars in general were rare in Mianyang, forty-five out of the fifty-six women entrepreneurs had their own cars, most of them foreign imports. Of course, this in itself does not indicate any kind of corruption, but it can underscore a popular perception of the connections between wealth, political power, and cars.[17]

In 2008 China, when most of the research for this chapter was conducted, officials (and their sons and daughters) who had access to particular kinds of expensive foreign cars (Toyota Prados, Mercedes, Audi sedans) were criticized. Yet, as private citizens started to be able to purchase their own cars, it became increasingly *what* officials did with their cars and *when* that became subjects of popular critique.[18] For example, public (official) cars' disregard for traffic regulations was a constant and commented upon sight around Kunming city in 2008.

> What is that white Mercedes doing driving the wrong way up the bus lane?
> Oh, it is a 'public' (official) car.
> Who are those black Audis driving at twice the speed limit on the ring road?
> Official cars.
> Who are those black Audis passing in a no passing zone?
> Official cars.

Official cars' violation of rules of the road served as a mundane metaphor for corruption. Moreover, official cars' indifference to the law was especially ironic given that in the lead-up to the Beijing Olympics during 2008, there was an official "civility" (*wenming*) campaign intended to produce "civilized citizens" (*wenming shimin*). This movement—broadly promulgated on billboards, neighborhood blackboards, and posters— emphasized "Kunming citizens' ten public don'ts" (*Kunming shimin shibu gongyue*), the first of which was "don't violate traffic regulations" (*bujun fanyi jiaotong guize*).

Since the most notorious offenders appeared to be the so-called "public" cars and their drivers, "public" cars did not seem "public" (*gong*), nor did their drivers appear to be "citizens" (*shimin*) who were supposed to adhere to traffic laws. Certainly, not all officials violated the law, but because official cars are clearly designated by their official license plates, any time an official car *did* violate traffic rules, it was obvious to all that it was an official.[19]

Official disregard for the road also appeared as a marker of corruption in cartoons. For example, in one cartoon, an official, marked by his imperial, Yellow Emperor-style costume, drives a car with a "special power license plate" (*tequan chepai*). The "emperor"-like official is driving over a book titled "Traffic Regulations" (*jiaotong fagui*). Another man, presumably a lower-ranking official in a green pinstripe suit and pink tie—connoting a kind of crass wealth—says respectfully and deferentially: "It does not matter if you run over these!" (*Nin yale mei guanxi*!). In other words, since you are a higher-ranking official, you can do whatever you want.

"Transgression" has often been celebrated as a way in which the less powerful attempt to challenge or invert socioeconomic hierarchies (see Stallybrass and White 1986: 17–18) and disciplined spaces and places (Cresswell 1996). With regards to cars in particular, it has been working or lower class youths who use cars to violate both the rules and restrictions of the state and their parents.[20] For example, in Norway and Sweden, working-class youths use cars as vehicles of resistance to and freedom from middle-class norms of behavior (Garvey 2001; O'Dell 2001). In the United States, low-income Latino youths also use low riders to symbolically and spatially challenge a racist society and the spatial strictures of police surveillance (Bright 1995; Best 2006; Chappell, Chapter 7, this volume).

In and around Kunming city, some younger men have begun to engage in (illegal) street drag racing (*saiche*) or "drifting" (*piaoyi*)—sliding through turns on mountain roads—both a form of transgression against official regulation (see Roth, this volume).[21] However, many of these young men are well-off professionals, like my friend John, and do their racing or drifting late at night on deserted stretches of road. Usually, the only people watching are other racers or car fans.

Transgression, as I discuss it here differs from the type enacted by the Scandinavian and American working- and lower-class youths, as well as by elite young Chinese late night drag racers. The traffic transgressors in this context are mostly male, middle-aged officials. Their transgressions are blatant—done during the day on crowded streets, or on highways when hundreds of people can observe them. In other words, it is *those in power* who are transgressing expected, regulated behaviors of space and place. And it is precisely because they have power to do so that they may do so without fear of repercussion. It is this blatant disregard for rules that everybody else is expected to follow that regular citizens cite as one marker of corruption.[22]

A second critique of corruption in 2008 was expressed in two popular sayings: "public cars become private cars" (*gong che dang si che* 公车当私车) or "public cars, private use" (*gong che si yong* 公车私用). For example, my friend John with the silver sports coupe—who appeared at the opening of this chapter when I quoted him as wanting friends "to go be corrupt"—worked for a major bank. His job there was to recruit new clients and retain old ones primarily by entertaining them. This usually involved hosting older men, both businessmen and officials (or the new hybrid businessman-official) at restaurants and clubs. "I have to drink way too much for my job," he told me. "Sometimes I just stumble home and then collapse in the hallway."

John's line of work is satirized in another cartoon in which two men stagger out of a restaurant. The younger man says drunkenly to the older one:

> "Secretary Li, you have no skill [as a driver], let … me … drive" (*Li chu, ni mei benr, hai shi wo… kai … che*).
> The older man replies, even more drunkenly:
> "Don't tease me, even if I lack skill, I … will as usual … drive … home …" (*bie dou le, mei benr, wo … ye zhaoyang … kai … hui … qv …*).

In the cartoon, Secretary Li's personified car 'looks on' with concern. We viewers, who are positioned as another car, perhaps the younger man's, also watch fretfully (and with wry amusement). This cartoon formed part of an official anti-corruption campaign, of which there have been many. Here, the government itself recognizes the popular critique of corruption through vehicle metaphors that attempt to persuade the public that something is being done about it.[23]

Ordinary people are suspicious of the entertainment activities of officials which they view as "corrupt" because the latter use public cars to enjoy themselves in private places, off hours, presumably at public expense.[24] However, as Uretsky (2008) and Osburg (2013) have observed, officials, businessmen, and businessmen-officials establish and cement networking relationships (关系 *guanxi*) at restaurants, bars, and karaoke (*kala OK*) clubs. Men spend time there eating, drinking, and sometimes "playing" with "kala OK girls" who perform songs and other services. The officials consider this to be an essential part of their work, but to workaday, commonfolk, officials appear to be doing little more than fooling around.

Whereas both cars and entertainment were once the exclusive domain of officials, now, young men like John who can afford their own cars mimic the terms and actions of corruption. They drive private cars to scenic places, and go out to eat, drink, and "play" with young women. What used to be the exclusive domain of officials—having access to cars and having access to places to enjoy oneself with colleagues or friends—what was considered "corrupt"—has now been taken on by China's emerging elite and middle-class youth. This popular, satiric use of "going to go be corrupt" indicates that both people's practices have changed and that the content of what constitutes "corruption" has changed. Whereas during the Cultural Revolution (1966–1976), "romance" and "relaxation" were considered forms of "bourgeois" corruption, now corruption constitutes transgression, misappropriation of funds and resources, embezzlement, and fraud (see Qiu 2006; Kinkely 2007; Barboza 2008).

As "corruption" changes, so too does the meaning of "public" and "private." Whereas "private" was once considered "bourgeois" (and therefore anti-communist), as more of the economy has been privatized, "private," especially in the form of private property—homes, apartments, cars—has come to take on more positive meanings. Young, well-off men like John, are not the only ones to purchase cars. With an emerging (upper) middle class (Zhang 2008, 2010), middle-aged couples are also buying cars. Since the mid 1990s, when individuals were first allowed to purchase cars, car ownership has increased exponentially in China, to the extent that "China is quickly becoming a car-dependent society" (Appleyard et al. 2007: 5). By 2009 the number of new car sales in China surpassed the number of new car sales in the United States.[25]

In this context of rising car consumption, "private cars" (*siche*) have come to have a positive valence in distinction to the "public cars" of officials. In another cartoon, two small private cars daintily sip gas out of wine glasses, while a giant, official SUV guzzles gas out of a barrel. The private cars represent a decent-sized, modest, or moral, consumption of resources, while the public, official, monstrous SUV consumes an unequal share.

Whereas the public views official cars as representing the state, the new upper,- middle-class car consumers I interviewed in 2008 described their private cars as being like a second child (somewhat like the way citizens of the former Yugoslavia personified the Fića as kin, see Živković, this volume). A private car must be "raised" (*yang che* 养车), as one would raise a child (*yang haizi* 养孩子). Cars must be cared for as one might a child—they must be fed and cleaned. Some cars, like some spoiled children, would "eat" too much (*chi you* 吃油; *hao you* 好油). And cars needed to be looked after. An large auto supply and repair shop I visited several times was called "Auto Nanny" (*Che baomu* 车保姆).

While the word *gong* (public) has long held positive connotations, by contrast to the negative references of *si* (private), these valences are shifting as privatization intensifies during China's reform era. In the Mao era (1949–1976), *gong* was associated, at least ideally and in state discourse (but I would argue in individual discourse as well), with all that was positive—the public, the people, righteousness, etc.—and *si* was associated with all that was considered negative—the private, the individual, the bourgeoisie, selfishness, etc. However, during the reform era, the meanings of the two categories, public and private, have been basically reversed. G*ong* has come to be linked to corruption, excess, and transgression in unofficial discourse, while *si* is associated with ethics, modesty, and following the law. I have tabularized this reversal below.

Mao Era (Ideal) Discourse		Reform Era (Unofficial) Discourse	
公	私	公	私
gong	*si*	*gong*	*si*
public	private	public	private
the people	the individual	the state	the individual
proletarian	bourgeois	official	unofficial
righteous	mean	corrupt	ethical
shared	hoarded	excessive	modest
fair	selfish	transgressive	law-abiding

In her engaging comparative discussion of metaphors of "public" and "private" in the United States, Hungary and Poland, Susan Gal (2005) observed that Americans and Eastern Europeans conceptualize these terms differently. Americans, she suggests, understand "public" and "private" spatially. For example, the street is a "public" space, whereas the home is considered a "private" space. Eastern Europeans by contrast, think of "public" and "private" in terms of persons. "We," the regular people, are "the private," while "they," the officials, are "the public." In China, people conceptualize "public" and "private" in terms of a tri-part constellation of persons, space/place, and time. Similar to Eastern Europe, there certainly exists the "us" and "them" division, where "we" the regular people, the "old hundred names" (*laobaixing*) constitute the unofficial, the non-public, and "they," the officials, constitute "the public." Yet, especially since the growth of the market economy orchestrated by the Communist Party, a distinction between "public" and "private" spaces and places has arisen. There are spaces and places that are clearly marked as "public"—Party and government offices, plazas, parks, schools, streets, official cars. Other spaces and places are now "private"—privately-run restaurants, shops, new condominiums, and new individually-owned cars. A third more nebulous domain, that of time, has also come into play.[26] Indeed, the popular adage, "public cars, private use" (*gong che si yong*) can be more fully understood if we include time as a dimension of "public" and "private." When a public official drives or is driven in his official car to a private restaurant or karaoke club (private) at night, during unofficial or "private" hours, he or she is seen to be inappropriately mixing public and private categories of space and time. Or, when an official drives his official, public car with his family inside it (private) to go sweep his family's ancestral tombs (private) on grave sweeping day (arguably a "public" holiday, but one during which one tends to "private" family matters), he is also considered to be mixing public and private inappropriately. It is this transgressive combination of person, space/place and time that is then criticized by ordinary people (whom we might normally think of as "the public") as corrupt.

Conclusion

Margaroni and Yiannopoulou claim that a "striking convergence between the postmodern politics of mobility and a *politics of metaphor*" is taking place at the moment and they urge scholars to analyze "instances of how discourse and material manifestations of movement interact" (2006: 10–11, italics in original).[27] Similarly, Bal has argued that we adopt the neologism "to metaphor," which verb form captures the work of carrying over or bridging meaning to "express" a situation (Bal 2006: 159, 163–65). These points are well taken. Vehicles provide exactly the theoretical capacity to which they refer: vehicles provide empirical and theoretical entrée into ways in which various scales of the moral may be conveyed, transported, and uncovered across semantic domains.

At least since the 1940s in China, people have been *metaphored* as cars in various forms of media, or cars have been *metaphored* as people as a way of critiquing corruption. In a 1946 cartoon, the body of a poor, naked man carries the well-to-do "public servant;" in a 2008 cartoon, an anthropomorphized official "public car" sports utility vehicle guzzles gas, drinking up resources at public expense. While the derogatory metaphors "people as cars" and "cars as people" have been in consistent use, the socioeconomic context and specific symbolic valences of these metaphors have changed dramatically.

In China's current transition to a market economy, young men like John have become able to afford their own sports coupes. Their call to action, "Let's go F.B.!," is a caricature of vehicle-officials now inflected with a positive valence, or at least a morally equivocal one. To go out and "be corrupt" suggests that it has now become at least somewhat acceptable for people to have a good time in public, but perhaps it has also diluted the popular critique of corruption. Yet, despite the growing number of private cars on the roads, cars are still seen as symbols of official corruption. Public commentary and cartoon critiques—Official Li as an emperor, as a drunken cadre, as the SUV itself—express contradictions between the ideals and the practices of life in contemporary China, between public and private, righteousness and corruption, fairness and selfishness.

NOTES

1. The main Chinese ideograph for corruption, 腐 *fu*, which initially referred to rotten meat, later came to refer to other things, practices, or thoughts that were considered rotten or degenerate. "腐 爛也。从肉，府聲。*Fu*: rotten. From meat, sound: *fu*" (Xu 2004: vol. 1, 588).
2. "Going to go be corrupt" (*qv fubai*) in a playful sense is used now not only in relation to going places in cars, but as a way of saying "going out." Still, I will argue here that there is a particularly strong valence between cars and corruption.
3. In this short chapter I do not attempt to be comprehensive. I have not examined all cartoons, films, novels, and popular sayings from 1940 to the present; that project has yet to be done. Here I am simply using key examples to highlight the connection between cars and corruption. Moreover, there is a vast literature on corruption, especially in political science. For a working bibliography on corruption see Michael Johnston's web page: http://people.colgate.edu/mjohnston/personal.htm. His page also includes a list of public interest and other organizations that monitor corruption around the world.
4. Quinn gives two examples of speakers who use metaphors to explain something that they do not understand: non-engineers who try to explain electricity through analogies of water or crowds; or children who explain marriage by using analogies of playmates or friends. These are interesting examples, but they are both cases of non-experts trying to explain something out of their purview, not examples of people who are trying to explain or describe a situation from their own lives (Quinn 1997: 151–52).

5. Quinn expresses skepticism over the explanatory power of metaphor: "In the course of their use in ordinary talk, then, metaphors typically do not give rise to new understandings; rather, they reinforce existing understandings by clarifying them. This is not to say that the kind of thinking involved in metaphor usage can never lead to new understandings" (Quinn 1997: 151).
6. 鄭氏 《六藝論》： 黃帝佐官又七人， 奚仲造車。From Zeng Shi, *Liu yi lun*, dating to the Han dynasty period (206 BC to 220 AD).
7. Here I use "Chinese" to refer to the written language, and "Mandarin" to refer to the official spoken language.
8. In his book *The Aesthetics of Comics*, David Carrier writes: "Comics in my view are essentially a composite art: when they are successful, they have verbal and visual elements seamlessly combined" (Carrier 2000: 4). By "verbal" here he means "textual"—(these are often conflated in languages that use phonetic writing systems). He raises the question: "If experience of words as words differs in kind from the experience of images as images, then how can images and the words in [text] balloons and below the images ever constitute a genuine unity?" He suggests that the unity of image and text in comics offer a unity to the reader/viewer analogous to the "unity of mind and body" (Carrier 2000: 72–73). Carrier acknowledges in passing that Chinese text/calligraphy may be read aesthetically (visually) (72), but he does not dwell on the difference between ideographic and phonetic text.
9. There were reported incidents of people throwing things at the cars of elites and foreigners. For example, Derk Bodde, in his memoir of living in Beijing (Peking) through the revolution in 1949, records: "There have been some unpleasant incidents here lately. An American military officer, for example, was cut on the face when the window of his car was hit by a stone. Two or three other stonings have also been reported. The police, however, seem to be genuinely anxious that such incidents should not recur" (Bodde 1950: 174). In her article situating the Sanmao cartoons within the early history of cartoons in China, Mary Ann Farquhar notes that after the war with Japan ended, internal Chinese "privilege and corruption become the target" of Zhang Leping's Sanmao series (1948; Farquhar 1995: 152). For writing on other revolutionary Chinese comics see Chesneaux (1973).
10. Geremie Barmé gives an example of another film, *Sentries under the Neon Lights* (Nihongdengxiade shaobing) made almost twenty years later, but set on the eve of the Communist "liberation" of Shanghai: "a swank convertible comes careering down the street, driven by a brash American (or, rather, a lanky Chinese actor with a plasticine nose imitating a brash Yank). Forced to halt by the soldiers after threatening to drive through the crowd, the foreign interloper is confounded by the pedestrians' militant anger, given a stern lecture and sent packing. This is a paradigmatic moment, for it encapsulates much of the public attitude toward both the car and things foreign in China throughout the twentieth century" (Barmé 2002: 177).

11. In 1953 officials were ranked into 26 grades. The ranking determined not only pay, but also to what kinds of privileges and information an official had access. For example, only officials of rank 14 or above could travel by plane or by soft seat on a train (Chang 1991: 181).
12. There were some exceptions of individuals other than officials who had cars. A colleague from Shanghai tells me that a father's friend, a U.S.-trained engineer, was able to keep his private car until the Cultural Revolution (1966–1976).
13. Chang (1991: 143). Chang notes that the first anti-corruption campaign, aimed at Communist Party members, occurred in 1951, only two years after Communist victory (Chang 1991: 182).
14. In Eastern Europe, cars were available for individual consumption earlier. Particular kinds of private cars then became nostalgically associated with the socialist era. See Marko Živković's discussion (this volume) of the Fića (Fiat) in the former Yugoslavia and Daphne Berdahl's discussion (2001) of the Trabi (Trabant) in the former German Democratic Republic (East Germany).
15. According to Transparency International's "Corruption Perceptions Index 2009," China is ranked number 79 out of 180 countries. New Zealand and Denmark top the list as the least corrupt, and war-torn Iraq, Sudan, Myanmar, Afghanistan, and Somalia comprise the bottom. The United States is listed at number 19, after Japan and the United Kingdom. See http://www.transparency.org/policy_research/surveys_indices/cpi/2009/cpi_2009_table, accessed July 12, 2010.
16. Michael Johnston and Yufan Hao have identified privilege (*tequan*) as a key marker of corruption during the Mao era. See Johnston and Hao (1995); also Johnston (2001).
17. (Chen 2008: 112–25). Of the 56 women, 7 did not report their income, 16 made less than 1 million yuan, 15 made between 1 million and 9.99 million yuan, 7 made between 10 million and 99.99 million, and 11 made over 100 million yuan (Chen 2008: 115).
18. Most of the ethnographic research for this chapter was conducted in 2008 with some follow-up research conducted in the summer of 2012. Research funding was provided by the National Endowment for Humanities, a Charles A. Dana research associate professorship and a Luce Foundation Trinity College Faculty research grant.
19. I have written more about this traffic civility campaign elsewhere (see Notar 2010).
20. Sarah Jain analyzes another variation on this theme presented in a six-minute online BMW ad called "Star," where a lower-class chauffeur takes Madonna (and her stuntwoman) for a transgressive, violent ride (see Jain 2006).
21. They have been inspired in part by the Japanese *manga* and *anime* series about racers, *Initial D* (头文字D), later made into a Hong Kong movie.
22. In his work, James Fernandez has taken us from metaphor as "the essential figure of speech" to the relationship between metaphor and ritual action (Fer-

nandez 1977: 101). Here I am looking at mundane, not ritual contexts, but Fernandez's discussion of performative metaphor aids me in thinking about driving as a performative, symbolic act. Thus, Official Li driving his black SUV at breakneck speed the wrong way up the bus lane is a performance that says to all who observe it: "I can do this and you cannot." Kristin Monroe (2012) has begun to examine traffic transgressions in Beirut, Lebanon as representing what many people see as an ineffective state. In China, conversely, transgression in traffic illustrates the power of those associated with the state.
23. This cartoon also illustrates the interesting phenomenon of lower-level officials driving themselves. During the Mao era, if an official had access to a car, he or she would be chauffeured.
24. For film images of the karaoke club scene, see Jia Zhangke's *The World* (Shijie) and *Xiao Wu*.
25. "China Overtakes U.S. as World's Biggest Car Market" *The Guardian*.
26. Abraham Joshua Heschel has made the point that while time is unique—one moment is like no other—it can never be "owned," like an object or a place, for time is inherently shared ([1951] 2005).
27. Whether or not politics in China can be termed "postmodern" is a whole other issue that I will not get into here.

REFERENCES

Appleyard, Bruce, Zheng Yeqing, Rob Watson, Laura Bruce, Rachel Sohmer, Xuanyi Li, and Jingjing Qian. 2007. *Smart Cities: Solutions for China's Rapid Urbanization.* New York: NRDC (National Resources Defense Council).

"Auto Boom." 2009. *Beijing Review* 52, no. 28: 32–33.

Bagley, Robert. 1999. "Shang Archaeology." In *The Cambridge History of Ancient China*, edited by E. L. Shaughnessy, 124–230. Cambridge: Cambridge University Press.

Bal, Mieke. 2006. "Metaphoring: Making a Niche of Negative Space." In *Metaphoricity and the Politics of Mobility.* Special issue of Thamyris/Intersecting 12, edited by Maria Margaroni and Effie Yiannopoulou, 159–79. Amsterdam and New York: Rodopi.

Barboza, David. 2008. "Chinese Officials Accused of Embezzlement." *The New York Times,* Aug. 29. http://www.nytimes.com/2008/08/29/world/asia/29china.html, accessed August 29, 2008.

Barmé, Geremie R. 2002. "Engines of Revolution: Car Cultures in China." In *Autopia: Cars and Culture,* edited by Peter Wollen and Joe Kerr, 177–90. London: Reaktion Books.

Ben-Amos, Dan. 2000. "Metaphor." *Journal of Linguistic Anthropology* 9, nos. 1–2: 152–54.

Berdahl, Daphne. 2001. "'Go, Trabi Go!': Reflections on a Car and Its Symbolization over Time." *Anthropology and Humanism* 25, no. 2: 131–41.

Best, Amy L. 2006. *Fast Cars, Cool Rides: The Accelerating World of Youth and Their Cars.* New York: New York University Press.

Bodde, Derk. 1950. *Peking Diary: A Year of Revolution.* New York: Henry Schuman, Inc.

Bright, Brenda Jo. 1995. "Remappings: Los Angeles Low Riders." In *Looking High and Low: Art and Cultural Identity,* edited by Brenda Jo Bright and Liza Bakewell, 89–123. Tucson: University of Arizona Press.

Carrier, David. 2000. *The Aesthetics of Comics.* University Park: Pennsylvania State University.

Chang, Jung [Zhang, Rong]. 1991. *Wild Swans: Three Daughters of China.* New York: Anchor Books/Doubleday.

Chen, Minglu. 2008. "Entrepreneurial Women: Personal Wealth, Local Politics and Tradition." In *The New Rich in China: Future Rulers, Present Lives,* edited by David Goodman, 112–25. New York: Routledge.

Chesneaux, Jean. 1973. *The People's Comic Book.* Translated by Frances Frenaye. Garden City, NY: Anchor Press.

"China Overtakes U.S. as World's Biggest Car Market." 2010. *The Guardian,* January 8. http://www.theguardian.com/business/2010/jan/08/china-us-car-sales-overtakes, accessed August 3, 2010.

Transparency International. 2009. "Corruption Perceptions Index 2009." http://www.transparency.org/policy_research/surveys_indices/cpi/2009/cpi_2009_table, accessed July 12, 2010.

Cresswell, Tim. 1996. *In Place/Out of Place: Geography, Ideology, and Transgression.* Minneapolis and London: University of Minnesota Press.

———. 2002. "Introduction: Theorizing Place." In *Mobilizing Place, Placing Mobility: The Politics of Representation in a Globalized World.* Special issue of Thymaris/Intersecting 9, edited by Ginette Verstraete and Tim Cresswell, 11–32. Amsterdam and New York: Rodopi Press.

Croll, Elisabeth. 2006. *China's New Consumers: Social Development and Domestic Demand.* New York: Routledge.

Dant, Tim. 2005. "The Driver-Car." Reprinted in *Automobilities,* edited by Mike Featherstone, Nigel Thrift, and John Urry, 61–80. London: Sage.

Edensor, Tim. 2005. "Automobility and National Identity: Representation, Geography and Driving Practice." Reprinted in *Automobilities,* edited by Mike Featherstone, Nigel Thrift, and John Urry, 101–20. London: Sage.

Farquhar, Mary Ann. 1995. "*Sanmao:* Cartoons and Chinese Pop Culture." In *Asian Popular Culture,* edited by John A. Lent, 139–58. Boulder, CO: Westview Press.

———. 1999. *Children's Literature in China.* Armonk, NY: M. E. Sharpe.

Fernandez, James W. 1977. "The Performance of Ritual Metaphors." In *The Social Use of Metaphor: Essays on the Anthropology of Rhetoric,* edited by J. David Sapir and J. Christopher Crocker, 100–31. Philadelphia: University of Pennsylvania Press.

Fernandez, James W. 1991. "Introduction: Confluents of Inquiry." In *Beyond Metaphor: The Theory of Tropes in Anthropology*, edited by James W. Fernandez, 1–13. Stanford, CA: Stanford University Press.

Gal, Susan. 2002. "Semiotics of the Public/Private Distinction." *Differences* 12, no. 1: 77–95.

———. 2005. "Language Ideologies Compared: Metaphors of Public/Private." *Journal of Linguistic Anthropology* 15, no. 1: 23–37.

Gartman, David. 2005. "Three Ages of the Automobile: The Cultural Logics of the Car." Reprinted in *Automobilities*, edited by Mike Featherstone, Nigel Thrift, and John Urry, 169–96. London: Sage.

Garvey, Pauline. 2001. "Driving, Drinking and Daring in Norway." In *Car Cultures*, edited by Daniel Miller, 133–52. New York: Berg.

Goodman, David, ed. 2008. *The New Rich in China: Future Rulers, Present Lives*. New York: Routledge.

Hasty, Jennifer. 2005. "The Pleasures of Corruption: Desire and Discipline in Ghanaian Political Culture." *Cultural Anthropology* 20, no. 2: 271–301.

Heschel, Abraham Joshua. [1951] 2005. *The Sabbath*. New York: Farrar, Straus and Giroux.

Howe, James. 1977. "Carrying the Village: Cuna Political Metaphors." In *The Social Use of Metaphor: Essays on the Anthropology of Rhetoric*, edited by J. David Sapir and J. Christopher Crocker, 132–63. Philadelphia: University of Pennsylvania Press.

Hsing, You-tien. 2008. "Socialist Land Masters: The Territorial Politics of Accumulation." In *Privatizing China: Socialism from Afar*, edited by Li Zhang and Aihwa Ong, 57–70. Ithaca, NY: Cornell University Press.

Jain, Sarah. 2006. "Urban Violence: Luxury in Made Space." In *Mobile Technologies of the City*, edited by Mimi Sheller and John Urry, 61–75. New York: Routledge.

Johnston, Michael. 2001. "Corruption in China: Old Ways, New Realities and a Troubled Future." http://people.colgate.eud/mjohnston/MJ percent20papers percent2001/currhist.pdf, accessed July 31, 2010.

Johnston, Michael, and Yufan Hao. 1995. "China's Surge of Corruption." *Journal of Democracy* 6, no. 4: 30–94.

Katz, Jack. 2000. *How Emotions Work*. Chicago: University of Chicago Press.

Kinkley, Jeffrey C. 2007. *Corruption and Realism in Late Socialist China: The Return of the Political Novel*. Stanford, CA: Stanford University Press.

Lakoff, George, and Mark Turner. 1989. *More than Cool Reason: A Field Guide to Poetic Metaphor*. Chicago: The University of Chicago Press.

Lemonnier, Pierre. 2012. *Mundane Objects: Materiality and Non-Verbal Communication*. Walnut Creek, CA: Left Coast Press.

Liang Shih-chiu (梁實秋), ed. 1972. A New Practical Chinese-English Dictionary (最新實用漢英辭典). Taipei: The Far East Book Co, Ltd (遠東圖書公司).

Lu, L. 1993. "Chariot and horse burials in ancient China." *Antiquity* 67: 824–38.

"Luxury Car Sales Continue to Grow." 2010. *China Car Times*, July 23. http://www.chinacartimes.com/2010/07/23/luxury-car-sales-continue-to-grow/, accessed August 3, 2010.

Manser, Martin H., Zhu Yuan, Wang Liangbi, Ren Yongchang, Wu Jingrong, Mei Ping, Ren Xiaoping, and Shi Qinan, eds. [1986] 2007. *Concise English-Chinese Chinese-English Dictionary*, 3d ed. Beijing: The Commerce Press; Hong Kong: Oxford University Press.

Margaroni, Maria, and Effie Yiannopoulou. 2006. "Theorizing Metaphoricity, Reconceptualizing Politics." In *Metaphoricity and the Politics of Mobility*. Special issue of Thamyris/Intersecting 12, edited by Maria Margaroni and Effie Yiannopoulou, 9–24. Amsterdam and New York: Rodopi.

Miller, Daniel, ed. 2001. *Car Cultures*. New York: Berg.

Monroe, Kristin V. 2012. "Stop and Go: Traffic Control and State Power in Beirut, Lebanon." *Anthropology News* 53, no. 9: 8.

Notar, Beth E. 2010. "Performing Civility or 'Flooring It'!: Competing Discourses of Mobility in Urban China." Panel: Circulating the City: Traffic. American Anthropological Association Annual Meetings. New Orleans.

O'Dell, Tom. 2001. "*Raggare* and the Panic of Mobility: Modernity and Everyday Life in Sweden." In *Car Cultures*, edited by Daniel Miller, 105–32. New York: Berg.

Osburg, John. 2013. *Anxious Wealth: Money and Morality Among China's New Rich*. Stanford: Stanford University Press.

Qiu Xiaolong. 2006. *A Case of Two Cities*. New York: St. Martin's Minotaur.

Quinn, Naomi. 1991. "The Cultural Basis of Metaphor." In *Beyond Metaphor: The Theory of Tropes in Anthropology*, edited by James W. Fernandez, 56–93. Stanford, CA: Stanford University Press.

———. 1997. "Research on Shared Task Solutions." In *A Cognitive Theory of Cultural Meaning*, edited by Claudia Strauss and Naomi Quinn, 137–88. Cambridge: Cambridge University Press.

Roth, Joshua Hotaka. 2012. "Heartfelt Driving: Discourses on Manners, Safety, and Emotions in Japan's Era of Mass Motorization" *Journal of Asian Studies* 71, no. 1: 171–92.

Sapir, David J. 1977. "The Anatomy of Metaphor." In *The Social Use of Metaphor: Essays on the Anthropology of Rhetoric*, edited by David J. Sapir and J. Christopher Crocker, 3–32. Philadelphia: University of Pennsylvania Press.

Siegelbaum, Lewis H. 2008. *Cars for Comrades: The Life of the Soviet Automobile*. Ithaca and London: Cornell University Press.

Scoggin, Mary. 2001. "Wine in the Writing, Truth in the Rhetoric: Three Levels of Irony in a Chinese Essay Genre." In *Irony in Action: Anthropology, Practice, and the Moral Imagination*, edited by James W. Fernandez and Mary Taylor Huber, 145–71. Chicago and London: University of Chicago Press.

Shaughnessy, E. L. 1988. "Historical Perspectives on the Introduction of the Chariot into China." *Harvard Journal of Asiatic Studies* 48:189–237.

Smith, N., and C. Katz. 1993. "Grounding Metaphor: Towards a Spatialized Poetics." In *Place and the Politics of Identity*, edited by M. Keith and S. Pile, 67–83. London: Routledge.

Stallybrass, Peter, and A. White. 1987. *The Politics and Poetics of Transgression*. Ithaca, NY: Cornell University Press.

Transparency International. 2009. *Corruption Perceptions Index 2009*. http://www.transparency.org/research/cpi/overview, accessed July 12, 2010.

Turner, Victor. 1967. *The Forest of Symbols*. Ithaca, NY: Cornell University Press.

Urry, John. 2005. "The 'System' of Automobility." Reprinted in *Automobilities*, edited by Mike Featherstone, Nigel Thrift, and John Urry, 25–40. London: Sage.

Uretsky, Elenah. 2008. "Mobile Men with Money: The Socio-cultural and Politico-Economic Context of 'High-Risk' Behaviour among Wealthy Businessmen and Government Officials in Urban China." *Culture, Health and Sexuality* 10, no. 8: 801–14.

Virilio, Paul. 1986. *Speed and Politics: An Essay on Dromology*. Semiotext(e) Foreign Agents Series. New York: Columbia University Press.

Wang Ping, and Ge Xin, dir. 1964. *Sentries under the Neon Lights* (Nihongdengxiade shaobing). Tianma Studio.

Xu shen (許慎). [Eastern Han, c.] 2004. 说文解字今释 (Shuowen jiezi jin shi). Tang Kejing, zhuan (湯可敬撰). Zhou Pingjun, shending (周ping鈞審訂), 4th ed. Changsha: Yuelu shushe (岳麓書社).

Young, Diana. 2001. "The Life and Death of Cars: Private Vehicles on the Pitjantjatjara Lands, South Australia." In *Car Cultures*, edited by Daniel Miller, 35–57. New York: Berg.

Zhang Leping. 1948. *Sanmao Liulang ji, diyi ji* 三毛流浪记，第一集 (Sanmao the Vagabond, vol. 1). Shanghai: Shanghai dagong bao guan 上海大公報館.

Zhang, Li. 2008. "Private Homes, Distinct Lifestyles: Performing a New Middle Class." In *Privatizing China: Socialism from Afar*, edited by Li Zhang and Aihwa Ong. Ithaca, NY: Cornell University Press.

———. 2010. *In Search of Paradise: Middle-Class Living in a Chinese Metropolis*. Ithaca, NY: Cornell University Press.

Zheng Junli, dir. 1949. *Crows and Sparrows* (Wuya yu maque). Shanghai: Kunlun Studio (The Peak Film Industries Corp., Ltd).

Zhongguo Shehui Kexueyuan Kaogu Yanjiusuo Anyangdui (CASS, I. o. A., Anyang Team). 1988. "The horse-chariot pit of Shang period at southwest of Guojiazhuang, Anyang" (Anyang Guojiazhuang xinan de yindai chemakeng). *Archaeology* (Kaogu): 882–93.

CHAPTER 7

Barrio Metaxis
Ambivalent Aesthetics in Mexican American Lowrider Cars

Ben Chappell

Lowriders are cars customized within a particular tradition of popular aesthetics identified with Mexican Americans. The characteristic modifications of a lowrider include replacing the suspension with shortened springs and hydraulic cylinders powered by additional batteries in order to raise and lower the car at the driver's will. Hydraulics, along with particular custom wheels, are the most basic markers of lowrider style, but lowrider cars are also typically decorated with elaborate custom paint jobs and accessorized interiors. Such adornments constitute a distinctive lowrider aesthetic, the boundaries of which are subjects of debate among participants in lowriding (also called lowriders). Such debates notwithstanding, certain general tendencies are conventional in lowrider style: a broad palate of colors, use of multi-layered lacquer, a baroque elaboration of fine detail in either abstract or figurative forms, chrome and gold plating, and so on. As lowriders continue to make customization decisions, and as their cars are evaluated at competitive car shows and neighborhood cruising sites, their collective, emergent aesthetic characterizes lowriding as a mode or genre of automobility.

Thus, as lowriding is a living tradition, its aesthetic is dynamic but can be rendered coherent by certain persistent sensibilities. In this chapter, based on fieldwork with lowriders in Texas as well as over fifteen years of following lowriding from a research perspective, I unpack one component of the lowrider aesthetic sensibility, a kind of ambivalence or duality.[1] I adopt the term "metaxis" to describe this principle, and to emphasize the simultaneity of a "both-and" logic that it represents. More than a finite iconography of specific images or a particular figurative style (although it appears both alongside and through these things), metaxis names a particular relation that is highlighted in lowrider style. Below I present examples of a metaxis relation drawn from my fieldwork and other ethnographic as well as cultural-studies literature in order to illuminate how lowrider aesthetics functions, and to imagine how it is related to the shared history and memory of urban Mexican Americans.

Lowriding as Art and Sign

Outsiders have long interpreted lowriders as trivial if not offensive tokens of bad taste, or even as dangerous symptoms of violent street culture—by one account, "lowrider" originated in California as a pejorative term used by police for street youths. Regardless of the authenticity of this origin story, "lowrider" remains closely resonant with "gang" in the public imaginary. Those who advocate for a less dismissive conception of lowriders in public often counter this "negative" depiction by emphasizing their artistry. Indeed, the art world has embraced lowrider aesthetics in events like the show at Boston's Institute for Contemporary Art titled *Customized: Art Inspired by Hot Rods, Low Riders, and American Car Culture* (Donnelly 2000). In addition, curators of an international art exhibition in the Museum of the City of Mexico invited a couple from Dallas to show their well-known lowrider "La Carcacha," a '48 Fleetline that was the 1997 Lowrider Bomb of the Year (Lopez 2000a).[2] The exhibition of a lowrider as representative of Mexican American art would not be surprising to those conversant with Chicano/a studies, but the extent to which the gallery embraced a custom car as a work of art was relatively unprecedented. Titled, "The Gold Returns to Mexico City," an article in the May 2000 issue of *Lowrider Magazine* (*LRM*) reports on La Carcacha's trip south, stating that "Frank and Rosie Requeña are the first Chicanos to show their lowrider as official artwork" (2000a: 55). Editor Lonnie Lopez expands on this theme in the editorial of the same issue:

> People from all walks of life are taking note of the lowrider lifestyle and the custom vehicles they create. The lowrider is an artistic expression that can no longer be ignored or denied; the lowrider has caught the eye of many intellectuals who study cultures and subcultures. They are now trying to understand who the people are who create these fantastic vehicles that boggle the imagination. (Lopez 2000b)

Such art-world overtures and a popular willingness to legitimize lowriding as art represent a laudable effort to situate lowriders as coeval cultural producers with credentialed artists, and to undo an ascription of triviality that historically has articulated the cultural production of minoritized people together with popular culture. If the legitimation came in an exoticizing flavor, that did not appear to be a concern to the editors of *LRM*. Yet making the claim that lowriders have the capacity to function effectively within the conventional parameters of legitimate art risks situating them at a distance from the primary participants in lowriding, the mechanics, painters, and vehicle owners who created and carry on the tradition. When such a vindication relies on high-art criteria for significance it raises a serious question about whether we are still discussing the same phenomenon.[3] As Raúl Homero Villa has influentially argued, the *barrio* communities out of which lowriding emerged have produced their own cultural criteria and priorities, a repertoire of collective memory, vocabulary, iconography, and a web of related cultural forms that Villa terms "barriology," taking the name from the quizzes that used to be features of the underground Chicano magazine *Con Safos* (Villa 2000). The notion of barriology contrasts with individualist constructs of artistic inspiration or insight by linking the popular knowledge and cultural resources available to people by virtue of their connection to specific Chicano/a *barrios* to the history of racialization, class immobility, and general, spatialized administration of Mexican Americans in the United States. As such, barriology is also "freighted" with the ambivalences of the concept of a *barrio* itself—simultaneously a homespace, locus of community, and source of identity; and a site of struggle and marginalization that some denizens wish to resist or escape.

At issue is whether a lowrider is simply a car functioning as art and thus a vehicle for aesthetics, or whether it must be understood as the expression of a particular aesthetic. A more recent illustration of the tension between barriological and art-world production appeared in the exhibition *La Vida Lowrider* at the Petersen Automotive Museum in downtown Los Angeles, which emphasized in part the capacity of a car to serve as an expressive medium.[4] Hence, alongside a number of cars that were well-known in lowrider circles such as Gypsy Rose (Figure 7.1), the exhibit included a truck decorated by San Antonio, Texas painter Vincent Valdez under the patronage of recording artist and Dukes car club member Ry Cooder (Figure 7.2).

The truck had been customized by Cooder's clubmates, the Ruelas brothers, and the mural depicted scenes from the conflicted history of the "barrioization" of the Chavez Ravine neighborhood, also the subject of Cooder's album *Chavez Ravine* (George 2007). While the images on the truck amounted to an impressive piece of work in narrative, political mural art mixed with social history, they simultaneously represented a

Figure 7.1. "Gypsy Rose" on display at the Petersen Automotive Museum. Photo: Petersen Automotive Museum, Los Angeles.

noticeable aesthetic break with other the cars in the exhibition, presumably built and decorated by those principally committed to the lowrider scene, as opposed to "art" as such. Valdez, an art school graduate with a record of gallery exhibition, worked with oil paint, in essence treating the truck's surface like a canvas rather than layering lacquer finish as found on a typical lowrider. Beyond the materials, Valdez's mural deployed a detailed, realist, figurative style that contrasts with the baroque elaboration and mythically idealized or cartoonishly exaggerated figures that typically adorn a lowrider. In the Petersen exhibition, a lowrider ice cream truck decorated by L.A. artist Mr. Cartoon demonstrates the difference (Figure 7.3).

Such contrasts harken to a perennial point of debate among intellectuals engaged with "the popular," or "the folk," similar to the disagreement between Zora Neale Hurston and W. E. B. DuBois over the Fisk Jubilee Singers' performances of "spirituals," which Paul Gilroy discusses in *The Black Atlantic*. Hurston attacked the "musicians' tricks" deployed by the singers as not being genuine representations of the folk performances that preceded them, a posture which Gilroy interprets as a defense of

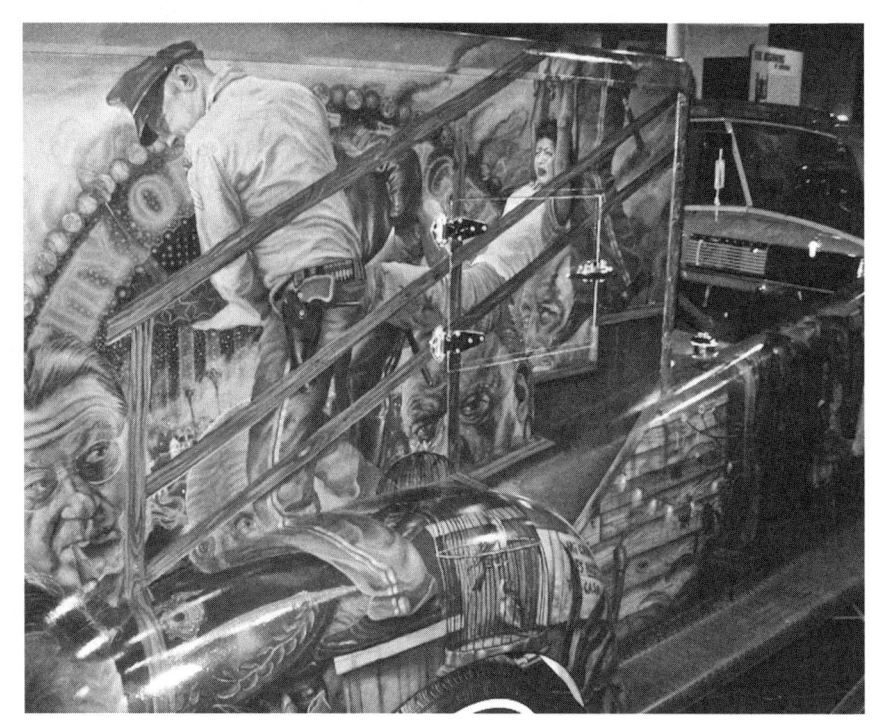

Figure 7.2. "Chavez Ravine" on display at the Petersen Automotive Museum. Photo: Petersen Automotive Museum, Los Angeles.

a bounded and reified notion of black authenticity (1993: 92). Gilroy's point is well taken: to situate an absolute touchstone of authenticity in the irretrievable past renders the very "folk," whom an intellectual may be trying to legitimize, as ahistorical. But short of freezing a notion of the folkloric authentic in amber, Hurston's complaint also implies that as forms ascend a scale of publicly recognized cultural value, something may well be lost.

My point in discussing the Petersen exhibition is not to fix any particular aesthetic boundaries as defining the quintessence of lowrider authenticity, since as I have noted, every individual lowrider is likely to have specific and varying ideas of what this is. Even less would I wish to discount Valdez's work or Cooder's participation in lowriding. Certainly, the Chavez Ravine truck was celebrated in the pages of *Lowrider Magazine*, and the show's curator Denise Sandoval is one of the recognized academic experts on lowriding. Yet the noticeable aesthetic contrast between Cooder's truck and the others on display bears attention. One implicit point made by the exhibition was that the commissioned car (into which Cooder told *Lowrider Magazine* he had invested six fig-

Figure 7.3. Mr. Cartoon's Lowrider Ice Cream Truck on display at the Petersen Automotive Museum. Photo: Petersen Automotive Museum, Los Angeles.

ures) achieved what other cars gesture toward, and which accords with a central argument of this book—that vehicles could be art, that they held rich potential as vehicles of representation as well as transportation, and that they could convey stories, situations, and relationships that would be widely recognized as being of substance.[5]

Without taking up the question of authenticity, I would propose that the contrasting aesthetics in the Petersen exhibition mark a distinction between two potentially overlapping modes of artistic practice: one that situates the *barrio* as an object of contemplation and representation, for which the car serves as a conventional medium among others; and another that, as a process of production, constitutes a *barrio* subjectivity—the car as an embodiment, not only a reflection, of a particular sociosemiotic context. I recognize that the work of this chapter, the work of scholarly representation, is more related to the first of these modes than to the second. In the course of that work I will gesture toward some reference points of legitimation that would mean little to lowriders themselves. Therefore I cannot advocate that lowriding belongs only within the mode of *barrio* production and should stay there, but along with Hurston, I suspect that something may be lost if they are conflated as instances of the same thing.

I bring that suspicion also to the more general discussion of vehicles as metaphors in this volume. Contrary to what is implied by the discourse that seeks to vindicate lowriders as good enough to be art, what is at issue is not just whether lowriders will be seen positively or negatively. Instead the pressing question is whether lowriders may be taken by "us" in the academy and the gallery on something like their own terms, rather being squeezed into our own familiar categories. Put another way, what we can learn from lowriders? The answer to that question that I will try to draw out of the examples below lies not only in the fact that lowriders are a medium of representation, but also in a tendency or sensibility in the way they represent this aesthetic of ambivalence that I am calling metaxis. I find the term useful to mark a break from conventional understandings of metaphor. As a literary device, metaphor speaks to the passage of meaning across a boundary between domains. Such deployments of metaphor have characterized some of the prior writing on lowriders, figuring them as "cathedrals on wheels" (Ortíz-Torres 2000) or the drivers as "car charros" in the tradition of Mexican cattle culture (Vigil 1991). To call a car a metaphor in this sense is to suggest that it represents something other than "carness" proper—for instance, it looks like a car, but it is really a piece of art. Or conversely, it is decorated like a mansion, even though it is really a car. But who is to say what real carness is, anyway? In a stratified society, where consumption manifests identity and status and automobiles represent the consumer commodity par excellence, such a question is political. So therefore is the issue of in which domain of significance meaning may be found autochthonously and into which other domain it must be made to migrate.

Metaxis describes a notion of simultaneous duality, an alternative to the passage of meaning. Metaxis was defined by the Theatre of the Oppressed theorist Augusto Boal as "the state of belonging completely and simultaneously to two different, automonous worlds" (1995: 43, cited in Linds 2006). For Boal, these worlds are the domains of materiality and ideality: "the image of reality and the reality of the image" (ibid.). In this, he echoes but also departs from the Platonic *metaxu*, speaking of the middle ground occupied by spirits between humans and gods. Independently of Boal, Shields deploys metaxis to refer to an ideology of double existence characteristic of virtuality in computer-mediated experience (2003). Metaxis for Shields is often attributed to "virtual reality," an experiential state of being simultaneously in both the world of the concrete and that of the virtual, or more generically, of information.

On the scale of this essay, I will not succeed at synthesizing these diverse senses of the term or at doing their distinctions justice. Neither does my usage necessarily follow any one of them, but in an experimental spirit I take up metaxis to mark a relationship of doubleness that I find running through lowrider aesthetics and barriology more generally. Metaxis speaks to a position not only wavering between poles or options, but one that levels their relationship and embraces their simultaneity, an unresolved but tightly bound dialectic. Hence "ambivalence" is literally what metaxis describes, but without the negative connotation that it carries in English in the United States, where singular points of reference are much preferred in matters of definition, taxonomy, evaluation, identity, and so forth. Metaxis is ambivalence in the literal sense of being both-valent, not in the common sense of being unsettled, confused, or incapable of making a decision that must ultimately be made. My characterization of the handful of images addressed in this chapter should specifically not be taken as support for any interpretation of barrio aesthetics as expressive of a developmental lack or psychological pathology as compared with a "normal" which is mature enough to make a choice and get off the fence. In what follows, I discuss examples of metaxis to show how barriological cultural forms function not only to represent what they are not, but as "objectifications" (Miller 1994: 54n1) of ambivalent and even contradictory relations that characterize their social contexts.

Remember the Alamo

In the spring of 2000, I attended the Centro Cultural Aztlán's 18th annual lowrider festival, in Rosedale Park, San Antonio, Texas. At that point I was midway through my first major fieldwork on lowriders, which had taken me to a variety of sites from garages to local weekend cruising strips. This local car show contrasted with lowrider "supershows," the high-dollar touring spectacles sponsored by *LRM,* in that mainly locals were displaying in the park, and not every car was completely finished. Indeed, some of the cars in the park that day barely rated "custom" status: for instance, a Chevy El Camino that showed no customization whatsoever except a flag with the logo of the San Antonio Spurs professional basketball team stuck into the window. The owner had parked amidst the lowriders and spread a collection of Spurs basketball memorabilia on the hood. At the top was a newspaper clipping featuring him as "the Spurs' biggest fan." He had lots of autographed pictures, not only of star players, but also of the mother of David Robinson, the Spurs' hall-of-fame pivot-man. The owner chattered eagerly to passersby about the value of his collection, how it had gone up since the championship, and how he was praying for another title to improve his investment more. Bystanders complimented him, but there was no question of whether he would be competing for one of the car show trophies. A car used to display the owner's admittedly impressive collection of basketball memorabilia was not in itself a lowrider. Still, the Spurs car illustrated that the event presented an opportunity to represent and engage with local identities.

Nearby was a more accomplished lowrider, a truck with a full-hood airbrushed mural that incorporated the slogan "Remember the Alamo," and an image of the historic battle (Figure 7.4). Considering how Richard Flores has depicted the Alamo as a "master symbol of modernity" (2002), which in turn signifies not only a nationalist but a colonial project of Anglo hegemony in Texas, this mural carried a substantial measure of ambivalence in the Chicano/a space of the lowrider car show. Indeed, the use of the Alamo image approached the polar opposite of the Chicano/a-Mexican cultural nationalism that is more widespread in lowrider murals, represented for example in mytho-heroic indigenous warriors and princesses, Aztec calendars, and other imagery. "Remem-

Figure 7.4. Alamo truck mural, San Antonio, Texas. Photo: Ben Chappell.

bering the Alamo" has become a rallying point for a nationalist politics that in part reacts against identity-based liberation movements, and calls U.S. citizens to hold the line of their national boundary against broader hemispheric identifications. As a student in Texas, I was struck by how the observance of the state's independence day often occasioned a showdown of demonstrations between the Young Conservatives of Texas and the *Movimiento Estudiantil Chicana/Chicano de Aztlán*. The impression left by those events, and by visits to the shrine-like Alamo itself gave a distinct sense of being in a post-colonial society, the wounds of which were far from healed.

Yet a closer look at the Alamo mural revealed levels of complexity that kept it from posing a wholesale embrace of Texas nationalism and rejection of Mexican points of reference. The presentation of the familiar shape of the Alamo chapel required a perspective from outside its walls. This meant that the mural shared a vantage point with a diorama of the battle of the Alamo in the *Galería de la Historia* of the Caracol museum in Mexico City, which presents the scene as the victorious battle of the Alamo, the defeat of Texan insurgents by the Mexican State.

On the other hand, the truck mural depicted a large Lone Star flag, replacing what is historically likely to have been a Mexican tricolor bearing "1836" to denote loyalty to the constitution of that year. This detail shifts the image into line with the triumphalist narrative of Texas independence, turning it back into an Anglo story, even though people of Mexican descent fought on both sides of that conflict.

I was unable to track down the owner of the Alamo truck to discuss the image but noted the artist's signature, which appeared on the mural in a graffiti-tag style with the logo "Chicano Art-Works" and the slogan "winning the battle to make art." As the focus of my research turned to everyday cruising with car clubs in Austin, I spent less time in San Antonio and never found the owner of the vehicle to ask about his intentions. It was at another car show later in Austin that I ran across a Chicano Art-Works booth where the airbrush specialist named Moodie was selling his original T-shirts. I asked him about the Alamo mural and he said, "Yeah, that's me—winning the battle to make art." Moodie asked me if I had noticed a tiny stick-figure soldier that, like the artist himself, had a long braid down his back. He had painted himself into the mural as a soldier in Santa Ana's army, charging to attack Davy Crockett and the other characters of the Texas epic inside the Alamo walls.

When I tried to discuss the politics of this Alamo imagery in San Antonio, Moodie wasn't interested in going there, though he seemed to appreciate my attention to the details of his work. Without pinpointing the political motivations of either the car's owner who commissioned the mural or the artist who executed it, however, it is still possible to identify within the mural an aesthetic that embraced ambivalence. While participating in a general public-cultural representation of San Antonio as the "Alamo City," the mural represented not a simple or unproblematic participation so much as a negotiated one. Its polysemy refashioned the slogan "Remember the Alamo" from its use as a triumphalist battle cry, accenting it with Moodie's signature, his self-insertion, and the outside-the-walls perspective in order to make it resonate with other, more everyday battles, and the ongoing contradictions of the position of Mexican people in U.S. modernity.

We are suggesting in this section of the volume that cars seem to lend themselves to convey moral equivocality. As Daniel Miller found in Trinidad, the automobile can serve as a site for the aesthetic objectification of central contradictions of modernity (1994: 132–33). Miller argues that the custom aesthetics of automotive surfaces he saw in Trinidad—interior upholstery, exterior paint and wheels, and the accessorization and decoration of both—expressed a tension also salient across a broader swath of Trinidadian life, between cultural principles of transcendence and transience. Transcendence speaks to the elaboration of domestic space and an emphasis on family relations as the loci of ties and traditional practices held to be stable and timeless. In Trinidad, this principle revolved around values encapsulated in the festival of Christmas. Transience, by way of contrast, emphasizes individualism, free mobility, and public display, all qualities associated more with the festival of Carnival (Miller 2001: 20–21).

Miller characterizes this duality as fundamental to the conditions and contradictions of modernity in Trinidad. While there are stereotypes about specific identities associated with the extreme embrace of either pole, modern subjects are in fact compelled simultaneously toward both. The values portrayed as transcendent in Christmas rituals and everyday domestic spaces rely on particular relations of property ownership, while the freedoms promised by transience are equally constrained by such relations. Hence the car, as an object and focus of practices amenable to both components of the duality of transcendence and transience, becomes "the classic instrument of modernity" (Miller 1994: 245), enabling people to live the contradiction. This characterization of automotive aesthetics as an objectification of a general condition of modernity leads Miller to conclude that inflections on this moral dualism that are tied to specific identities—e.g., ethnicity or gender—are in fact epiphenomenal to the modern condition, more than expressions of a unique social position (2001: 21).

Surely, custom cars only bring to the fore and accentuate tensions present in all automobiles, such as the way in which vehicles are inhabitable, interior environments that can also move and occupy other spaces. But differences in automotive aesthetics, which amount to different emphases and priorities in automotive practices such as customization, underscore how the stakes involved in such scalar spatial arrangements are hardly the same across social continua. How could they be, when urban cartography has played a major role, from the days of segregation to red-lining and "weed-and-seed" police programs, in the management of a race- and class-stratified society? That is to say, how can a car that is strongly identified with *barrio* space and community be the functional equivalent of one that gives the impression of belonging in and with other spaces, such as an affluent suburb? By turning from a particular example of lowrider aesthetics to an image that recurs widely within barriological cultural production, I will suggest why it is important to consider aesthetic principles such as the embrace of metaxis in relation to particular histories and communities, in this case the particular experience of urban Mexican Americans, including the relationship between *barrios* and the city at large.

Figure 7.5. Smile now/cry later truck, Austin, Texas. Photo: Ben Chappell.

Smile Now, Cry Later

The motif of comedy and tragedy masks, or more often, of laughing and crying clown faces, is the visual version of a slogan, Smile Now/Cry Later, that recurs throughout the popular/folkloric repertoire of barriology (Figure 7.5). Lowrider murals are one medium for this. Smile Now/Cry Later also appears in popular drawings such as those published in *LRM* or the affiliated magazine *Lowrider Arte,* in T-shirts, tattoos, and other visual media. "Smile Now, Cry Later" is the title and refrain of an R&B ballad recorded by the San Antonio Chicano band Sonny and the Sunglows in 1966, part of the genre known as "oldies" that holds a special place for lowriders. Since then, numerous groups have recorded songs based on the phrase. The popularity of Smile Now/Cry Later images in Chicano prison tattooing and its undeniable appeal within the *cholo* street culture has caused the image to be interpreted by some authorities as a "gang sign."

Since not everyone who identifies the Smile Now/Cry Later image with aesthetic affect is necessarily involved in a gang, it falls to sympathetic researchers to offer an alternative interpretation. Marie "Keta" Miranda (2003) refers to Smile Now/Cry Later while describing an encounter between academic and participant interpretations of barriology. Miranda tells the story of how the young, female, Latina gang members who were subjects of her research project attended a session about gang studies at the annual meeting of the National Association of Chicana and Chicano Studies. Smile Now/Cry Later came up in a presentation by the accomplished linguistic anthropologist Norma Mendoza-Denton, and the homegirls immediately recognized the image but contested the point of reference with which the scholar made sense of it. Mendoza-Denton showed a version of the two masks when presenting drawings from letters she had received from interlocutors in her fieldwork in order to portray the symbology of barrio culture:

> When Mendoza-Denton held up a drawing of two masks, one of the girls stated: "Smile Now, Cry Later."
> Mendoza-Denton: "The symbol of Tragedy and Comedy."
> Another girl: "No, it's the oldies song, 'Smile Now, Cry Later.'" (Miranda 2003: 118)

Miranda describes this encounter as an intervention by the homegirls, "clarifying the origins" of the symbol, and includes it in slightly longer discussion in which she contrasts generalizing academic language with what she implies is the more grounded and specific discourse of the homegirls. The "girls" follow up Mendoza-Denton's presentation by presenting a slide show and recorded song that represent their lifeworld in a dense fabric of images, without synthesizing arguments. Giving credit to the complexity of the situation, Miranda goes on to characterize the rare cross-talk at this academic session as a "jubilant co-discursivity" (2003: 119), which does not reveal any fundamental antagonism to the work of "sympathetic ethnographers," in which category she includes herself and presumably Mendoza-Denton. In her own, later book on Latina gang members, Mendoza-Denton goes on to problematize her relation to research subjects and their expressed assumptions that she would have the insight of "insider" status due to her Latina background, an idea she specifically disavows due to differences in their experiences (2008).

As in the discussion above of the divergent aesthetics presented in lowriders at the Petersen exhibit, my point here is not to adjudicate between two claims about the significance of Smile Now/Cry Later. While Miranda suggests that the homegirls bore a more organic connection to the image than outside scholars do, the main point I draw from this story is that interpretation is a contextualizing gesture. What caused Mendoza-Denton's and the homegirls' interpretations of Smile Now/Cry Later to diverge were the contexts in which they situated the work as relevant, which in turn suggests something about the audiences for which such interpretations were intended. This was not really an empirical question about origins, but a matter of aesthetics. The question was which contextualization yielded the most satisfying effect for its audience.

By referring to the classical resonance of the comedy and tragedy masks, Mendoza-Denton voiced a conventional, and in some ways, still very much needed anthropological move to situate "The Other" within the domain of the human, with which an academic audience might share a common point of reference to make understanding possible. Ethnographers of urban Latinos can attest that this gesture remains timely, even urgent, in the context of efforts to situate urban people of color—especially with recourse to the stigma of the "gang" label—as undeserving of rights, subject to heightened police surveillance and control, deportable, and so on (Chappell 2006). The popularization of cultural relativism notwithstanding, an impulse to assert the humanity of cultural others remains relevant. Yet by arguing that this classical reference was incorrect, and that the sign "actually" represented the oldies song by Sonny and the Sunglows, the homegirls articulated a preference for the specific cultural memory of barriology, not classical humanism, as the web of significance around the masks. Beyond the specific origin of the song in Texas, which the homegirls may not have even known about, the "oldies" genre enjoys a history as the traditionally preferred music within the Chicano/a street culture of which lowriders and Smile Now/Cry Later are also part. This is barriological memory with a particular geography: while no less mobile in some ways than the classical reference, it was also manifested in deeply local ways. Thus, what Miranda found to be "fully grounded" in the homegirls' interpretation was not necessarily an absolute meaning, but recognition of local and collective memory as the condition for aesthetic impact on a viewer.

An effect that I propose both the Alamo mural and Smile Now/Cry Later generate for those who identify with barriological signs is a sense of "fit," the perhaps unarticulated feeling that an aesthetic form belongs within a particular cultural repertoire and hence is tied to a particular social context. In Kathleen Stewart's elaboration of the notion of a structure of feeling (Williams 1977) as an emergent affective field, which characterizes the circulation of public culture, she comments on moments of recognition in which circumstances and events can "snap into place," becoming briefly comprehensible before melting back into a generally emergent state (Stewart 2007). There is a tantalizing convergence between this idea of snapping into place and the term used by lowriders during my fieldwork to describe a satisfying aesthetic display: "tight." What is crucial about understanding visual culture in these aesthetic terms is that it gestures toward a significance that is specific in its sociocultural location and performative iteration, without being precise in the sense of conforming closely to established, exclusive boundaries between possible meanings. Various meanings of Smile Now/Cry Later remain plausible—its referent could be to a kind of aloof masculinity which reserves the expression of pain and sadness for private moments, or to a jaded retrospective view on carefree youth gone by, or to a sense of tragic inevitability to the temporal limits of happiness. Many other explanations are plausible, but all such textual interpretations only approximate the impact of a "tight" visual trope of metaxis, which already carries weight for those who identify with barriology even while the jury remains out on what it "actually means."

I cannot argue that an aesthetic of metaxis is the quintessential characteristic of barriological expressive culture, much less of Mexican American culture in general. I do, however, propose that it offers a way to understand the layers of polysemy and apparent contrast that occur in lowrider aesthetics, lending coherence to such juxtapositions as a portrait of Emiliano Zapata, the hero of the rural southern revolution in Mexico, with miniaturized chandeliers, fountains, and other accoutrements of luxury (Figure 7.6); or that of another vehicle customized as a memorial for a deceased loved one also decorated with images of cartoon Martians.

What may appear as jarring, incoherent, or inconsistent to the analyst in search of an essential explanation asserts a "both-and" logic that

Figure 7.6. Zapata/luxury truck, Houston, Texas. Photo: Ben Chappell.

resonates with the shared memory of prior significations. Metaxis characterizes a range of images that might differ in content while presenting a similar relation.

Barriology and Non-Unitary Subjects

I have tried to show that the aesthetics of lowrider mural art harbors a tendency to embrace or accept ambivalence, and that this is part of what generates an aesthetic effect of recognition that renders particular murals as fitting within a larger cultural repertoire of barriology. Moreover, I have called this relation of ambivalence, metaxis, in order to emphasize that it objectifies a simultaneous coexistence of what are typically conceived as distinct domains. My understanding of the significance of the Alamo and of Smile Now/Cry Later is aesthetic, not strictly iconographic, because I do not think it is the presence of identifiable, representational figures alone that makes an image work as barriology, though that is part of it. Rather, such figures presented in a particular way join other aspects of barrio expressive culture in that they carry the affective capability to satisfy expectation among certain conditioned audiences, that is to say, to "fit."

Barriological metaxis itself resonates with a tradition of Chicana/o Studies scholarship and popular cultural practice that embraces a nonunitary subject. Perhaps the most influential of Chicana writers to present this idea is Gloria Anzaldúa, whose borderlands "new mestiza" subjectivity is fluid, polyvocal, and multiply-identified (1987).[6] Indeed, the quintessential Latino/a experience of metaxis is perhaps the ambivalent concept of *mestizaje*, the cultural and genetic admixture of Iberian and indigenous heritage following the conquest, which carries both trauma and celebration as its permanent legacies. The project of locating Latino/a subjectivity without resort to an essential foundation continues decades after the publication of Anzaldúa's *Borderlands/La Frontera* with work like Antiono Viego's call to a Lacanian Latino Studies (2007). Within this discourse, Yvonne Yarbro-Bejarano compellingly distinguishes between performances of unresolved duality and those that seek to appropriate multiplicity in the controlling interest of a kind of political project that presumes coherence and continuity to be normative (2006: 85). It is within a politics that demands unity that the metaxis of *mestizaje* gets tamed into a national idea, even considering the tragic dualism of its traumatic origins in the conquest and rape of the indigenous population by the Spanish. A *mestizo* national idea not only fed the consolidation of the Mexican state but enabled intellectuals like Octavio Paz to contemplate such unities (albeit complex ones) as the "Mexican man" with his "soul" (1961). For all the depth with which Paz was able to think about the Mexican soul, when he visited Los Angeles and saw some *pachucos* embodying a metaxic barriology, they freaked him out. *Pachucos*, the participants in an early Mexican American street culture that remains a source of barriological memory, occupied a contradictory social position that challenged even the construction of the Mexican *mestizo* nation.[7] To Mexicans like Paz, *pachucos* in the United States as represented by figures like the World War II-era zoot-suiter were culturally denuded, unable to claim any of the nobility of a Mexican national identity.

On the other hand, many Anglos viewed *pachucos* as a threat to a social order constructed around Anglo normativity and minoritized and working-class populations that knew their place. Even as Paz saw *pachucos* as having forgotten or abandoned their essential identity, discourses of essential Mexican savagery became a focus of moral panics within the United States. Epochal events like the 1942–1943 Sleepy Lagoon trial, at which twenty-two Mexican American youths were collectively charged with murder after a tragic fight at a *pachuco* party (seventeen were ultimately indicted), were saturated with discourses of violence as an inherent racial trait. An L.A. sheriff department deputy who testified in the trial, Lieutenant Edward Duran Ayres, was an active proponent of such pseudo-anthropology that also played to wartime racial logics, stating that a "total disregard for human life has always been universal throughout the Americas among the Indian population, which of course is well known to everyone." Ayres attributed this essential violence to "oriental characteristics" present as the deep genetic heritage of Mexicans (Griffith 1948: 212–13). As Antonio Viego notes in some detail, such attributions fall within a long history in which Chicanos were constructed as criminal subjects via discourses of psychology and genetics (2007: 138). All of these instances may be understood as making use of singular identification as a technique of oppression.

Thus in *pachucos* we see innovators of the cultural repertoire I have been calling barriology, who were denigrated from at least two sides at once—cast as insufficiently Mexican and American, found lacking both in the failure to embrace one essential identity and in the failure to escape another one. Marcos Sánchez-Tranquilino and John Tagg describe how *pachuco* aesthetics emerged as a response to this predicament.

> Pachuco culture was an assemblage, built from machines for which they never read the manuals. It was a cultural affirmation not by nostalgic return to an imaginary original wholeness and past, but by appropriation, transgression, reassemblage, breaking and restructuring the laws of language: in the speech of Caló and *pochismos*, but also in the languages of the body, gesture, hair, tattoos, dress, and dance; and in the languages of the space, the city, the barrio, the street. Paz was offended and saw only negativity: a grotesque and anarchic language that said nothing and everything: a failure of memory or assimilation. The refusal to choose made no sense. (1992: 559; cf. Alvarez 2008)

This ambivalence made no sense for an essentialist subjectivity, but barriology did make aesthetic sense of indeterminacy, or better yet, it made sense *with* indeterminacy. Short of offering an explanation or resolution of the contradictions that Mexican Americans face as a result of their historical positioning, barriological aesthetics objectifies this position in forms that are iconic with it.

Theoretical work building on non-unitary subjectivity carries implications for how we understand the politics of identity and expressive culture. For instance, Chela Sandoval has developed an influential notion of fluid political subjectivity as "oppositional consciousness," a critical, perpetual differentiation which refuses to accept the identities proffered by society and shifts boundary lines to form alliances against oppression (Sandoval 2000). Alternately, drawing on Norma Alarcón's survey of various positions on difference, the differential, and *différance* (1996, cited in Muñoz 1999: 7), José Muñoz refers to "identities in difference" (Muñoz 1999: 22). While these concepts are clearly relevant for understanding popular practices such as lowriding, I am not sure that "consciousness" or indeed "identity" captures or exhausts the ways in which metaxis overlaps with the political in everyday cultural productions. Metaxis is evident within lowrider style and other projects of affective work as an aesthetic principle before or without the realization of a "consciousness" and as a production, not necessarily an expression, of identity.

It is admittedly problematic to conflate the differential theories of identity developed largely out of Chicana women's and queer experience with lowrider aesthetics, since lowriding is heavily dominated by masculine normativity and serves as a means of masculinity for many of its participants in ways that would repress the very forms of difference that Anzaldúa, Alarcón, Sandoval, Muñoz, and others focus on. Still, I risk this juxtaposition not to deny that non-unitary subject formation occurs on conflicted ground, but to take note of what I think is a crucial point of commonality among the critical stances affected by various kinds of differential identity. That area of overlap is the situation of materiality as a centrally important site for identifying practices, not only for reflection of or reference to prior consciousness. Whether the differences embraced by, for example, lowrider metaxis and Anzaldúa's "new *mestiza*" are in fact compatible and can be worked by historical actors into a non-oppressive community is an open question that will be answered by those who live these identities rather than merely commenting on them.

Nevertheless, the lesson offered by the embodied queer performances of politics that are Muñoz's principal subject as well as material car aesthetics is that materiality is amenable to the unresolved dialectic of metaxis. This is a plausible explanation for why material aesthetic forms, e.g., vehicles, carry more compelling significance than even "strategic" essentialisms. It is not material existence itself but imagined wholes, such as the nation, that are called into crisis by images of duality such as the co-presence of Mexican and U.S. flags in an immigrant-rights march. The requirement of modern nationalism that one must choose a primary allegiance in order to achieve coherent subjectivity does not always hold against historical experiences such as those of American citizens "repatriated" to a Mexico they barely knew during the Great Depression only to receive a draft notice from Uncle Sam when they were needed by the United States for the war (cf. Rivas-Rodriguez 2005). The emphasis on metaxis in popular and high-art cultural production recenters significance on these experiences and the limits of unified identities that they expose. The everyday traffic in aesthetic affect is one site in which such struggles continue. The elaborated visuality of lowriders accentuates how cars, as decorable surfaces ubiquitous in U.S. society, take part in this cultural-political process.

NOTES

1. For a report on the larger ethnographic project, see Chappell (2012). For a survey of the literature on lowriding, see Chappell (2013).
2. A "bomb" is what lowriders call a custom car built from an older vehicle, usually a pre-1950s model.
3. Susan Stewart cogently models such a question about whether identical visual forms can both be identified as "graffiti" if produced under different contexts, such as commissioned work on designated walls as opposed to clandestine and unauthorized writing (1994).
4. The exhibition ran from October 2007 to June 2008, but a description with photographs remains on the Petersen website at http://petersen.org/exhibitions/la-vida-lowrider-cruising-the-city-of-angels.
5. Other credentialed artists engage with lowriders in order to explore the possibilities of blending "high" and "low" modes of production and criteria of value. Rubén Ortíz-Torres, whose installations include objects such as leaf blowers and riding lawn mowers customized in lowrider style as well as full lowrider vehicles, went through a kind of apprenticeship with lowrider car clubs, submitting his custom car work for their critique (Chavoya 2000). Colombian-American photographer and installation artist Liz Cohen has taken inspiration from lowrider customization and glamour photography for her project that involves both building a car and posing as a bikini model in front of it (Irwen 2006).
6. Indeed, duality and multiplicity are perennial tropes within Chicana/o historiography and cultural criticism, as in Ramón Saldívar's "dialectic of difference" (1990), George Sánchez's "ambivalent Americanism" (1995), and others.
7. On *pachucos* and zoot-suiters, see also Alvarez (2008), Ramírez (2009), and Noriega (2001).

REFERENCES

Alarcón, Norma. 1996. "Conjugating Subjects in an Age of Multiculturalism." In *Mapping Multiculturalism*, edited by Avery Gordon and Christopher Newfield. Minneapolis: University of Minnesota Press.

Alvarez, Luís. 2008. *The Power of the Zoot: Youth Culture and Resistance During World War II*. Berkeley: University of California Press.

Anzaldúa, Gloria. 1987. *Borderlands/La Frontera: The New Mestiza*. San Francisco: Aunt Lute.

Boal, Augusto. 1995. *The Rainbow of Desire: The Boal Method of Theatre and Therapy.* Translated by A. Jackson. London: Routledge.

Chappell, Ben. 2006. "Rehearsals of the Sovereign." *Cultural Dynamics* 18, no. 3: 313–34.

———. 2012. *Lowrider Space: Aesthetics and Politics of Mexican American Custom Cars.* Austin: University of Texas Press.

———. 2013. "Lowriders." In *Oxford Online Bibliography in Latino Studies,* edited by Ilan Stavans. New York: Oxford University Press. http://www.oxfordbibliographies.com/obo/page/latino-studies, accessed June 29, 2013.

Chavoya, C. Ondine. 2000. "Rubén Ortiz Torres: Style Politics and Hydraulic Hijinx." In *Customized: Art Inspired by Hot Rods, Low Riders and American Car Culture,* edited by N. Donnelly, 43–47. New York: Henry N. Abrams.

Donnelly, Nora, ed. 2000. *Customized: Art Inspired by Hot Rods, Low Riders and American Car Culture.* New York: Henry N. Abrams.

Flores, Richard. 2002. *Remembering the Alamo: Memory, Modernity, and the Master Symbol.* Austin: University of Texas Press.

George, Lynell. 2007. "Driven to Distraction." *Los Angeles Times,* September 16, online edition, http://articles.latimes.com/2007/sep/16/entertainment/ca-valdez16, accessed June 29, 2013.

Gilroy, Paul. 1993. *The Black Atlantic: Modernity and Double Consciousness.* Cambridge, MA: Harvard University Press.

Griffith, Beatrice. 1948. *American Me.* Boston: Houghton-Mifflin.

Irwin, Megan. 2006. "Hard Body: Liz Cohen's Infiltrating the Lowrider World–and Calling It Art." *Phoenix New Times,* October 5, online edition, http://www.phoenixnewtimes.com/2006-10-05/news/hard-body, accessed June 29, 2013.

Linds, Warren. 2006. "Metaxis: Dancing (in) the In-between." In *A Boal Companion: Dialogues on Theatre and Cultural Politics,* edited by J. Cohen-Cruz and M. Shchutzman, 114–24. New York: Routledge.

Lopez, Lonnie. 2000a. Editorial. *Lowrider Magazine,* May.

———. 2000b. "The Gold Returns to Mexico City." *Lowrider Magazine,* May.

Mendoza, Ruben. 2000. "Cruising Art and Culture in Aztlán: Lowriding in the Mexican American Southwest." In *U.S. Latino Literatures and Cultures: Transnational Perspectives,* edited by F. A. Lomelí and K. Ikas, 3–35. Heidelberg, Germany: Universitätsverlag C. Winter.

Mendoza-Denton, Norma. 2008. *Homegirls: Language and Cultural Practice Among Latina Youth Gangs.* Malden, MA: Blackwell.

Miller, Daniel. 1994. *Modernity–An Ethnographic Approach: Dualism and Mass Culture in Trinidad.* Oxford: Berg.

———. 2001. "Driven Societies." In *Car Cultures,* edited by Daniel Miller, 1–34. Oxford: Berg.

Miranda, Marie. 2003. *Homegirls in the Public Sphere.* Austin: University of Texas Press.

Muñoz, José Esteban. 1999. *Disidentifications: Queers of Color and the Performance of Politics.* Minneapolis: University of Minnesota Press.

Noriega, Chon. 2001. "Fashion Crimes." *Aztlán* 26, no. 1: 1–13.
Ortíz-Torres, Rubén. 2000. "Cathedrals on Wheels." In *Customized: Art Inspired by Hot Rods, Low Riders and American Car Culture,* edited by N. Donnelly, 37–38. New York: Henry N. Abrams.
Ramírez, Catherine. 2009. *The Woman in the Zoot Suit: Gender, Nationalism, and the Cultural Politics of Memory.* Durham, NC: Duke University Press.
Rivas-Rodriguez, Maggie. 2005. *Mexican Americans and World War II.* Austin: University of Texas Press.
Saldívar, Ramón. 1990. *Chicano Narrative: The Dialectics of Difference.* Madison: University of Wisconsin Press.
Sánchez-Tranquilino, Marcos, and John Tagg. 1992. "The Pachuco's Flayed Hide: Mobility, Identity, and *buenas garras*." In *Cultural Studies,* edited by L. Grossberg, C. Nelson, and P. A. Treichler, 566–70. New York: Routledge.
Sánchez, George. 1995. *Becoming Mexican American: Ethnicity, Culture and Identity in Chicano Los Angeles, 1900–1945.* New York: Oxford University Press.
Sandoval, Chela. 2000. *Methodology of the Oppressed.* Minneapolis: University of Minnesota Press.
Shields, Rob. 2003. *The Virtual.* London: Routledge.
Stewart, Kathleen. 2007. *Ordinary Affects.* Durham, NC: Duke University Press.
Stewart, Susan. 1994. *Crimes of Writing: Problems in the Containment of Representation.* Durham, NC: Duke University Press.
Viego, Antonio. 2007. *Dead Subjects: Toward a Politics of Loss in Latino Studies.* Durham, NC: Duke University Press.
Vigil, James Diego. 1991. "Car Charros: Cruising and Lowriding in the Barrios of East Los Angeles." *Latino Studies Journal* 2, no. 2: 71–79.
Villa, Raúl Homero. 2000. *Barrio Logos: Space and Place in Urban Chicano Literature and Culture.* Austin: University of Texas Press.
Williams, Raymond. 1977. *Marxism and Literature.* Oxford: Oxford University Press.
Yarbro-Bejarano, Yvonne. 2006. "Gloria Anzaldúa's *Borderlands/La Frontera*: Cultural Studies, 'Difference,' and the Non-unitary Subject." In *The Chicana/o Cultural Studies Reader,* edited by Angie Chabram-Dernersesian, 81–92. New York: Routledge.

CHAPTER 8

Driving into the Light
Traversing Life and Death in a Lynching Reenactment by African-Americans

Mark Auslander

Since 2005, a multiracial group of activists has gathered each July to reenact the mass killing of four young African-Americans. Hundreds of supporters watch the amateur performers reenact the key events associated with the lynching; in the late afternoon, at the culminating moment of the reenactment, a sedan arrives at an isolated bridge, carrying the four African-American victims and a driver, playing the role of a local white farmer. A group of reenactors, playing Klansmen, emerges from the woods and wrestles the screaming victims out of the automobile and down the embankment, where they are repeatedly shot in front of the audience. In this chapter, I explore some of the nightmarish and redemptive possibilities afforded by the composite body of car-driver-passenger, especially as a potent signifier of double consciousness for African-American men and women. I examine a seemingly minor enigma associated with the annual reenactment of a notorious 1946 mass lynching in a small Georgia town.

My puzzle is this: Each year, the urban-based sponsors of the reenactment, who include some of the most prominent African-American political figures in the State of Georgia, insist that the automobile that carries the victims to their reenacted death should be a period-authentic vintage vehicle, to provide maximum verisimilitude to this horrific performance. Yet most years, the local African-American organizers have quietly arranged for a locally owned 1977 Lincoln Town Car to be used. The choice is inevitably challenging, since this particular car is notoriously unreliable, and there is considerable anxiety each year over whether or not its engine will actually turn over at the crucial moment. Yet, this specific car is well loved by the local African-American participants, who passionately insist each year on using it, if at all possible. Why, given the reenactors' avowed commitment to a "smooth-running" and "accurate" reenactment, do they so often make use of this trouble-prone vehicle?

Cars and Race in the Deep South

To appreciate and make sense of the emotive power condensed in this "sign vehicle," it is helpful to begin by reviewing the wider racialized associations of automobiles in this rural community and in comparable communities throughout the Deep South. In African-American rural Georgia communities, automobiles feature prominently in popular narratives that foreground experiences of alienated or reconstituted personhood, especially on the frontier between life and death. Stories about feared legendary white sheriffs and deputies often center on their vehicles, which would follow black men or linger ominously near their places of dwelling or relaxation. The interior of the police vehicle is often recalled as a terrifying place, where beatings were administered and death threats uttered. Richard, an African-American man in his early eighties, recalls one particularly memorable night in the early 1950s, in which two deputies detained him on suspicion of involvement in a bootlegging operation rivaling that run by the county's white sheriff:

> Well, they threw me in the back, and told me they were gonna take me on a little ride. Let me tell you, that's not a place you ever wanna be. One of them said, best make peace with your maker now, boy ... Got in next to me, and started going at me with his stick ... The other deputy, the one driving, started laughing, "Do I see somebody resisting arrest?" ... Well, at a curve they threw me out, told me it was my lucky day, that I had a message to deliver to my boss. About not creating any more trouble in the county. "You understand, boy?" Made my home on foot somehow. Never told my wife what happened. But I never forgot that night or the inside of that cruiser.

Cars often function as switch-points between different temporal eras, enabling seemingly abrupt forms of narrative time travel. Many times, I have heard African-American informants share stories about escapes from slavery, recounting tales handed down through the generations. Halfway through, a story about running through a corn field during "slavery times," will effortlessly morph into a tale about escaping from a post-slavery chain gang. Such a break is generally signaled by the presence of an automobile. In the words of George, a skilled story teller in his late seventies:

> And you'd be running, running, keeping low, and then you'd freeze cause you'd suddenly be in the light ... the headlights, from the posse, you know. You'd dive down, face in the ground, till the cars passed. And then you're up, running. You can hear the engines, and you're running for the tree-line.

Such narratives poetically play with the structural continuities between legal chattel slavery and post-emancipation forms of racialized penal control in the South, often termed "slavery by another name" (Blackmon 2008).

Cars often figure prominently in oral narratives of white multitudes driving to witnessing lynchings. Nathan, a 60-year-old African-American man recalls stories heard from his uncles and his grandfather:

> And they had a regular traffic jam, all driving in their big sedans to see the deed being done. Those crackers so proud of their cars, driving the whole family for the celebration, like a regular Saturday night barbecue. Driving home with body parts, like trophies from a deer hunt. That's how they did it.

At the same time, cars are often figured as sites of heroic black masculinity and positive capacity. Narratives of remembered interstate travel within African-American-owned cars during the Jim Crow era often center on miraculous concealment, hiding men threatened with lynching in the trunk and driving them through the night to safety in a northern state. Fathers and grandfathers, it is recalled, would keep a shotgun under the driver's seat when driving across Mississippi to visit kin in Arkansas. Robert, a man in his seventies, explains:

> My Daddy was never looking for a fight. He took it easy whenever he could. He had one of those green books [The Negro Motorist's Green Books] explaining where it was safe to get food, get fuel, stay for the night. But he wasn't anyone's fool. He knew there were times that the only way to protect himself and his family was with a ten gauge. And he was ready to use it, I believe. Nobody was going to put a scratch on his sedan, believe you me.

Pride in one's automobiles is of course hardly limited to African-American men, or even to males in American society, but to this day there is arguably a particular intensity to the pride many black men take in their cars, born in part of the long histories of oppression and structural violence embedded in the American experience (see Živković, Notar, and Chappel, this volume). Nathan recalls his elders' stories about their cars:

> When your people have been kept down for so long, driving a fine motor vehicle—well it was saying "I am somebody." Still is. Driving through the neighborhood you were saying, I'm a man, nobody can

take that away from me. That's how, in the thirties and forties especially, you were known. You had a fine automobile, you were known for that.

Although cars are frequently associated with intense racialized difference, the interiors of cars are often figured narratively as microcosmic spaces in which conventional differences broke down, where the color line temporarily dissolved or was at least radically reconfigured. Many African-Americans recall that the most meaningful conversation they've ever had with a white person took place within the relative privacy of a car. Those who have worked as chauffeurs for white employers emphasize unexpected moments when normal relations of hierarchy and deference broke down, and intensely personal confidences were shared in both directions. As Allen, an African-American man in his late eighties recalled laughingly, "Oh yes, it was a regular 'Driving Miss Daisy' moment you could say: for that drive at least, we were best friends."

In turn, Thomas, a white musical producer in his fifties, recalls how he fell in love with the blues and with soul music as a schoolboy:

> My daddy hated desegregation so much he put me in a Christian academy clear across the other side of the Mississippi Delta; every day he had his chauffeur drive me there and back. But it backfired you see, since we just listened to black music every drive and I realized all I wanted to do was spend time with black musicians. My Daddy never did get over that!

Motor vehicles in the Deep South thus carry a particularly charged set of racial associations, as equivocal mobile arenas in which racial difference was both reinforced and undone, in which racial violence was inflicted and in which moral personhood could be redeemed and refashioned.

The Moore's Ford Lynching

All of these dimensions of automotive symbolism—including the conflation of emotional intimacy and the threat of violence—converge in popular memories in Georgia of the violent events of the early postwar period. The summer of 1946 saw extensive incidents of racial violence across the Deep South, much of it directed against returning African-American servicemen, who were widely thought by white segregationists to pose a direct threat to the established order of racial relations in the region. White-perpetrated racial violence was especially intense in Georgia, as a bitter gubernatorial election battle revolved around the question of the U.S. Supreme Court decision (*Smith v. Allwright*) authorizing black participation in the Democratic Party primary process. During that summer, at least four separate lynchings took place in Georgia alone (a lynching is not only a hanging, but may be said to refer to any illegal murder by a vigilante mob by whatever violent means. The only African-American brave enough to vote in one district, for example, was shot to death.)[1] Of these racial killings, the most notorious was the mass murder at Moore's Ford, about sixty miles northeast of Atlanta. The location was partly overdetermined; Walton County was Georgia's leading cotton producing county, where the contoured landscape kept out mechanical cotton pickers and where direct white control over black farm labor was thus especially vital. As historical sociologists Tolnay and Beck argue (1995), lynching can be understood as part of a system of labor control, strongly correlated with the intensity of cotton cultivation.

Although the struggle over the vote and the local political ecology framed the killings, the precise details of the Moore's Ford lynchings powerfully illustrate the complex webs of affiliation, opposition, resistance, and complicity that characterized the racial micro-politics of the Jim Crow South. On July 14, 1946, Roger Malcom, an African-American sharecropper, and his employer, a white farmer named Barney Hester, had a violent altercation. Malcom suspected Hester of having an affair with Dorothy Murray Malcom, Malcom's girlfriend (sometimes referred to as his common law wife), who like Malcom had been working for the white farmer's family. Hester, some report, was attempting to whip Malcom for beating Dorothy. Malcom stabbed the white farmer with a knife and then fled until he was apprehended by local whites. Hester in time recovered from his wounds, but at the time it was widely expected that he would die. Malcom was held in the county jail in Monroe for eleven days, during which time local white supremacists, including prominent Klansman, evidently laid plans for his lynching.

On July 25, Loy Harrison, a local white farmer who was the employer of Malcom's girlfriend's brother, George Dorsey, bailed Malcom out of jail, explaining that he was going to drive Malcolm to his farm where he could work to pay off his bail. (Harrison, like other wealthy white farmers, frequently employed coerced black laborers in this penal-related system, which was to some extent a structural continuation of plantation slavery.)

Also riding in the vehicle were Dorothy, George Dorsey, and Dorsey's girlfriend Mae Murray. George Dorsey was a U.S. Army veteran, recently returned from service in the Pacific. Harrison drove his car on a circuitous route, bringing it eventually to the isolated bridge over the Apalachee River at Moore's Ford, on the border of Walton and Oconee counties. There, the vehicle was stopped by twelve to fifteen armed white men who violently removed the four young African-Americans from the car and hung a noose around Roger Malcom's neck. Within minutes all four African-Americans who had been dragged down the embankment were dead, their bodies pierced by scores of bullet holes. There is some evidence that the white murderers may have initially planned on killing only Roger Malcom but that, when one of the African-American women spoke to the white ringleader by name, the Klansman decided to kill all four of them.

The case attracted national attention, first in the black press and then in the national mainstream media. A large reward was offered for information. President Harry Truman was so disturbed about the killing of a returning serviceman that he ordered an extensive FBI investigation. Later, Truman asserted that the murder was the final factor leading to his order to desegregate the U.S. Armed Forces. However, no indictments were ever brought in the case, which remains officially unsolved to this day.

The case returned to prominence in 1991, when a white witness came forth to describe details in the killings (although he did not identify any of the living perpetrators). Largely as a result of the press coverage, a multiracial group of local community members was formed. "The Moore's Ford Memorial Committee" sought both justice and reconciliation, and over the years it has sponsored public hearings, scholarship banquets, and film screenings. Yet many activists continued to be deeply frustrated that in contrast to other cold cases of the civil rights era, no indictments or prosecutions ever resulted.

The Moore's Ford Reenactment, 2005–2010

In spring 2005, senior figures in the Southern Christian Leadership Conference proposed that a reenactment of the Moore's Ford lynching be staged. As one activist declared at the time, "We need some shock therapy to move things forward. White folks are just in a state of denial on this case, and this'll be something nobody can ignore." Another avowed, "White folks love their Civil War reenactments, which is mainly one big fantasy about the Lost Cause being so noble, so why not reenact some real history for a change?" Many expressed hope that a reenactment would encourage long-intimidated witnesses to come forward and officially identify the surviving killers.

Working with several prominent African-American politicians, local African-American community members quickly organized a reenactment event that was to take place during the next July on the fifty-ninth anniversary of the Moore's Ford killings.

Although hurriedly put together, the July 2005 reenactment captured national press attention, including a prominent article in the *New York Times* and some CNN coverage. In some respects this was the most dramatically interesting of all the reenactments; at the last minute, the white people who had volunteered to play the murdering Klansman backed out, so a group of African-American men had to play the white killers. Some wore white cloth coverings over their heads, while others wore store-bought white masks. The daylong event roughly followed the path of the 1946 events; it began in downtown Monroe in the sanctuary of the First African Baptist Church for a commemorative rally, where prominent civil rights activists including Rev. Joseph E. Lowry and Rev. Jesse Jackson spoke. The group then drove by motorcade to the site of the Hester farm where the initial stabbing took place, then to jail in downtown Monroe where Roger Malcom was bailed out, and then to the Moore's Ford bridge where the massacre was staged. At each stop, two African-American organizers narrated the unfolding events via megaphone.

No attempt was made to costume the reenactors in period dress or use period-appropriate automobiles. As a number of people observed at the time, the most authentic thing about the first reenactment was the use of actual (emptied) firearms by the men playing the Klansmen. In initial years, the Klansman wore signs or headbands saying "KKK"; since 2008 they have simply worn white T-shirts.

The reenactment has since become an annual event, attended by many hundreds of spectators. From 2006 onward, white persons, many of them Atlanta-based peace and justice activists, have been recruited to play the Klansmen. In most cases, the African-American victims have been played by local African-American residents of Walton County, some of them distant kin to the murdered victims. None of the performers have had professional acting experience. Since recruiting white men has been difficult, the Klansmen have often been played by white female peace activists, often with considerable verve and skill.

The most ominous moment in the whole process, each year, is the moment when the car stops just in front of the bridge and Klansmen appear. The lead Klansman marches across the bridge, pounds on the hood of the car, and shouts, "We want that nigger!" Klansmen previously hidden in the woods rush at the car, and drag the four African-Americans down the embankment to the glade where they are "shot" repeatedly, as fire crackers are lit off, and fake blood is poured over the prone victims.

Each year brings some changes to the performance, changes that are always attended by a degree of controversy. In recent years, the reenactment concluded as a local African-American woman sang "Precious Lord," Dr. Martin Luther King, Jr.'s favorite hymn, over the prone bodies[2]:

> Precious Lord, take my hand
> Lead me on, let me stand
> I am tired, I am weak, I am worn
> Through the storm, through the night
> Lead me on to the light
> Take my hand precious Lord, lead me home

As she sang, scores of onlookers at this point rushed forward to photograph the "dead" bodies lying on the ground, in a moment that, to some troubled viewers, recalled the long, gruesome history of photography of spectacle lynchings from the 1880s onward.

The culmination of the reenactments in 2006 and 2007, extensively photographed and televised, was the staged cutting out of the abdomen of the actress playing Dorothy Murray Malcom of her seven-month-old fetus, which was triumphantly held up by a Klansman. In the audience, I could hear a person say, "White man the devil." Another person said, "Worse'n the devil." In 2008, 2009, and 2010 the display of the bloody fetus was performed in a more muted fashion, in part because of protests by white feminist participants, who were worried that excessive focus on the fetus played into local anti-abortion politics.

The Question of the Car

Considerable controversy also swirls each year around the car used to drive the victims to their deaths. Since 2005, the car nearly always used has belonged to a low-income African-American man in his fifties, whom I will call William Mason. William has family roots in Walton county, but he grew up on the streets of Atlanta and was an active gang member, he recalls, in his youth. William proudly explains that the year before the first reenactment he spied this old, 1977 Ford Lincoln Town Car sitting up on blocks in the front yard of a local white man, and that he gradually persuaded the owner to sell it to him. As William delightedly tells the story, "That white man never did think I'd ever get it running again; that's why I got it for practically nothing!"

At the first reenactment, William played the role of the white farmer Loy Harrison, and drove the town car to the bridge, carrying the four African-American victims. It should be noted that William was the only one of the fifteen African-Americans playing white people who did not wear a white mask that year. When I asked him why he wore no mask, he said, "Think about it man, I'm in the car!" (His comment seems to suggest that at least in this context, the car is the structural equivalent of a mask.)

William has taken considerable pride in the fact that his vehicle is usually called upon for this purpose. In 2008, he remarked, "I'm so proud of my car. Its taken me through many a dark, long night ... Now it's gonna carry us all back across that bridge. We're gonna drive the truth back into the light." As noted above, each year there's a good deal of anxiety over whether or not the car will actually start; it often stalls out at the jail, and only William's mechanical ingenuity is able to get the engine to turn over, as the vehicle begins its fateful journey to the bridge ten miles away. William, by the way, has refused numerous offers to buy the car. "It belongs in the reenactment," he says. "That's why it came to me I think."

William notes a proud lineage of automotive ownership in his own family. His grandfather famously owned the first black-owned vehicle in the county, a truck that was closely associated with him for four decades:

> That truck could hold up over anything—mud, rain, ice. One time some cracker tried to run it off the road but it just kept right on going. Grandfather, you know, he had sharecroppers, had fourteen families living on his land. He looked after them though, not like a white man. Never took more shares than was his to take. He could do that since he had his own truck, could take cotton, produce ... wherever it needed to go, not depending on anybody. That's how he took care of everyone.

After his grandfather's death, William notes sadly, one of his aunts was "conned out of that truck by a white woman who offered her a fraction of its worth." The value of the Lincoln Town Car, he emphasizes, is all the greater in light of the loss of the truck. "Well, we lost the truck, but we sure got this fine sedan back, that's what I say."

At the start of summer 2009, the Atlanta-based African-American politician who ultimately sponsors the reenactment stated that that year there would be a historically realistic car. "People need to see the way this really was," he said. "No ghetto cruisers that can barely start ... This is going to be a vintage car. I'll personally pay for renting one from any movie studio. Whatever it takes!" Initially, William agreed that his car would not be used. As a committed member of the multiracial Moore's Ford memorial committee, he was aware that many of the organization's white members were vehemently opposed to the memorial, which they believe fundamentally undercuts efforts at cross-racial reconciliation. William had hoped to maintain neutrality and maintain peace in the group by not offering up his car.

Yet, the local Walton County organizers continued to show a deep attachment William's car and simply were not interested in period-specific verisimilitude. Nick, who has been researching the case since the 1960s

Figure 8.1. Moore's Ford reenactment, July 2009. Photo: Ellen Schattschneider.

and who serves as the leading local organizer, in early July 2009 quietly visited William and prevailed on him to lend his car. William found it impossible to refuse his long-time friend, whom he had known since childhood. Thus, his Lincoln Town Car once again occupied pride of place in the July 2009 reenactment (Figure 8.1). In 2010, the car's starter was too expensive to replace, and at the last moment a local African-American funeral home lent a 1962 Buick, which, Nick explained to me, "was as close as we could get to William's car." As of this writing, William, Nick, and their close friends insist that in 2011, William's Town Car will once again be used.

Toward an Explanation: Why the 1977 Town Car?

Why, even when the option existed of hiring a 1930s vintage sedan, have the local organizers insisted on using William's much more recent car, or, failing that car, a car that reminds them of William's vehicle? Nick, the principal local organizer, explained to me:

> Well, [William], you see. He's one of us.... He has kin all over the county. People know him and they know that car of his. This thing,

this lynching, it burned a hole right into the soul of this county ... For us, it didn't just happen once. It happens again and again. People see William's car, they just know this thing happened to real people, not somebody in the history books. It could happen again to anybody, if we don't hold together.

Suggestively, though, local activists feel that historical verisimilitude is vital in all cinematic renditions of the lynching. They were all concerned about the historical mistakes in Keith Beauchamp's recent docudrama on the Moore's Ford 1946 lynching, *Murder in Black and White*, which incorrectly depicted the victims riding in the back of a pickup truck as opposed to a 1930s style sedan. As James, a man in his sixties, remarked after a screening:

> I understand Keith wanted to show, oh, black people had to ride in the back of the truck, like they were cattle or something. But you know it wasn't always that way, sometimes, so much of the time, there was something that seemed like kindness back then, you thought, all right, this man is going to take care of me, he's putting me right inside his car and just talking to me ... Of course, you never knew where he was taking you. That was the point about life back then, you never knew ... So I think the movie misses that part, somehow, by putting them in the back of the truck.

What precisely makes the reenactment different than a filmic version of the killings? Why is direct mimesis not critical for the participants in the reenactment? My provisional understanding is that the annual reenactment largely recalls the logic and structure of the medieval mystery play, in which each year, local community members played roles in the Gospel story, culminating in the reenacted crucifixion of Jesus and in his resurrection and apotheosis. The apprehended identities of the local performers was an important feature of the mystery play, emphasizing that each one of us was intimately implicated in the grand narrative of Christ's martyrdom and rebirth.

Similarly, the organizers of the modern reenactment, recalling a latter day Cavalry, strive to avoid any appearance of distance between the 1946 tragedy and the present moment. As Alice, who sometimes plays one of the murdered women, told me:

> I can't tell you all the pain I feel inside of me, knowing what happened to those poor souls that day. When I'm lying down there in the mud by the bridge, it's like no time has passed. This could happen to anyone, my brother, my son, my grandchildren. This thing, it happened then, but its still happening.

Similarly, Jane, who for two years played the other murdered woman, the pregnant Dorothy Malcom, explains that she does this to honor the memory of her own son, who was slain on the streets of Atlanta ten years earlier in a black-on-black drug-related shooting. "All this killing, this lynching, it haunts us still. That's why we need to be here, to bear witness, to remember. Otherwise the killing just keeps on going on," she said. For her, the doll of the fetus is closely associated with her own lost son. The unredeemed horror of these violent events remains as raw for many black community members as it was in 1946. A vintage vehicle of the 1930s would place the story too firmly in "the past," and undercut its relevance to contemporary experiences of suffering and injustice.

Like many of her fellow reenactors, Jane rejects the idea of a permanent stone memorial to the victims at the bridge site:

> I don't know, a memorial, a monument? Maybe someday. But not now. Not yet. That would mean this story is finished, over. But it isn't over. You can't have "closure." You can't have "healing" the way some folks want. Not when the surviving *known perpetrators* are still walking around free in the county. Not when there has never been an indictment in this cold case. There is nothing "over" about this story. We're still seeking justice (emphasis in original).

In this complex ritual and emotional field, William's car functions as a highly evocative sign vehicle, "bridging" different temporal epochs, from slavery time, to Jim Crow, to the present day, as it approaches the potent threshold space of the Moore's Ford bridge (see Živković, this volume). Its prominent rust spots give it a patina of age but it does not extend beyond the immediate horizon of memory. It is still the kind of car that could drive on local highways without attracting much notice, and in that sense the vehicle helps to reinforce the point that African-Americans are still subjected to random acts of violence at the hands of law enforcement and persons unknown.

The fact that it is a Lincoln Town Car, so closely associated with masculine prowess and mastery, helps as well, for this is a narrative so closely bound up in the dangerous emotional terrain of intertwined white and African-American masculinity under Jim Crow. The white and black men in the stories were intimately bound together, through shared labor and a common landscape, through complex kinship ties and shared desire for the same women, by ambivalent friendships stretching back into childhood, and by the curious intimacy of physical violence. Many African-American reenactors explain that they are motivated by an intense curiosity to "figure out" what motivated the perpetrators, to understand how a "man could behave in such a way" and to understand "just what the victims felt like on that day." The Town Car, which passed from white to black ownership on the eve of the first reenactment is thus a potent signifier of an equivocal, double consciousness, allowing for reenactors to try out, in effect, "black" and "white" subject positions. As William recalls,

> I learned a lot that day in 2005, when I drove the sedan to the bridge, being a white man you know? I got to thinking as I was driving, why would I do this, why would be driving these young couples to their deaths, right into the ambush? I got to thinking like a white man, how I depended more on my white neighbors than anything else, even being a big planter. I found myself behind the wheel, feeling and acting like him. So I learned something that day.

At the same time, the widely known fact that a local African American man, in the grand trickster tradition, got it off a white man for "practically nothing," gives the car added resonance, helping it evoke both the original white-owned 1946 car and the fact that the reenactment is "ours," that is to say, it is an African-American-controlled event. No vintage automobile rented from outside of Walton County would be able to conflate local racial histories of ownership in quite the same way, or allow for such contradictory experiences of a double moral consciousness, evoking dominant and subordinate perspectives by participants and audience members.

I have also become convinced that the suspense each year surrounding the question of whether or not William's town car will actually start has become an integral component of the overall ritual drama. William, who works as a local fix-it man and gardener, is a quintessential *bricoleur*, widely celebrated for his last minute capacity to pull off unexpected repairs (see Živković, this volume). Each year, the crowd holds its collective breath at the jail, as William tinkers under the hood under the car, and exhales a breath of relief when the engine roars back to life. (This is one of the many paradoxical mimetic features of the ceremony: hundreds of African-Americans gathered to protest, in effect, a history of racial violence, are nonetheless relieved that the lynching will go off as scheduled.) In some respects, the mimetic killings at the bridge each year recall the logic of ritual sacrifice, through which an entire community reinvigorates itself through the bloodletting of a scapegoat. All sacrifices entail a degree of suspense: Will the spear strike cleanly? Will the beast fall on its right flank? The drama of the mercurial Town Car engine "works" in this sense and helps to fuel the necessary collective catharsis once the deed is done.

In addition, the multilayered associations of this particular vehicle render it highly useful for the subtle work of witnessing to which the reenactment is dedicated. In his *Remnants of Auschwitz*, Giorgio Agamben contemplates the paradoxical necessity and impossibility of witnessing the true immoral nature of the death camps (1999). As the ultimate expression of the Foucauldian bio-political, Auschwitz was oriented not simply to the mechanical mass production of death, but rather toward the production of the "living dead" (Agamben 1999: 44), those who had entered into a state of seeming or actual acquiescence to their fate, numbed to all worldly concerns. How, wonders Agamben, can one ethically convey the condition of living death, daring to speak for those whose very consciousness had been largely neutralized even as they breathed and walked? How does one avoid the Nazi condemnation and ridicule of the victim while still remaining sensitive to the complex lines of complicity and choice faced by those who could not, and cannot, speak for themselves?

The Moore's Ford reenactors grapple each year with comparable ethical challenges. They strive to honor the dead, to reveal unspeakable moments of terror, while at the same time acknowledging that the ultimate experience of terror, as known by victim and perpetrator alike, are beyond representation. As Nick remarks, "No one can know what they felt that day, only God can know that. But we have to try, we have to try."

At the same time, the participants struggle with the related mysteries of death and life everlasting. As Samuel, who regularly plays the role of his distant cousin George Dorsey, wondered in 2008 as he stood up out of the mud, "We come back to life, we come back to life." The reenactors pass through horror each year, and each year must find a way back into the flow of conventional, everyday life.

Finally, the use of a locally-owned vehicle resonates with the local participants' emphasis on proximately-controlled movement through history. I once asked Nick why the ceremony had to involve driving for several hours across the county. Why couldn't everyone simply gather at the river's edge for the reenactment of the ambush and massacre? Nick responded:

> We need everyone to understand how our people truly suffered, what they really endured, all across this county. Can't do that in just one place. You need to be moving, back and forth, across all this land, all this history. So we stop, we drive on, we stop, and each time we stop, you see another part of the story, another stage in what unfolded here … That's why we need to drive together in the motorcade, together, following this story, all the way from its start, right to its finish. We're traveling together, through our history.

In Nick's suggestive phrasing, we may discern a further echo of the logic of the medieval pageant of the mystery play, which similarly involved ambulation across a proximate, sacralized landscape. During the York mystery play cycle of the fourteenth and fifteenth centuries, for example, performances spanned the entirety of Creation from Genesis to Doomsday. Participants travelled on specially outfitted wagons, periodically stopping to perform plays at designated sites, or "stages," as they were then called.[3] The Lincoln Town Car in the early twenty-first century functions as a comparable kind of vehicular "stage," conveying the community through a landscape that is simultaneously proximate and mythic, and allowing as it does a performance of a narrative of martyrdom and promise across time and space.

Hence, the multiple resonances of William's claim, "We're gonna drive the truth back into the light." This particular automobile, which exists suspended between the right now of this life and the back-then of the lynching, lets the participants and witnesses move back and forth between the hidden past and visible present. The car's powerful, if mercurial, engine, evokes the unstoppable energy of the collective quest for truth. The obvious fact that the vehicle is not a vintage make and model allows for a kind of ethics of deferral that does not claim to show everything just as it would have looked, but nevertheless aims to get at something essential about the nature of human monstrosity, human courage, human hope.

Both white-owned and black-owned, the Town Car reminds us that we are all bound together by the endless repeating story of martyrdom, from whose moral force none of us are exempt. In its capacity to drive forward, against all odds, this cherished, rusting vehicle reminds us that no story is ever finished, no life exhausted by physical death. For there is always another bridge to cross, another land to reach. William's car thus encapsulates the promise of the beloved hymn sung each year over the prone bodies as they are impossibly suspended between death and life:

> *Through the storm, through the night*
> *Lead me on to the light*
> *Take my hand precious Lord, lead me home.*

NOTES

1. While many lynchings in the United States involved hanging, other methods of murder were frequently used, including shooting and burning alive. The 1946 incident at Moore's Ford, in which four persons were shot to death, is often termed "the last mass lynching in America" (Wexler 2003).
2. Dr. King's final words, on the balcony of the Lorainne Hotel on which he was killed, are reported to have been a request that "Precious Lord" be per-

formed at a rally that evening (Branch 2006: 766). The hymm, by Thomas Dorsey, was sung at Dr. King's funeral (Armada 1988).
3. The term used for these performance sites, "stages," was the origin of the theatrical term "stage." On the cosmology and performance of the York mystery plays, see Clifford 1984, Taylor 2006, Rogerson 2011.

REFERENCES

Agamben, Grigorio. 1999. *Remnants of Auschwitz*: *The Witness and the Archive.* Translated by Daniel Heller-Roazen. New York: Zone Books.

Armada, B.J. 1998. "Memorial Agon: An Interpretive Tour of the National Civil Rights Museum." *Southern Journal of Communication* 63:235–43.

Blackmon, Douglas A. 2008. *Slavery by Another Name: The Re-Enslavement of Black People in America from the Civil War to World War II.* New York: Doubleday.

Branch, Taylor. 2006. *At Canann's Edge: America in the King Years, 1965–68.* Atlanta, GA: Simon and Schuster.

Clifford, Davidson. 1984. *From Creation to Doom: The York Cycle of Mystery Plays.* New York: AMS Press.

Taylor, Jeffery H. 2006. *Four Levels of Meaning in the York Cycle of Mystery Plays: A Study in Medieval Allegory.* Lewiston, NY: Edwin Mellen Press.

Tolnay, Stewart, and E. M. Beck. 1995. *A Festival of Violence: An Analysis of Southern Lynchings, 1882–1930.* Champagne-Urbana: University of Illinois Press.

Wexler, Laura. 2003. *Fire in a Canebrake: The Last Mass Lynching in America.* New York: Scribner.

Rogerson, Margaret. 2011. *The York Mystery Plays: Performance in the City.* Rochester, NY; York Medieval Press.

AFTERWORD

Quo Vadis?

James W. Fernandez

The Figurative Imagination

In the foregoing collection of essays, our editors, David Lipset and Richard Handler present to the reader valuable and informative work on the figurative imagination[1]—inspiring work, in fact, at least for this an-tropeologist. Indeed, it is a fundamental collection since, as all authors recognize, the vehicular is fundamental in the figurative imagination itself, as it is fundamental, as Lipset reminds us, to the Greek etymology of the term metaphor, that principle mediator of figurative thought: "to transfer from one place to another." As a member of the original metaphor mafia of the late sixties and early seventies,[2] I want to discuss how these various chapters have further moved my understanding of this body of thought, and, indeed, my own moral imagination! I cannot possibly, of course, give an adequate reading to all the hares started up in my mind and imagination by these very interesting essays. But I think it important to recognize several things I learned, or re-learned, upon reading them.

In my Africanist years, before turning to ethnography in Europe, my object of study in the various parts of that continent were African religious movements. I frequently pondered that central trope of "movement," that "metaphor of metaphoricity," as Lipset calls it, or, in Živković's parlance, that "metaphor of metaphors." I frequently pondered "what it means to be moved" in religious experience and, more generally, in the dynamics of all social and cultural experience (Fernandez 1964, 1977). And this concern with the moving, emotional dynamics of the figurative imagination in inspiring or resisting social movement has remained a constant interest ever since. That interest, and the questions it raises, I find addressed and rewarded in this collection, especially by its location of movement directly in the various vehicular embodiments of human experience. In this Afterword, to restate it, I wish to ponder, taking my cue from the book's title, something of the many things this collection teaches us about movement and particularly about movement in the moral imagination, that imagination concerned with the better and the worse in the human condition and principally in human relations.

Of course, the automobile itself has become so ubiquitous a contrivance of exhilaration and frustration in modernity, and so emotionally powerful and ever present a trope for expressing and explaining ourselves and our situation to ourselves, the fact that so many of our authors are mainly concerned with that particular vehicle is also part of this collection's strength. The exhilaration found in motoring is obvious enough as the generations of automobile advertising emphasizing the speedy conquest of space and distance makes clear (see also Roth, this volume). The frustrations of motoring are less obvious, perhaps, although the great destruction of human lives brought about by this blunt instrument is frequently enough lamented as a hidden immorality of the car craze. The true frustration, of course, is found in the present dreadful overpopulation of horseless carriages, such that the morning and evening commutes to work or to home, whether on the Eisenhower or the Kennedy in Chicago, the A1 or A3 in Paris, or the M30 in Madrid, indeed on the so-called "express"-ways of practically any large city, have become, ironically, a nightmare of stop-and-go, mostly stop, traffic. Indeed the car trope has come to take on the contrary meaning of frustrating immobility. The downside and dysfunction of the automobile in modern life has become such that it hardly surprises when graduate students coming into our profession bedevil our moral imaginations by writing essays about the social immorality of auto-mobility in a truly civilized society.[3] The pedestrian-izing of large chunks of the city centers of Europe is another expression of the rethinking of the pedestrian/auto driver agreement on "the rules of the road," the social contract of auto-mobility fashioned over the years and detailed by Richard Handler in his chapter.

To be sure, there are cultures that live in a water world, or figure themselves to be Her Majesty's masters of it. Our inspirational editor, David Lipset, first intrigued us into this collection with Charon's Boat and the Titanic before inveigling our imaginations into the water world of the lower Sepik and the embodiments of the all-purpose canoe metaphor in the employ of the seaside Murik living there. Charon's Boat, of course, is the master redemptive vehicle of human mortality in the West, ferrying us across to immortality, predicating, at whatever cost to the passengers, perpetuity upon life's inevitable finality. What greater movement of the human imagination could there be than that from finality to perpetuity? Even an old rusty town car, as Mark Auslander so persuasively shows us in Chapter 8, a decrepit car central to a southern reenactment of a tragic lynching and repeatedly and miraculously cranked up year after year to take its central part in the drama, can carry the black participants across from martyrdom to resurrection.

But not all vehicles can carry us so surely to the sweet or bitter by and by. The *Titanic*, on the other hand, has become a trope, a great ironic metaphor as *The Onion* put it in Lipset's first communication to us, of human frailty, futility, and lack of foresight. Over and over again the *Titanic*s of human ambition and accomplishment are sunk or exploded before our very eyes turning a vehicle of our inventive conquest of time and space and of the water world or space beyond it into a sunken or shattered signifier of finality and futility and of the ultimate impossibility of human realization, the ultimate perfidy of the perfectionism we imagine! Again, even graduate students in anthropology aware of the hidden icebergs of thought upon which anthropological theory could so easily founder have employed it (Anonymous 1954).

The Variety of Vehicles

Ben Chappell (Chapter 7) shifts our attention to quite another vehicle of affective transformation, the Mexican-American lowrider. Here, we have quite the opposite of that rusty resistance to, indeed embodiment of, "time's winged chariot," the time-worn Southern Town Car so central to the lynching reenactment. Here we have, rather, a highly focused customized aesthetic creation, and a museum-collection-worthy contribution to American car culture, despite its distinctly subaltern status in the American hierarchy of valued cultures and valued productions. Chappell explores this ambivalence, this tension, between the pretensions of these cars, their irritating swaggering presence we might say, recalling the zootsuiters of the 1940s, in contrast to the scorn with which they have been so often regarded in mainstream culture.

They may be deprecated in that larger conquest culture of the Southwest, but they cannot be ignored. For as carefully created cars slowly making their way down public streets, they make an in-your-face, in-your-eye, in-your-ear statement, these elaborately and carefully fashioned vehicles of Mexican-American pride and protest. They are icons, indeed, emblematic of our unhappy hierarchies and, for the most part, the class immobility of ethnic differentiation. Chappell prefers to use the term metaxis rather than metaphor, for these aesthetic vehicles of the lower classes, on the basis that metaphor is understood mainly as the transfer of meaning from one thing to another thing that it is not. Metaxis recognizes rather, he argues, the doubleness of experience, the "simultaneous duality," the both/and experience of the artful object. Of course, within trope theory the interactionist view of metaphor (Black 1962) argues for a similar kind of simultaneity in tropological assertions of relationships of difference, a kind of "mutuality of making sense," a vice-versa-ness, as Wayland puts it in Chapter 3.[4]

Old rusty Town Cars and spiffily re-engineered and glowingly repainted lowriders make for a contrasting enrichment to our understanding of the vast domain of vehicular potency and potentiality that the moral imagination has at its disposal—and of some of the crucial status changes and moral transformations that can take place within that domain. There is much and varied enrichment of our apprehension of the corporeal in vehicular form in this collection. Beth Notar in her well documented study (Chapter 6) of the relationship of cars and corruption in Chinese society, just on the verge of entering into a fully car-dominated culture, further enlightens our moral imagination. Not that the corruption, of the young, particularly that which can occur in car courtship, is not a readily available association for most Americans. What is interesting in China is the degree to which vehicle possession and use has long been associated with official corruption and bureaucratic over-privilege. Indeed, as Notar points out, the very old reference in Chinese to the aristocracy and to officialdom as "vehicle people" (*che ren*) well captures that association and the ever possible transgressions and abuses of privilege present in it. Movement itself would seem to have, at least the person's capacity to command the various means of movement, an implicitly moral component insofar as it can lead to a sense of distributive injustices of power and privilege, to greater and lesser mobility, as it were, in society.

If it is not a moral component directly implicit in the car trope, at the least it is the gendered associations of car usage in Japan that, in Chapter 4, Joshua Roth brings to our attention. He alerts us especially to the way that the car as gendered metaphor can integrate in a self-interested way different existing discourses on speed, safety, and manners. In a highly mannered society like the Japanese, with its marked dichotomy in gender roles, the car, with its centrifugal valences, has become especially available for an affirmative expression of masculine prowess. But the difference in the range of cars available, fast cars and slow cars, can yet act to integrate traditional readings into car culture such that, and rather paradoxically, women's traditional homebound centripedality can still be confirmed by car choice and driving manners, that is to say in "who gives way to whom both at the literal and figurative crossroads of life."

If the moral order in society is not always in important part expressed in a society's distribution and facilitation of the centrifugal and centripetal impulses of its members accompanied by rules as to "whom gives way to whom" in social circulation, then I don't know what is.

The gender element arises as well in Wayland's work (Chapter 3) on that other great vehicle of modern times, airplanes (restored World War II aircraft in his essay) and their association through name and nose-art imagery, with women. Wayland asks the important, indeed necessary, question about what ideological work is done by these metaphoric associations between different domains of experience, the domain of flying machines and the domain of women. And he answers this question comprehensively: the association masculinizes the aviator and makes masculine work out of aircraft building and flying; it hierarchizes the male role not only in control over the vehicle so metaphorized, but in social relations more generally; it predicates the quirkiness and complexity of women upon the airplane and vice versa and thus acknowledges the need for special affectionate and attentive care and patience to both; and finally, it works as metaphor, metaphor that both reveals and conceals. It reveals these meanings but it conceals, for example, the deadly destructiveness of these vehicles of war. We cannot forget that the pilot of the bomber who dropped the atomic bomb, "Little Boy," upon Hiroshima, instantaneously cremating thousands of civilians relatively uninvolved in Japanese militarism, named the plane after his nurturing mother, Enola Gay. What work does such euphemistic personification accomplish as regards distracting or confusing the vigilance of the moral imagination from the instantaneous obliteration, that hideous hecatomb of "collateral" obliteration that was Hiroshima?

Marko Živković (Chapter 5) moves the moral imagination in a different direction. He takes us for a "metaphoric ride" back to a nostalgically imagined community, the former Yugoslavia in its heyday. The vehicle for that ride is the little chain driven Yugoslav car,[5] the Fića, entirely of local manufacture, though not produced since the collapse of that country several decades ago now. "Riding along" with him in his essay, we get into a vehicle not part of a rising political-economic giant like China, or a reigning political-economic giant like Japan, but in a now fractured polity and struggling economy, post-war Serbia. Here, the restored Fića, but even more the act of its restoration, becomes a repository of associations in bitter times of better times. It becomes a nostalgic time-binder, a mnemonic that serves as a reminder of those heady years of that unitary mediating East-West state, Yugoslavia, bivalent, as it was, on both sides of the Iron Curtain. It evokes a Yugoslavia, that, however jury-rigged, was at least "ours" prior to the devastating civil wars of the late 1980s and

1990s, and before, the now dismembered set of polities that are effectively, more or less, "theirs" or of "their" imposition or creation.

That little car is clearly a time-binder and evocative enough to bring tears to a former Yugoslav's eyes.[6] Somehow, by tropic power no doubt, the long hours of careful restoration efforts on the Fića put into it by its devotees have made of it an icon of nation-state nostalgia. Its devoted restoration moreover, as Živković points out, becomes a kind of healing ritual for the dismemberment this former nation-state has suffered, and for the "integrity," in the various senses of the word, that has been lost. The little car thus becomes itself a sign-vehicle of emotions in which there is manifestly a moving moral message. We can even believe that in a present-day Fića's restoration there is evocation of the virtues that the former socialist state once pretended to, if it did not actually, achieve. One might even ask: are the communitarian ideals of the socialist moral order what the Fića conveys, however poorly such values may have been formerly realized?

Two Challenges to Our Halting Habitus

We have been moving in this Afterword in a direction contrary to the organization of the volume. Rather than beginning as it does with our two inspirational editors, or better perhaps, *agents provocateurs,* Handler and Lipset, I want to end here with them and several central issues raised in their arguments. They put forth two fruitful provocations relevant to the place and momentum of figurative investigation in ethnography and thought. These provocations can also serve us as a lead on to a concluding comment or two on the moral imagination. To be sure there is also an interesting complementarity in the essays of our two editors. They bring us insight about embodiment processes and the vehicular construction and vicissitudes of human agency from the very outer reaches and from the very inner reaches of our anthropological and ethnographical concerns: Richard Handler works from within our burgeoning car culture, as only Erving Goffman could explore it, and David Lipset works from without our own lifeways or *habitus* by exploring a canoe culture challenged by modernity, the changing culture of the Murik, of the far-off Sepik River in New Guinea, that long-hallowed destination for anthropological inquiry.

But more than this complementarity of treatments each editor in a different way raises an issue that touches on the *quo vadis,* or future path, question. For this author, that is the question of the future prospects of the figurative approach in anthropology, and of where this sensibility and this approach, this *trope*ology, is going in ethnological theory and ethnographical method. Handler raises the question, for me at least, of the degree to which figurative understanding is not just explanatory and clarifying in one of our great theorists, Erving Goffman, but basic to social thought and cultural creation generally. Lipset raises the question of how a discipline, like ours, which as we have long recognized bridges the sciences and the humanities, can, in focusing on the figurative, continue to bridge fruitfully those distinctly different commitments to interpretation and explanation.

In respect to Handler's revealing essay, we encounter once again the Goffmansesque insights into the place of self-presentation and self-preservation in everyday life. We are shown how these processes can be figuratively highlighted by reference to the emerging car/pedestrian culture and the long struggle between these two differently vectored constituencies, car people and pedestrians, in establishing the "rules of the road."

As for me, I have always primarily associated Goffman with the subtleties of the framing of human interaction, framing being, not incidentally, crucial to trope theory as well. It was Goffman's contribution to inform us about the polyvalences of the theatrical frame or trope of "front stage" and "back stage," and especially about the "face work" of the *persona* in negotiating these frames. Most importantly, Goffman pointed us unsparingly at the prevailing differences between platitudes and attitudes and at, the essential face-tiousness, if not two-facedness, of human interaction. Indeed, Goffman himself brings to us a special kind of moral imagination at work in and on the performances of the human situation. This is particularly so in respect to the superficial sincerities so often associated with morality and moral postures of any kind. In his way Goffman was, in my mind, one of the great ironists of inquiry, mischievous might even be the word, in his examining of the intricacies of exposure and concealment, expression and self-protection, other interest and self-interest in the interacting ego! Above all, he was a theorist whose moral imagination was possessed by a strong sense of human vulnerability, probably sharpened in insight, like Kafka, by his own sense of vulnerability.

In the end, of course, the Goffmanesque moral imagination is preoccupied, like so many, with the protections available to that vulnerability—with how society, in the form of the person, protects itself against the vulnerability present in various kinds of interactive breakdown, that is to say, working within the vehicle trope, the "collisions" of everyday life between inter-actors to which they are especially exposed. Among the virtues of the Handler essay is to show us Goffman's vehicular conception of the vectoral in human life—the imagining of the inter-actor as a kind of carapaced, hard-shelled though fragile vehicle—would beetle be the word with the VW (and Kafka) in mind? He shows us, in the guise of the vehicular, Goffman's vectored and vulnerable actor morally intent upon creating and following the "rules of the road" so as to avoid the exposure of that vulnerability to the so-often deeply distressful "collisions" of social interaction and its undesired intimacies. This use of the vehicular trope, the jaywalking trope particularly, enables us to imagine the street-smart and street-stupid moralities and immoralities of daily interaction in a particularly consequential way—consequential because we are brought to contemplate and appreciate, under the influence of this imaginative vehicular reformulation of a body-present social life, the distressing consequences for the vulnerable persona of "social collision."

There is much more in Handler's essay than this central argument. An illuminating picture emerges in his essay, as indicated, of the decades-long struggle between pedestrians and drivers to resolve their mutual but antagonistic rights as regards "the rules of the road." It is a struggle that tells us something about the evolution of social control generally in society and the degree to which it is always morally charged with possible threats to the rights and the living breathing *persona* of the various actors in interaction. We also come to see the way that the moral value of freedom of action, in so many ways a neoliberal value, has became attached to the car, giving to it a kind of ethical invulnerability to our misgivings about it even in the face of the pollution, energy dependency, personal isolation, roadway mayhem, and social congestion it creates.

If Handler invites us through Goffman to consider the moral imagination of human vulnerability in social interaction—the imagination of Erving Goffman expressed in vehicular form—David Lipset invites us to consider the vulnerabilities of the moral imaginations of the Murik of the Sepik Estuary. Their fate is actually caught up in the negotiation between two moral imaginations. For they are caught up in the dilemma between the satisfactions of their former ways and their present, very modern, practices and challenges, particularly the challenges to a seaside people of rising seas levels. Lipset has made Bourdieu's *habitus* a central term for these lifeways, but his dependency upon this trope is only partial. For one thing, he causes us to reflect upon our own moral imaginations as anthropologists caught between, could we call them, the different *habitus* of the social sciences and the humanities? The Murik dilemma is that between the traditions of their canoe culture, on the one hand, and an invasive modernity not only of outboard motors, airplanes and all the mesmerizing vehicular means and mechanisms of a techno-digital world, but also the threats of global warming and of rising seas levels. The latter very directly impinge upon them and challenge their former mytho-poetic mastery of their water world, a mastery so often achieved by putting the canoe trope at the very center of their thoughts and of their seafaring bodies. This was the mastery they achieved in their former water world of oceanic travel (Lipset 2011).

In such a water world as that of the Murik, canoes were bound to be not only good to travel with, but essential to think with. Lipset gives us a thick description, indeed of their figuratively enriched thinking, not only as regards their past traditions, but about their associated attempts at re-enactment of the old time masteries under the duress of changing times. Since metaphor rises again and again in his fine-grained ethnographic account, canoes being predicated here upon houses, there upon drums, or upon political leaders, upon dancers etc., etc., one comes to see, metonymically perhaps, how important a part of the whole culture and the whole person the canoe was. One wonders at the metonymics of it all, the mastery once obtained by this skein of tight part-whole contiguities of the, at one time, self-contained and confidently confined but yet moving tribal life!

But there remains this major question in Lipset's essay that is relevant to all anthropologists and anthropology. It arises from our indeterminate condition as a discipline that is, to say the least, problematically bridged between humanistic and scientific orientations, a discipline deploying both the logic of the sciences and the logic of the humanities in its interpretations and explanations (Northrup 1947). We have all been witness and frequently enough in our annual meetings, to the confrontation, in absolutistic form, between these allegiances to one or another orientation, to one or another investigative and interpretive vehicle for our thought.

In this respect David Lipset sets all of us interested in the figurative a challenge. In his essay, dedicated to revealing what he calls the "dense relational-differential interplay" of action on the ground and in which he brings forth the many local valences of the canoe trope both traditional and modern, he addresses this interdisciplinary issue by bringing into question the "abstractionist" approach. In working through the associative and the contiguous details of the canoe trope in detail he contrasts this ethnographic approach with much if not most metaphor theory and semiotics "motivated," as he says, by abstract or perhaps bureaucratic[7] "desire for intellectual and scientific mastery." This approach of abstraction he finds characteristic of such linguists as Jakobson (1956), whom he mentions, and most surely of cognitive linguists such as Lakoff and Johnson (1981).[8]

There is, indeed, in respect to the figurative, an anthropological tradition that seeks to master the materials by discovering and producing the elemental vectors of transformation, the structures of interactive implication of metaphoric and metonymic assertion and predication. Explanations of scientific and schematic type have been often sought, which is to say explanations as parsimonious, and as simply and clearly stated as possible.

But of course the commitment to the investigators' abstractions and explanations of the abstractionist type, however illuminating, will always be problematic for an ethnographically oriented anthropology insofar as such abstraction works at a considerable remove from the complex and so often ambiguous ethnographic experience and materials themselves and often enough in a manner alienating to and distancing from the ethnographic experience, surely from that focused upon the "relational/differential interplay." The lifeway abstraction that Lipset himself weaves provocatively through his materials, Bourdieu's *habitus,* stimulating to our understanding as it may be, still falls short, in his view, in its pragmatism, in grasping the discontinuities and vulnerabilities, the on-the-ground moral *aporia* and paradoxical discontinuities of life, as the Murik, passing the boundary from a once more integrated canoe and canoe-body mastered world into modernity, seek to adapt their once masterful canoe-bodies to modern circumstances and especially the rising sea-levels and destructive tides accompanying global warming.

It is never, and would not be, easy to ever provide an unambiguous all-purpose solution to the enduring science/humanism dilemma in anthropology, the recurrent betwixt-ness and between-ness of our always transitional profession. It seems to be an inevitable and ever present inchoate in any form of study and discipline exposed to and indeed dedicated to science yet so exposed to the contrarieties of the human condition. But perhaps some sort of compromise arrangement of interests is possible, an arrangement of the kind that Lipset suggests: that of seeking to anchor the complexity of ethnographic field data in some subtle if incompletely defined abstraction, like *habitus,* while making clear at the same time, as Lipset does, the ever presence of oceanic uncertainty in the field experience and field situation itself, hence its inadequacies in seeking to so life-jacket the existential.

What is clear enough is that we anthropologists, in some respects not too different from the Murik perhaps, are caught up in various kinds of dilemmas between, as is well-known, participation and observation, between engagement and reformulation, between the past circumstances of the complex contrarieties of the experiences of field work itself and the present effort-full circumstance of communicative obligation to clarifying interpretation and explanation. Such a set of dilemmas almost inevitably produces what Lipset refers to as "methodological ambivalence" or a "halting habitus," if one wills, vulnerable always to only a partial confidence in the ostensibly enabling masteries of any abstracted effort at explanation. Perhaps we are as a body of scholars at once both earth bound pedestrian-like fieldworkers and ethnographers and fast moving ethnologists in search of spiffy explanatory vehicles, each with a separate momentum and a separate relation to the ground beneath our feet (or tires) searching, as the rubber hits the road, for some persuasive and clarifying rules of the road mutually acceptable in our differentiated selves. The reader may well want to "block that elaborated metaphor" seeking to make use of the figurative materials here available to us in this collection. It may not seem a saving trope. But it is the kind that surfaces from the deep in such an inchoate and vulnerable discipline as our own.

¿Quo vadis?

I was very early on in my first fieldwork among Fang in Western Equatorial Africa made aware of the vectoral in life ways (a vehicle by definition, after all, implies the vectoral). I was struck by their standard greeting to each other whenever they met outside immediate village circumstances, *Wa so ve*, "where are you coming from," *Wa ke ve*, "where are you going." Fang culture had been historically a migrant culture coming down historically from the extended vistas of the barren Sudanic brush lands into the lush, life-filled vitalities, and also dense and closed vistas, of the Equatorial Rain Forest. This greeting with its focus on the vectored nature of life made sense in the context of that historical itinerancy, and the limited inquiry provoking vistas of life in the Equatorial Forest. They were also a people who, because of the quick exhaustion of fertility characteristic of the equatorial soils, moved their bark house villages with some frequency in the sparsely populated but densely vegetated rain forests. Every twelve years or so they decamped in search of more fertile soils.

Other African peoples and European villagers in my experience have been more cautious in evoking the vectoral. This Fang greeting style also made it easier for me to understand why, in the religious movement I studied among them (Fernandez 1982), "The Path of Life and Death," was such a central trope, and why this religion promoted, through ingestion of the alkaloid, *ibogain*, dreams of supernatural journeys of salvation. I might have more thoroughly explored, by the way, the vehicular trope in that religion had I had the impetus and knowledge provided by this valuable collection.

Had I been asked to contribute a chapter, I might well have devoted it to the "soul-boat," the setting of a small candle, after initiation, in a large concave *okoume* leaf, then gently releasing this fragile vessel into a stream to make its way down and out to the equatorial ocean of the afterlife. There is something very vehicular in this rite as in the religion itself, indeed very probably in most religions, which so frequently offer, like Charon's Boat itself, a "way out of" or a "way across" the finalities of the human condition. And of course central to the moral imagination of Western Christendom is Peter's question to Jesus, *Quo vadis?* "To Jerusalem, to be crucified" was the answer, and, the faithful might add, to become, indeed, and however tortuously, *the way* of Christian life and *the vehicle* of human salvation.

But I want to use the saintly question not to evoke all that is vehicular and vectoral in the Christian moral imagination, but rather to think briefly and finally here about where we, that is those of us anthropologists who are interested in tropes and the moral imagination that they configure, are going in our work on the figuration of culture. We have surely come to a very good place in our understanding in this collection. But the way forward is not unambiguous. We may feel, certainly this author feels, that the figurative and its work on the moral imagination, however tortuous its multi-layered workings may sometimes be, are at the heart of cultural creation. But how widely shared that feeling is or can or will be, how stoutly it could stand up to the stark and seemingly anchored attractions of neuroscience for example, is a large question, and how it will be treated in future fieldwork and the work of ethnography is yet a question. *Quo vadis?*

I hope I have made my own view clear in respect to the incongruences of callings that bedevil us, humanistic and scientific, participant-observationist and abstractionist. The answer is that of many anthropologists: for us in anthropology, ethnographically anchored as we are, particularities always cast more light than do generalities on the human condition, but it is still in the interaction of these two dispensations, and in the tension between them, that the enrichments of our professional understanding reposes.

In any event, our own moral imaginations as anthropologists are challenged by this double identity of being true to our past field materials while adapting them to the present circumstance of more parsimonious and always possibly alienating requirements of ethnographic write-up and the even more parsimonious and alienating requirements of scientific-type presentation. And this time-binding of past and present is a challenge to our moral imaginations because the people of our former fieldwork are in many ways vulnerable to how we treat them whether in subsequent humanistic interpretation or in scientific explanation. That is to say, they are vulnerable to how we figure them out in our subsequent ethnography.

We do not escape the challenge of figuration—a moral challenge as I want here at the end to suggest—either in interpretation or explanation.

In the first place, we have the moral responsibility of attending carefully to their own figurations, to their canoe-bodies or their auto-bodies, and secondly, to our own configurations of their figurations, our interpreted conceptualizations of their consternated condition given vehicular directionality, for example. Can metaphorizing itself escape from being an act of the moral imagination? Can the car trope be put forth, for example, as an instance of overcoming the stalemate of human vulnerability by vehicular freedom without being morally aware of the multitudes they kill, the heavens they pollute, the self-satisfaction and social isolation and social inurement they produce? We do not escape that moral challenge as I think the preceding essays of this collection make clear.

Such can be the challenge but also the power of the tropes, their fun, their fascination, and their frailty, but also their seriousness and capacity to evoke and at once protect and give directionality to human vulnerability. Indeed the tropes can, as Marko Živković says, "take us for a ride," or "betray us down the garden path," but they can also carry us deeper into the at once cautious and innovative human condition. That is something that is surely accomplished in this at once creative and cautionary volume. But there is enrichment in this challenge, as there is enrichment in these collected essays. I have found in them restorative understanding of how figurations of directionality are understood and obtained in the human condition and its *simulacrum*, anthropology.

NOTES

1. Over the years, the course I have long offered on metaphor, since my Dartmouth years in the early seventies, has gradually changed its title from "'Metaphor Theory" to "Trope Theory" to, finally, "The Figurations of Social Thought and Action in Culture." Hence my featuring of "figuration" as the core term in this Afterword.
2. The Rosaldos, Renato and Michelle, David Sapir, Chris Crocker, Peter Seitel, myself, and others. Stanley Tambiah and Clifford Geertz from the sixties and though not subversive "Mafiosi of the Metaphoric" should certainly be cited as godfatherly presences in our early work on the contribution of the figurative to the construction of culture. The Mafia trope may be apt because there *was* something subversive and underworld about suddenly making so basic to our understanding the figurational component of social action and of cultural construction. For the most part, figuration had been previously considered as supplemental and peripheral to our straightforward terminological anchorage in ethnologic understanding and interpretive reasoning about, it as presumed, a seriously anchored culture and social action This subservience to "practical reason" begs many questions.

3. Cf. Joe Grim Feinberg, http://carbusters.org/2010/08/11/cars-can-never-run-cleanly-the-automobile-as-an-anti-social-form/, accessed June 12, 2012.
4. This vice versa-ness of metaphor is also seen in Lipset's chapter in his discussion of body as canoe/canoe as body.
5. Perhaps, taking what Živković tells us, *clunker* or *put-put* would be the apt American translation.
6. Tears to my own eyes as well let me say, since Živković's subtle study carries me back to our memorial session for our late colleague and friend Daphne Berdahl and her work on the East German Trabi—also a vehicular repository of images and feelings about another "imagined community," the former economically egalitarian if politically authoritarian and economically subordinate East Germany.
7. In the use of the term "bureaucratic," Lipset evokes the more or less direct and troublesome association of early anthropologists with colonial regimes anxious for the ethnographic data which might serve as facilitating to their bureaucratic task of administering the natives. The persistence of such bureaucratic roles taken by anthropologists as seen in service to the military in Vietnam and more recently in Afghanistan is an instance of that awkward if not questionably moral relationship to power as regards native well-being.
8. Tambiah's (1968) classic article parsing the metaphoric equivalences in Trobriand garden magic can also be seen as an abstractionist study except for its careful reproduction of many of the actual garden spells from Malinowksi's great ethnography, which Tambiah is engaged in explaining. And, in the interest of full disclosure, this author has as well used the vectors of the semantic differential to plot emotional movement accomplished by figurative predications on persons and things (Fernandez 1977). This is an abstractionist approach to the vehicular to be sure but always, as argued there and here, accompanied by the attempt to anchor abstraction as fully as possible in the ethnographic materials that one has experienced and is seeking to so model.

REFERENCES

Anonymous. 1954. "Wasn't It a Thought Titanic?" *American Anthropologist* 56, no. 5: 742.

Black, Max. 1962. *Models and Metaphors: Studies in Language and Philosophy.* Ithaca, NY: Cornell University Press.

Fernandez, J. W. 1964. "African Religious Movements, Types and Dynamics." *Journal of Modern African Studies* 3, no. 4: 428–46.

———. 1974. "The Mission of Metaphor in Expressive Culture." *Current Anthropology* 15, no. 2: 119–45.

———. 1977. "Poetry in Motion: Being Moved by Amusement, by Mockery, and by Mortality in the Asturian Countryside." *New Literary History* 8:459–83.

———. 1982. *Bwiti: An Ethnography of the Religious Imagination in Africa*. Princeton, NJ: Princeton University Press.

Lakoff, George, and Mark Johnson. 1981. *Metaphors We Live By*. Chicago: University of Chicago Press.

Lipset, David. 2011. "The Tides: Masculinity and Climate Change in Papua New Guinea," *Journal of the Royal Anthropological Institute (N.S.)* 17:20–43.

Northrup, F. S. C. 1947. *The Logic of the Sciences and the Humanities*. New York: Macmillan.

Tambiah, S. 1968. "The Magical Power of Words." *Man* (NS) 3, no. 2: 175–208.

CONTRIBUTORS

Mark Auslander is Associate Professor of Anthropology and Museum Studies at Central Washington University (Ellensburg, Washington) where he directs the university's Museum of Culture and Environment. He has undertaken research in Zambia and South Africa, and in African-American communities in the U.S. South. He is the author of *The Accidental Slaveowner: Revisiting a Myth of Race and Finding an American Family* (2011).

Ben Chappell is Associate Professor of American Studies at the University of Kansas. He is the author of *Lowrider Space: Aesthetics and Politics of Mexican American Custom Cars* (2012). His research on lowriders was recognized with awards from the Wenner-Gren Foundation; the Society for Urban, National, and Transnational/Global Anthropology; and the Foundation for Urban and Regional Studies.

James W. Fernandez is Professor Emeritus of Anthropology at the University of Chicago where he continues to teach "The Figuration of Social Thought and Action," the course which, in one form or another, has been the conveyance, not to say vehicle, of his thoughts on the rhetoric of social life for the last forty some years. He has taught at Dartmouth, Princeton, and Chicago and has done extended fieldwork in three parts of Africa: in Gabon, among Fang, in Natal, among Zulu, and in Togo/Ghana, among Ewe. In recent years he and his wife, also an anthropologist, have worked in Northern Spain.

Richard Handler is Professor of Anthropology at the University of Virginia, where he is Director of the Program in Global Development Studies. He has written extensively on nationalism and the politics of culture, museums, and the history of anthropology. His most recent book is *Critics against Culture: Anthropological Observers of Mass Society* (2005).

David Lipset is Professor of Anthropology at the University of Minnesota. He has conducted long-term fieldwork in Papua New Guinea since 1981. He is the author of two books, *Gregory Bateson: Legacy of a Scientist* (1982) and *Mangrove Man: Dialogics of Culture in the Sepik Estuary* (1997), as well as articles on a variety of topics relating to culture, change, and masculinity among the Murik Lakes people.

Beth E. Notar is Associate Professor and Chair of Anthropology at Trinity College, in Hartford, Connecticut. She is the author of *Displacing Desire: Travel and Popular Culture in China* (2007), which was selected by the American Library Association as an "outstanding academic title." Her research on cars in China has been funded by the Charles A. Dana Foundation, the Henry Luce Foundation, as well as the National Endowment for Humanities.

Joshua Hotaka Roth is Professor of Anthropology and Asian Studies at Mount Holyoke College. His book *Brokered Homeland: Japanese Brazilian Migrants in Japan* won the 2004 Book Award for Social Science from the Association for Asian American Studies. "Heartfelt Driving: Discourses on Manners, Safety, and Emotion in Japan's Era of Mass Motorization," an article based on more recent research, appears in *The Journal of Asian Studies*.

Kent Wayland is a lecturer in the Department of Engineering and Society, School of Engineering & Applied Science, University of Virginia. His recent work focuses on IT-based surveillance and transparency systems, including chapters in the edited volumes *Internet and Surveillance* (2012) and *Surveillance and Democracy* (2012).

Marko Živković is Associate Professor of Anthropology at the University of Alberta, Edmonton, Canada. He specializes in ex-Yugoslav political rhetorics, and in anthropology of performance, art, and science. He is the author of *Serbian Dreambook: National Imaginary in the Time of Milošević* (2011).

INDEX

accidents. *See under* traffic
airplanes
    and gender, 69–85
    nose art, 70–76
Alamo (San Antonio, Texas), 163–66
American Automobile Association, 25
Anzaldúa, Gloria, 172
Arapesh (Papua New Guinea), 62–63
Army Air Corps (U.S.), 77
Arunta (Australia), 13
Austronesians, 22–25
Auschwitz, 191
automobiles. *See under* cars
automobility, 7–8
Ayres, Edward Duran, 173

Balašević, Djordje, 112
barriology, 158, 168–72
Berdhal, Daphne, 112, 117
Black, Max, 40
Boal, Augusto, 162
boats, 3–5
Bong, Dick, 76
Bourdieu, Pierre, 21, 35, 203

canoes, 22–24, 26–36, 41–42
cars
    aesthetics of, 158–63, 166–67
    and corruption, 134, 137–47
    and gender, 69–70, 79, 89–90, 94–105, 174, 189–90
    and nationalism, 9–10
    and persons, 5, 116–17, 134–35, 146
    and racism, 179–81, 190–91
    and racing, 97–100, 102–3, 133, 143–44
    and repairs, 119, 124
    required equipment of, 58–59
    restoration of, 122–25
    as status symbols, 134–36, 140, 142
    as vehicular units, 49–50
    See also specific car makes and models
Caracol Museum (Mexico City), 165
Case of Two Cities, A (novel), 142
Centro Cultural Aztlán (San Antonio, Texas), 163
chariots, 136–37
Charon, 4, 10, 194–95, 205
Chavez Ravine (Los Angeles), 158
China Doll (airplane), 72–74, 78
Cohen, Liz, 175n5
Confederate Air Force, 69–70
Con Safos (periodical), 158
Cooder, Ry, 158, 160
Crocker, Christopher, 78–79
Crows and Sparrows (film), 140

Devil Z (car), 98–99
Ding Cong, 138
Dong Son drums, 24
Dorsey, George, 182–83
drivers
    education of, 55–59
    and gender, 89, 94–105
    reckless, 54–55, 89, 101–2

INDEX

Driving Miss Daisy (film), 181
Du Bois, W. E. B., 159
Durkheim, Emile, 13
Dyana (car), 121

elevators, 64n5
Engels, Friedrich, 1
Enola Gay (airplane), 85, 198

Fang (West Africa), 204–5
Fiat 600D (car), 111
Fiat 750 (car), 114–28, 198–99
Fića. *See under* Fiat 750
Fifi (airplane), 75–76
First African Baptist Church (Monroe, Georgia), 184
Fisk University Jubilee Singers, 159–60
Fortune, Reo, 62–63

George H. W. Bush, USS (ship), 70
Goffman, Erving, 48–52, 58, 63, 95, 200–201
Grable, Betty, 72
Greene, Graham, 111
Gypsy Rose (lowrider car), 157–58

habitus, 21, 31–32, 35, 41–42, 201–2
Heaven Above (novel), 141
Heaven's Wrath (novel), 142
Hiroshima, 198
horses, 53
Hurston, Zora Neale, 159–60

Indonesia, 24
Initial D (film), 150n21
Institute for Contemporary Art (Boston), 157

Jackson, Rev. Jesse, 184
jaywalkers, 53–55
Jung Chang, 140

Kafka, Franz, 64n2
K-car (car), 89–90, 94–97, 100–105
Kunming (Chinese city), 133, 143

La Carcacha (lowrider car), 157
Le Mans (auto race), 88
Lemonnier, Pierre, 134
Lincoln Town Car, 178, 185–92
Lowrey, Rev. Joseph, 184
Lowrider Magazine, 160, 168
lynching, 181–83

Madonna, 150n20
Malangan, 127
Malcolm, Dorothy, 182–83
Malcolm, Roger, 182–83
Maltbie, William, 61–62
Maori, 42
Mao Zedong, 140
Marinović, Milosav, 119, 124, 126
Marx, Karl, 1
Mazda RX-8 (car), 88–89
Mead, Margaret, 62
Mendoza-Denton, Norma, 168–169
Mercedes (car), 121, 127, 142
metaphor, 1–3, 13, 35–36, 40–41, 69, 79–84, 89–90, 113–18, 125–28, 134–37, 147–48, 162, 196–97
metaxis, 156–57, 162–63, 167–72, 174, 196–97
Miss Mitchell (airplane), 74
Moluccas, 22–23
Moodie (artist), 165–66
Moore's Ford (Georgia), 181–83
Moore's Ford Memorial Committee, 183
Movimiento Estudiantíl Chicana/Chicano de Aztlán, 165
Mr. Cartoon, 159
Murik (Papua New Guinea)
 canoes, 26–36, 41–42
 dances, 38
 lineages, 30

masks, 27–30
metaphors, 35–36, 40–41
moral agency, 32–33
mythology, 25–26
travel, 34–35
vehicle-bodies, 21–22, 32, 34
Murray, Mae, 182
Museum of Science and Technology (Belgrade), 123–24
Museum of the City of Mexico, 157

National Association of Chicana and Chicano Studies, 168
National Class, The (movie), 115
Nissan GT-R (car), 98
Nissan S30Z (car), 98

Ortíz-Torres, Rubén, 175n5

Papua New Guinea, 25, 41–42, 60–66
Paz, Octavio, 172
pedestrians, 48–49, 53–59, 91–96, 200
Peirce, Charles Sanders, 2, 137
Peterson Automotive Museum (Los Angeles), 158
Petty, George, 71
Preddy, George, 71
Pretty Dyana: A Gypsy Recycling Saga (film), 121

Robinson, David, 163
Roma, 121–22
Ross, Edward Alsworth, 52, 59
Royal Navy (British), 5

Sabac (Serbian town), 115, 119, 122
San Antonio Spurs (basketball team), 163–64
Sandoval, Denise, 160
Sanmao, 139–40
Sentries under the Neon Lights (film), 149n10

ships, 5–7, 69–70, 77, 79
Sleepy Lagoon trial, 172
Solomon Islands, 34
Somare, Sir Michael, 38, 40
Sonny and the Sunglows, 168–69
Southern Christian Leadership Conference, 183
speed, 56, 89, 100, 104
streets, 49, 53–55, 60
streetcars, 58, 90

Tanep, Vincent, 25
Tanimbar Islands, 23–24, 34
Titanic, RMS, 6–7, 195
Trabi (car), 112, 118
traffic
    accidents, 54–55, 91, 98–99
    control, 53–55, 91
    fatalities, 91
    rules, 49–50, 55–59, 92–99, 142–43
    safety, 89
Trinidad, 166
Truman, Harry, 183
Turner, Victor, 126, 134
Tuskegee Airmen, 71

Valdez, Vincent, 158–60
van Gennep, Arnold, 5
Vargas, Alberto, 71

Wagner, Roy, 60–61
Wangi (Sait headman, Papua New Guinea), 40
warbirds, 70–71
Warramunga (Australia), 3
Weber, Max, 64nn2–3
Wewak (city, Papua New Guinea), 36, 38
Wollunqua, 3
Women's Air Service Pilots (U.S.), 77

Yamuna, Felix, 40–41

Yellow Emperor (China), 136, 142, 143
Yellow Rose of Texas (airplane), 74, 78
Young Conservatives of Texas, 165

Yugonostalgia, 122

Zapata, Emiliano, 170
Zastava (Yugoslav factory), 115, 124